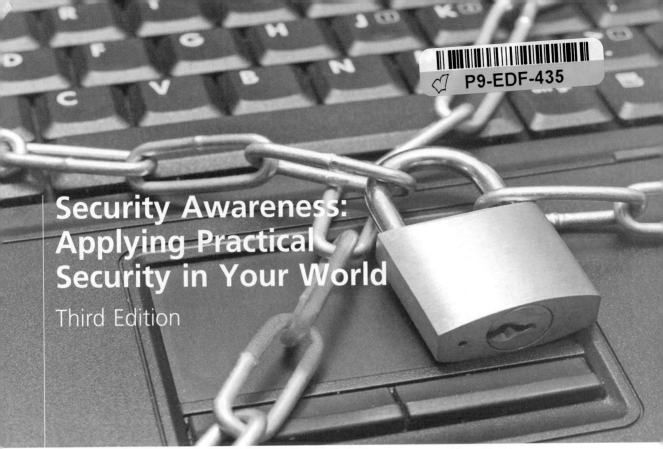

P9-EDF-435

Security Awareness: Applying Practical Security in Your World

Third Edition

15462

By Mark Ciampa, Ph.D.

COURSE TECHNOLOGY
CENGAGE Learning

Australia • Brazil • Japan • Korea • Mexico • Singapore • Spain • United Kingdom • United States

COURSE TECHNOLOGY
CENGAGE Learning™

Security Awareness: Applying Practical Security in Your World, Third Edition
Mark Ciampa

Vice President, Career and Professional Editorial: Dave Garza

Executive Editor: Stephen Helba

Managing Editor: Marah Bellegarde

Senior Product Manager: Michelle Ruelos Cannistraci

Developmental Editor: Deb Kaufmann

Editorial Assistant: Sarah Pickering

Vice President, Career and Professional Marketing: Jennifer McAvey

Marketing Director: Deborah S. Yarnell

Senior Marketing Manager: Erin Coffin

Marketing Coordinator: Shanna Gibbs

Production Director: Carolyn Miller

Production Manager: Andrew Crouth

Content Project Manager: Andrea Majot

Senior Art Director: Jack Pendleton

Cover Photo: Image copyright 2009. Used under license from Shutterstock.com

Production Technology Analyst: Tom Stover

Manufacturing Coordinator: Denise Powers

Copyeditor: Kathy Orrino

Proofreader: Harold Johnson

Compositor: International Typesetting and Composition

For product information and technology assistance, contact us at
Cengage Learning Customer & Sales Support, 1-800-354-9706

For permission to use material from this text or product, submit all requests online at **cengage.com/permissions**
Further permissions questions can be emailed to
permissionrequest@cengage.com

Microsoft® is a registered trademark of the Microsoft Corporation.

Library of Congress Control Number: 2009925012

ISBN-13: 978-1-435-45414-9
ISBN-10: 1-435-45414-6

Course Technology
20 Channel Center Street
Boston, MA 02210
USA

Cengage Learning is a leading provider of customized learning solutions with office locations around the globe, including Singapore, the United Kingdom, Australia, Mexico, Brazil, and Japan. Locate your local office at: **international.cengage.com/region**

Cengage Learning products are represented in Canada by Nelson Education, Ltd.

For your lifelong learning solutions, visit **course.cengage.com**

Visit our corporate website at **cengage.com**

Printed in the United States of America
1 2 3 4 5 6 7 12 11 10 09

Brief Contents

Table of Contents

Introduction

The single most important topic in the computer world continues to be *security*. **Over** 246 million data records of Americans containing personal information such as addresses, Social Security numbers, and credit card numbers have been exposed due to weak security. A computer connected to the Internet is probed by an attacker for weaknesses on average once every 39 seconds. Web pages that infect an Internet surfer's computer by just viewing the site and not even clicking on anything are increasing at a rate of over 6,000 new infected Web pages every day, or one every 14 seconds. Eighty percent of these pages belong to innocent companies and individuals who are unaware that their sites have been compromised. And the list goes on and on. Almost daily you hear about new attacks as well as warnings to keep your computer secure.

Yet knowing how to make a computer secure and keep it safe is a mystery to most computer users. What type of attacks will antivirus software prevent? What does a firewall do? How can I test my computer to be sure that it cannot be attacked through the Internet? How do I install software patches? Knowing how to keep a computer secure is a daunting task.

This book provides you with the tools you need to make your computer and wireless network secure. *Security Awareness: Applying Practical Security in Your World, Third Edition* presents a basic introduction to practical computer security for all users, from students to home users to business professionals. Security topics are introduced through a series of real-life user experiences, showing why computer security is necessary and providing the essential elements for making and keeping computers secure. Going beyond the concepts of computer security, you will gain practical skills on how to protect your computers and wireless networks from increasingly sophisticated attacks. You will also learn how an organization uses security, which will help you become a more secure employee.

Each chapter in the book contains hands-on projects that cover making computers secure. In addition, projects that show how to use and configure security hardware and software are included. These projects are designed to make what you learn come alive through actually performing the tasks. Besides the hands-on projects, each chapter provides realistic security case projects that put you in the role of a security consultant who works in different scenarios helping to solve the security problems of clients. Every chapter also includes review questions to reinforce your knowledge while helping you to apply practical security in your world.

Approach

The approach of *Security Awareness: Applying Practical Security in Your World, Third Edition* is hands-on and practical. You will learn all about the different attacks that a computer system faces today and how to make your computer secure. Because no previous in-depth knowledge of network, system hardware, or operating systems is required, you can begin immediately to learn the steps to keep attackers from infecting your computer.

Security Awareness is much more than a step-by-step approach for practical security. Because computer systems are as different as their users, you will also learn some basic concepts regarding computer security and the different types of attacks and defenses. This background will help you to apply your practical security knowledge to computers that are different from yours and to new computers, networks, and software. *Security Awareness: Applying Practical Security in*

Your World, Third Edition helps you learn what security is and how to use it to protect your computer today as well as in the future.

With the growth of online delivery of computer courses, it is essential that a textbook be flexible enough to be used in either the classroom or as part of an online Web course. This book is intended to meet the needs of students in a traditional classroom setting as well as in an online delivery of the course materials. Hands-on activities can be performed using equipment installed on a college campus or using personal computer equipment at home. All hands-on activities cover software that is included as part of the Windows operating system or is a free download from the Internet. This allows students to perform activities in a classroom computer lab with other classmates or alone in a home or apartment in an online course.

A specialized computer lab is not necessary in order to perform the hands-on activities in *Security Awareness: Applying Practical Security in Your World, Third Edition*. A standard computer lab with basic equipment can be easily used to learn about applying practical security.

Intended Audience

This book is intended to meet the needs of students and professionals who want to be able to protect their computers and networks from attacks. A basic working knowledge of computers is all that is required to use this book. The book's pedagogical features are designed to provide a truly interactive learning experience to help prepare you for the challenges of securing networks and computers. In addition to the information presented in the text, each chapter includes Hands-on Projects that guide you through implementing practical hardware, software, and network security step by step. Each chapter also contains a running case study that places you in the role of problem solver, requiring you to apply concepts presented in the chapter to achieve a successful solution.

Chapter Descriptions

The chapters in this book discuss the following topics:

Chapter 1, "Introduction to Security," explains what security is and why it is important and reveals who the attackers are and how they attack, in addition to outlining the basic defenses necessary for safeguarding a computer system.

Chapter 2, "Desktop Security," tells how to make a desktop or laptop computer secure by protecting the equipment and the data stored on it, as well as how to recover from an attack.

Chapter 3, "Internet Security," explains how attacks through the Internet can occur and what steps can be taken to reduce the risk of such attacks.

Chapter 4, "Personal Security," explains how attacks can steal personal information and what can be done to prevent them.

Chapter 5, "Wireless Network Security," describes how a wireless network works, the different types of wireless attacks, and how to secure a wireless network.

Chapter 6, "Enterprise Security," describes how an organization can implement a secure environment through business continuity and security policies.

Features

To aid you in fully understanding computer and network security, this book includes many features designed to enhance your learning experience.

- **Chapter Objectives.** Each chapter begins with a detailed list of the concepts to be mastered within that chapter. This list provides you with both a quick reference to the chapter's contents and a useful study aid.

- **Security in Your World.** Each chapter opens with a security-related vignette that introduces the chapter content and helps the reader to understand why these topics are important. These stories are continued throughout the chapter, providing additional information about real-life computer security.

- **Illustrations and Tables.** Numerous illustrations of security concepts and technologies help you visualize theories and concepts. In addition, the many tables provide details and comparisons of practical and theoretical information.

- **Hands-on Projects.** Although it is critical to understand the importance of security, nothing can substitute for real-world experience. To this end, each chapter provides several Hands-on Projects aimed at providing you with practical security experience. These projects use the Windows operating systems as well as software downloaded from the Internet.

- **Chapter Summaries.** Each chapter's text is followed by a summary of the concepts introduced in that chapter. These summaries provide a helpful way to review the ideas covered in each chapter.

- **Key Terms.** All of the terms in each chapter that were introduced with bold text are gathered in a Key Terms list with definitions at the end of the chapter, providing additional review and highlighting key concepts.

- **Review Questions.** The end-of-chapter assessment begins with a set of review questions that reinforce the ideas introduced in each chapter. These questions help you evaluate and apply the material you have learned.

- **Case Projects.** Located at the end of each chapter are several Case Projects. In these extensive exercises, you implement the skills and knowledge gained in the chapter through real design and implementation scenarios.

Text and Graphic Conventions

Wherever appropriate, additional information and exercises have been added to this book to help you better understand the topic at hand. Icons throughout the text alert you to additional materials. The icons used in this textbook are described below.

The Note icon draws your attention to additional helpful material related to the subject being described.

The Tip icon highlights helpful information based on the author's experience about how to approach a problem or what to do in real-life situations.

The Caution icon warns you about potential mistakes or pitfalls and explains how to avoid them.

Each hands-on activity in this book is preceded by the Hands-on icon and a description of the exercise that follows.

Case Project icons mark Case Projects, which are scenario-based assignments. In these extensive case examples, you are asked to implement independently what you have learned.

The Block Attacks icon identifies computer and network defenses that are designed to block attacks by creating a strong security perimeter much like a castle wall or moat.

The Update Defenses icon points out defenses that must be continually updated in order to remain effective.

The Minimize Losses icon illustrates action to be taken in advance of attacks in order to be ready to "pour water" on them when they come.

The Send Secure Information icon shows swift and strong proactive steps to be taken to thwart attackers.

Instructor's Materials

The following additional materials are available when this book is used in a classroom setting. All the supplements available with this book are provided to instructors on a single CD-ROM (ISBN: 1435454154). You can also retrieve these supplemental materials from the Course Technology Web site, *www.cengage.com/coursetechnology* by going to the page for this book, under "Download Instructor Files & Teaching Tools."

Electronic Instructor's Manual. The Instructor's Manual that accompanies this book includes the following items: additional instructional material to assist in class preparation, including suggestions for lecture topics; recommended lab activities; tips on setting up a lab for Hands-on Projects; and solutions to all end-of-chapter materials.

ExamView Test Bank. This cutting-edge Windows-based testing software helps instructors design and administer tests and pretests. In addition to generating tests that can be printed and administered, this full-featured program has an online testing component that allows students to take tests at the computer and have their exams automatically graded.

PowerPoint Presentations. This book comes with a set of Microsoft PowerPoint slides for each chapter. These slides are meant to be used as a teaching aid for classroom presentations, to be made available to students on the network for chapter review, or to be printed for classroom distribution. Instructors are also at liberty to add their own slides for other topics introduced.

Figure Files. All the figures in the book are reproduced on the Instructor's Resources CD. Similar to the PowerPoint presentations, they are included as a teaching aid for classroom presentation, to make available to students for review, or to be printed for classroom distribution.

Information Security Community Site

New to this edition is the Information Security Community Site. This site was created for students and instructors to find out about the latest information security news and technology. Visit *http://community.cengage.com/infosec* to:

- Learn what's new in information security through live news feeds, videos and podcasts.

- Browse our online catalog.

- Download student and instructor resources, such as additional labs, instructional videos and instructor materials.

- Connect with your peers and security experts through blogs and Ask the Author forums.

Acknowledgments

An entire team, and not just an author, is necessary to produce a book, and it was a privilege for me to be part of this team. The entire Cengage/Course Technology staff was always very helpful and worked very hard to create this finished product. I'm honored to be part of such an outstanding group of professionals, and to these people and everyone on the team I extend my sincere thanks.

Executive Editor Stephen Helba provided me with the opportunity to work on this project and also helped shaped the scope of this book. Senior Product Manager Michelle Ruelos Cannistraci was very helpful in keeping everything on track. Technical Editor John Bosco carefully reviewed the book and identified many corrections. And again special recognition goes to Developmental Editor Deb Kaufmann. Every project that I work on with Deb is a true delight. She takes care of all the tiny details, finds my errors, makes great suggestions, and somehow turns what I do into a book. Deb is truly the very best there is.

And finally, I want to again thank my wonderful wife, Susan, who is the greatest blessing of my life. As always, she was supportive, patient, and encouraging to me. Without her as my constant companion I could not have written this book.

Dedication

To my wife, Susan, my sons and daughters-in-law Brian, Amanda, Greg, and Megan, and my grandson Braden.

About the Author

Mark Ciampa is Assistant Professor of Computer Information Systems at Western Kentucky University in Bowling Green, Kentucky, and holds a Ph.D. in Digital Communication Systems from Indiana State University. Prior to this he was Associate Professor and served as the Director of Academic Computing at Volunteer State Community College in Gallatin, Tennessee, for 20 years. Mark has worked in the IT industry as a computer consultant for the U.S. Postal Service, the Tennessee Municipal Technical Advisory Service, and the University of Tennessee. He is also the author of many Cengage/Course Technology textbooks, including *Security+ Guide to Network Security Fundamentals 3ed*, *CWNA Guide to Wireless LANs 2ed*, *Guide to Wireless Communications*, and *Networking BASICS*.

Lab Requirements

To the User

This book should ideally be read in sequence, from beginning to end. However, each chapter is a self-contained unit, so after completing Chapter 1 the reader may elect to move to any subsequent chapter.

Hardware and Software Requirements

Following are the hardware and software requirements needed to perform the end-of-chapter Hands-on Projects:

- Microsoft Windows Vista or XP
- An Internet connection and Web browser
- Microsoft Office 2007 or Office 2003
- Microsoft Office Outlook

Specialized Requirements

Whenever possible, the needs for specialized requirements were kept to a minimum. The following chapter features specialized hardware:

- Chapter 5: Linksys WRT54G or WRT54G2

Free Downloadable Software is Required in the Following Chapters

Chapter 1:

- Microsoft Windows Malicious Software Removal Tool
- Secunia Online Software Inspector

Chapter 2:

- RootkitRevealer
- Irongeek Thumbscrew
- GRC Securable
- EICAR AntiVirus Test File
- Microsoft Baseline Security Analyzer (MBSA)

Chapter 4:

- KeePass Password Safe
- Keyboard Collector

Chapter 5:

- Sysinternals ShareEnum

Chapter 6:

- Directory Snoop
- Eraser
- Macrium Reflect

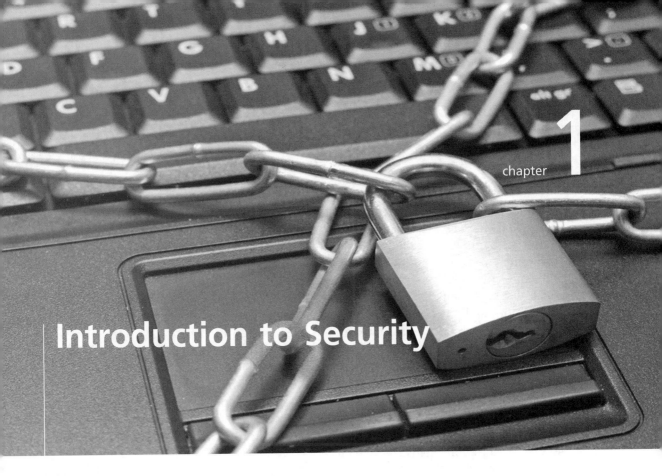

Introduction to Security

After completing this chapter you should be able to do the following:

- Describe the challenges of securing information
- Define information security and explain why it is important
- Identify the types of attackers that are common today
- List the basic steps of an attack
- Describe the steps in a defense and a comprehensive defense strategy

Security in Your World

"What are you studying now?" Susan asked Jackson. Susan and Jackson had first met at the college where they both were enrolled, and they occasionally studied together in the library. Jackson was majoring in Computer Information Systems. Susan liked to think of herself as being technically "savvy" since she owned the latest cell phone and laptop computer, so she often asked Jackson about his computer classes.

"I'm studying for my Introduction to Security test on Thursday," Jackson said. "Oh, security," Susan said. "Isn't that really overrated? I've never been attacked, and I'm on the computer all the time." "Well, if you've never been attacked then you've been very lucky," said Jackson. "Here, look at this." He moved his laptop computer that was connected to the college's wireless network so Susan could see the screen. Jackson opened a Web site that was a supplement to the security textbook he was studying and started scrolling down through some of the latest blog postings. "Apple Computers Need More Security," "Worm Attack on Unpatched Computers," "Eight Patches for Microsoft Software," "Wireless Computers Compromised," and "Personal Information Stolen" were just a few of the blog titles. "See," said Jackson, "It's not hype at all. These are real security problems that we all face—even you!"

"I have antivirus stuff on my computer so I'm safe from attacks," Susan said. Jackson smiled. "Well, that's not nearly enough to protect yourself today. There's other security software you need to have, and there are things that you shouldn't do on your computer. Remember the e-mail you received yesterday from the college that said to keep your account active you must click on the link and then enter your student ID and password?" Susan looked puzzled. "How did you know I got that e-mail?" "Susan," said Jackson, "Everybody at school got it. It was a hoax. That e-mail didn't come from the college but from an attacker who was trying to steal your password." "Oh, no! I typed in my password. Do those people have my password now?" Susan asked. "Yes, they do," warned Jackson. "You need to change it right away."

Susan closed her book in frustration. "How am I supposed to know what to do? Why is all this security stuff so hard? Can't there be just a button you click so your computer is safe?"

We live in a world where security is one of our primary concerns. Attacks of all sorts are on the rise. Suicide bombings, airplane hijackings, subway massacres, and guerrilla commando raids occur on an all-too-frequent basis. To protect their citizens from attacks, governments have implemented new types of security defenses, such as searching passengers who use public transportation and monitoring telephone calls. Individuals likewise have taken dramatic steps in order to be secure in their daily lives. The sale of home security systems increases each year, enrollment in self-defense classes is skyrocketing, and the number of firearm permits grows annually.

Just as physical terrorist attacks have escalated, so also have our computers and the information contained on them become prime targets for cyberattackers. An unprotected computer connected to the Internet is infected in a matter of minutes. Internet Web servers must resist thousands of attacks every day. Identity theft has skyrocketed.

Today, protecting our computers from attack has become critical. Although we have heard about attacks that can threaten our computers, most users are unsure about how to actually make their computers more secure. Ask yourself this question: If you were warned that a nasty Internet worm attack was to be released today, what would you do to protect your computer: Install a firewall? Use antivirus software? Download a patch? Unplug your Internet connection? Do nothing and hope for the best?

It is critical for all computer users today to be knowledgeable about computer security and to know what steps to take to defend against attacks. Applying practical security has never been more important than it is now. This chapter introduces computer security. It begins by explaining the types of computer attacks that occur today and the challenges of keeping computers safe. Next, you will learn what information security is and why it is important, and consider who is responsible for these attacks. Finally, the chapter looks at the steps in an attack and what defense strategies are needed.

Challenges of Securing Information

It might seem that computer information security should not be difficult and that there should be a single and straightforward solution to securing computers, much like putting a stronger lock on a door to deter thieves. However, there is no single simple solution to protecting computers and securing information. This can be seen through the different types of attacks that computer users face today as well as the difficulties in defending against these attacks.

Today's Security Attacks

The sheer number and variety of computer security attacks today are mind-numbing. A typical monthly security newsletter contained these types of warnings:

- A malicious program was introduced in the manufacturing process of a popular brand of digital photo frames that would infect the consumer's home computer. When a user inserted a portable storage device called a flash drive into the frame's Universal Serial Bus (USB) connector to transfer pictures to the frame for viewing, the malicious program was installed on the flash drive. When the flash drive was inserted into a computer, that computer became infected. This follows a growing trend of malicious programs being installed during the manufacturing process. In October 2007 a leading hard-disk drive maker acknowledged that a password-stealing program had infected a number of its disk drives shipped from a factory in China. In another incident, a computer virus snuck onto the hard drives of a limited number of Apple iPods during manufacture in 2006.

- An e-mail claiming to be from the United Nations (U.N.) "Nigerian Government Reimbursement Committee" is sent to unsuspecting users. The e-mail says that the user has been identified as a past recipient of the famous "Nigerian General" spam e-mail, in which the user is asked for his bank account number so a Nigerian General can temporarily hide funds from rebels. In return the user will be given ten percent of the money. However, the attackers use the bank account number to withdraw all the user's funds from the account. This current e-mail states that the recipient has been awarded the sum of $150,000 as reimbursement for their trouble and is asked to send their bank account number so the money can be deposited in their account. However, perpetrators of this new scam are the same as those behind the original scam and use the bank account numbers to steal users' funds.

- "Booby-trapped" Web pages are growing at an increasing rate. These pages infect any Web surfer's computer that simply visits the site and does not even click on anything or enter any information. Security watchers are finding over 6,000 new infected Web pages every day, or one every 14 seconds. Eighty percent of these pages belong to innocent companies and individuals who are unaware that their sites have been compromised.

- Although it is sometimes thought to be immune to attacks, Apple has shown that Mac computers too can be the victim of attackers and encourages its users to be more secure. Apple has issued an update to address 25 security flaws in its Mac OS X operating system, a decrease from a patch that fixed 45 security vulnerabilities the previous month. The most serious of the vulnerabilities could let attackers take control of unpatched systems. Apple has also recently updated two security guides for protecting OS X, one for servers (351 pages) and one for desktops (171 pages).

- Researchers at the University of Maryland attached four computers equipped with weak passwords to the Internet for 24 days to see what would happen. These computers were hit by an intrusion attempt on average once every 39 seconds or 2,244 attacks each day for a total of 270,000 attacks. Over 825 of the attacks were successful, enabling the attacker to access the computers.

The above partial list of successful attacks and weak defenses from just one monthly security newsletter is sobering. And security statistics bear witness to the continued success of attackers:

- TJX Company reported that over 45 million customer credit card and debit card numbers were stolen by attackers over an 18-month period and the cost to its organization was estimated to exceed $256 million. In addition, fraud losses to banks and other institutions that issued the stolen cards was an additional $68 million to $83 million.

- The number of security breaches that have exposed users' digital data to attackers continues to rise. Table 1-1 lists some of the major security breaches that occurred during a three-month period. According to the Privacy Rights Clearinghouse, from January 2005 through December 2008 over 246 million data records of Americans containing personal information such as address, Social Security number, and credit card numbers have been exposed due to weak security.

The Web site for the Privacy Rights Clearinghouse is located at www.privacyrights.org.

- Federal government agencies are required each year to test their systems for security vulnerabilities and develop remediation plans in the event that their computer systems are affected by major security attacks or outages. A recent report revealed that of 24 federal government agencies, the overall grade was only "C-", with eight agencies receiving a grade of "F".

Table 1-1 Selected security breaches involving personal information in a three-month period

Organization	Description of Security Breach	Number of Identities Exposed
University of North Dakota Alumni Association (Grand Forks, ND)	A laptop computer containing sensitive personal and financial information on alumni, donors, and others was stolen from a car. The information included individuals' credit card and Social Security numbers.	84,000
Medical Mutual of Ohio (Columbus, OH)	Eleven computer disks containing personal information on Ohio retirees and employees are lost because insufficient postage was placed on the envelopes containing the disks.	36,000
Baylor Health Care System Inc. (Dallas, TX)	A laptop computer containing limited health information on patients was stolen from an employee's car.	100,000
Arizona Department of Economic Security (Phoenix, AZ)	Hard drives that were stolen from a storage unit that contained names, addresses, phone numbers, and Social Security numbers for families.	40,000
Sinclair Community College (Dayton, OH)	The names and Social Security numbers of employees were left open to public view on the Internet for over one year.	1,000
University of Florida (Gainesville, FL)	Current and former dental patient information was accessed by an unauthorized attacker on a College of Dentistry computer server storing their personal information. Information stored on the server included names, addresses, birth dates, Social Security numbers, and dental procedure information for patients dating back to 1990.	330,000
Starbucks Corp. (Seattle, WA)	A laptop was stolen that contained names, addresses, and Social Security numbers of employees.	97,000
Florida Agency for Workforce Innovation (Tallahassee, FL)	Employment information and Social Security numbers were posted online while developing a new website.	259,193
Central California Appellate Program (Sacramento, CA)	A backup computer disk stored in a safe was taken by thieves who broke into a storage facility. The information on the disk contained Social Security numbers, tax identification numbers, addresses, telephone numbers, and e-mail addresses.	Unknown

NOTE

2007 was the first year that the Department of Homeland Security received a grade higher than "F".

Security attacks continue to be a major concern of all IT users, especially those responsible for protecting an organization's information.

Difficulties in Defending Against Attacks

The challenge of keeping computers secure has never been greater, not only because of the number of attacks but also because of the difficulties faced in defending against these attacks. These difficulties include:

- *Speed of attacks*. With modern tools at their disposal, attackers can quickly scan systems to find weaknesses and launch attacks with unprecedented speed. For example, a malicious program called the Slammer worm infected 75,000 computers in the first 11 minutes after it was released and the number of infections doubled every 8.5 seconds. At its peak Slammer was scanning 55 million computers per second looking for another computer to infect. Attack tools can initiate new attacks without any human initiative, thus increasing the speed at which systems are attacked.

- *Greater sophistication of attacks.* Attacks are becoming more complex, making it more difficult to detect and defend against. Attackers today use common Internet tools and protocols to send malicious data or commands to attack computers, making it difficult to distinguish an attack from legitimate traffic. Other attack tools vary their behavior so the same attack appears differently each time, further complicating detection.

- *Simplicity of attack tools.* In the past an attacker needed to have a technical knowledge of attack tools. Today, many attack tools are freely available and do not require any technical knowledge to use, as seen in Figure 1-1. Any attacker can easily obtain these tools through the Internet, and they increasingly have simple menu structures from which the attacker can simply pick the desired attack, as seen in Figure 1-2.

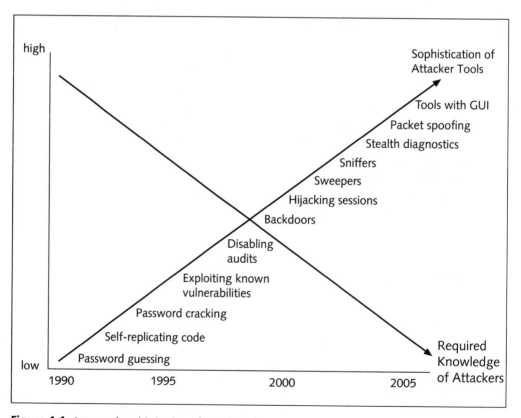

Figure 1-1 Increased sophistication of attack tools

Course Technology/Cengage Learning

Figure 1-2 Menu of attack tools

Course Technology/Cengage Learning

- *Quicker detection of vulnerabilities.* The number of system security vulnerabilities doubles each year. Today attackers are able to more quickly find these vulnerabilities before they are known to the security community. This has resulted in an increasing number of zero day attacks. While most attacks take advantage of vulnerabilities that someone has already uncovered, a **zero day attack** occurs when an attacker discovers and exploits a previously unknown flaw. Providing "zero days" of warning, a zero day attack can be especially crippling to networks and computers because the attack runs rampant while precious time is spent trying to identify the vulnerability.

- *Delays in patching products.* Software vendors are often overwhelmed trying to keep pace with updating their products against attacks from malicious attack programs (called **malware**). For example, software vendors who create defensive software to repel attacks usually look for tell-tale signs of the malware in order to block it. However, malware is being produced so rapidly that one software vendor receives over 200,000 submissions of potential malware each month. At this rate the vendors would have to update the software *every 10 minutes* in order to keep users protected. These delays in updating or "patching" products only add to the difficulties in defending against attacks.

- *Distributed attacks.* Instead of coming from one source, most attacks are now distributed and come from several different sources. Attackers can now use thousands of computers in an attack against a single computer or network. This "many against one" approach makes it impossible to stop an attack by identifying and blocking a single source.

- *User confusion.* Increasingly, users are called upon to make difficult security decisions regarding their computer systems, sometimes with little or no information to direct them. It is not uncommon for a user to be asked security questions such as *Is it okay to open this port? Is it safe to quarantine this attachment?* or *Do you want to permit your bank to install this add-in?* With little or no direction, users are inclined to answer "Yes" to these questions without understanding the implications.

Table 1-2 summarizes the reasons why it is difficult to defend against today's attacks.

Table 1-2   Difficulties in defending against attacks

Reason	Description
Speed of attacks	Attackers can launch attacks against millions of computers within minutes.
Greater sophistication of attacks	Attack tools vary their behavior so the same attack appears differently each time.
Simplicity of attack tools	Attacks no longer limited to highly skilled attackers.
Detect vulnerabilities quicker	Attackers can discover security holes in hardware or software more quickly.
Delay in patching	Vendors are overwhelmed trying to keep pace by updating their products against attacks.
Distributed attacks	Attackers use thousands of computers in an attack against a single computer or network.
User confusion	Users are required to make difficult security decisions with little or no instruction.

What Is Information Security?

Before it is possible to defend computers and their data against attacks it is necessary to understand what information security is. In addition, knowing why information security is important today and who the attackers are is beneficial.

Defining Information Security

In a general sense, security can be considered as a state of freedom from a danger or risk. For example, a nation experiences security when its military has the strength to protect its citizens from a hostile outside force. This state or condition of freedom exists because protective measures are established and maintained. However, the presence of the military does not guarantee that a nation will never be attacked; attacks from powerful outside forces might come at any time. The goal of national security is to be able to defend against these attacks and ensure that the nation will survive in the event of an attack.

The term **information security** is frequently used to describe the tasks of guarding information that is in a digital format. This digital information is typically manipulated by a microprocessor (such as on a personal computer), stored on a magnetic or optical storage device (like a hard drive or a DVD), and transmitted over a network (such as the Internet). Information security can be understood by examining its goals and how it is accomplished.

First, information security ensures that protective measures are properly implemented. Just as with national security, information security cannot completely prevent attacks or guarantee that a system is totally secure. Rather, information security creates a defense that attempts to ward off attacks and prevents the collapse of the system when an attack occurs. Thus, information security is *protection*.

Second, information security is intended to protect information that has value to people and organizations, and that value comes from the characteristics of the information. Three of the characteristics of information that must be protected by information security are:

1. *Confidentiality*—**Confidentiality** ensures that only authorized parties can view the information.

2. *Integrity*—**Integrity** ensures that the information is correct and no unauthorized person or malicious software has altered that data.

3. *Availability*—**Availability** ensures that data is accessible to authorized users.

Information security attempts to safeguard these three characteristics of information.

The confidentiality, integrity, and availability of information is known as CIA.

However, information security involves more than protecting the information itself. Because this information is stored on computer hardware, manipulated by software, and transmitted by communications, each of these areas must also be protected. The third objective of information security is to protect the integrity, confidentiality, and availability of information *on the devices that store, manipulate, and transmit the information*.

Information security is achieved through a combination of three entities. As shown in Figure 1-3 and Table 1-3, information, hardware, software, and communications are protected in three layers: products, people, and procedures. These three layers interact with each other. For example, procedures tell people how to use products to protect information. Thus, a more comprehensive definition of information security is *that which protects the integrity, confidentiality, and availability of information*.

Information Security Terminology

As with many advanced subjects, information security has its own set of terminology. The following scenario helps to illustrate information security terms and how they are used.

Suppose that Amanda wants to purchase a new stereo for her car. However, because several cars have been broken into near her apartment, she is concerned about someone stealing

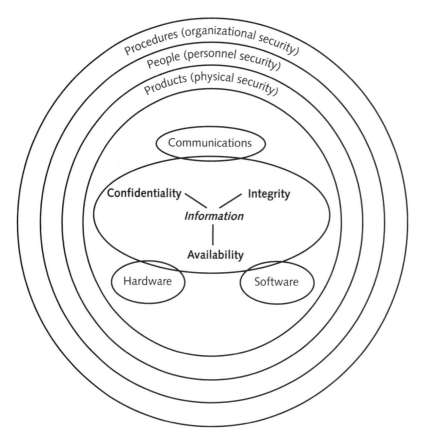

Figure 1-3 Information security components

Course Technology/Cengage Learning

Table 1-3 Information security layers

Layer	Description
Products	Form the physical security around the data. May be as basic as door locks or as complicated as special hardware or software.
People	Those who implement and properly use security products to protect data.
Procedures	Plans and policies established by an organization to ensure that people correctly use the products.

the stereo. Although she locks her car whenever she parks it, a hole in the fence surrounding her apartment complex makes it possible for someone to access the parking lot without restriction. Amanda's car and the threats to a car stereo are illustrated in Figure 1-4.

Amanda's new car stereo is an **asset**, which is defined as something that has a value. What Amanda is trying to protect her new car stereo from is a **threat**, which is an event or object that may defeat the security measures in place and result in a loss. Information security threats

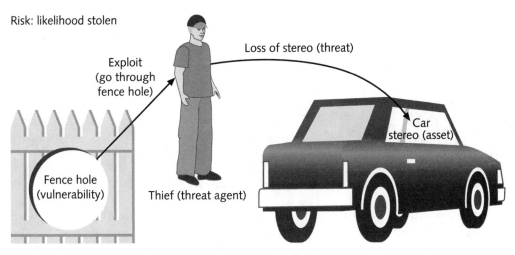

Figure 1-4 Information security components

Course Technology/Cengage Learning

are likewise events or actions that represent a danger to information. A threat by itself does not mean that security has been compromised; rather, it simply means that the potential for creating a loss is real. Although for Amanda the loss would be the theft of her stereo, in information security a loss can be the theft of information, a delay in information being transmitted, which results in a financial penalty, or the loss of good will or reputation.

A **threat agent** is a person or thing that has the power to carry out a threat. For Amanda the threat agent is a thief. In information security a threat agent could be a person attempting to break into a secure computer network. It could also be a force of nature such as a tornado or flood that could destroy computer equipment and thus destroy information, or it could be a virus that attacks a computer network.

Amanda wants to protect her new car stereo and is concerned about a hole in the fencing in her apartment's parking lot. The hole in the fencing is a **vulnerability** or weakness that allows a threat agent to bypass security. An example of a vulnerability that information security must deal with is a software defect in an operating system that allows an unauthorized user to gain access to a computer without a password.

If a thief can get to Amanda's car because of the hole in the fence, then that thief is taking advantage of the vulnerability. This is known as **exploiting** the security weakness. A hacker who knows an e-mail system does not scan attachments for a virus and sends infected e-mail messages to users is exploiting the vulnerability.

Amanda must decide if the risk of theft is too high for her to purchase the new stereo. A **risk** is the likelihood that the stereo will be stolen. In information security, a risk is the likelihood that a threat agent will exploit a vulnerability. Realistically, risk cannot ever be entirely eliminated; it would cost too much and take too long. Rather, some degree of risk must always be assumed. There are three options when dealing with risks: accept the risk, diminish the risk, or transfer the risk. In Amanda's case, she could accept the risk and buy the new stereo, knowing that the chances of it being stolen are high. Or she could diminish the risk by parking the car in a locked garage when possible and not letting anyone borrow her car keys. A third option is for Amanda to transfer the risk to someone else by purchasing additional car insurance. The insurance company then absorbs the loss and pays if the stereo is stolen. In information security most risks should be diminished if possible. Table 1-4 summarizes information security terms.

Security in Your World

"Oh, you just worry too much" said Ellen, Susan's roommate. After talking with Jackson about computer security Susan went back to her room and started looking at her computer to see if she had been attacked. "So what if one of these attackers got into your computer? What's the worst thing that can happen: Would they steal your music playlist? Really, what do you have that somebody would want?" Ellen laughed.

Susan said, "Jackson told me that there are all sorts of bad things that can happen if you're attacked." "Like what?" asked Ellen skeptically. "OK," said Susan, "Remember yesterday when you went online and bought that birthday present for your brother and used your debit card number? Jackson said that an attacker could intercept that and steal your debit card number and then use it." Ellen paused. She remembered that her aunt had her debit card number stolen and it took several months to get everything cleared up. "And what if an attacker got into your computer and just erased everything? Think of all the photos and stuff you have stored on your computer that you don't want to lose." "Well, OK," said Ellen. "What else?"

"Remember last year when the school thought your friend Mahmoud was downloading illegal stuff on the computer in his dorm room and wanted to kick him out of the dorm?" asked Susan. "It turned out it was his roommate who was doing that. Jackson said that these attackers can actually control your computer and download illegal stuff, but you might get in trouble for it because it happened on your computer." Ellen remembered how scared Mahmoud was that he was being accused of something he did not do, but had trouble convincing anyone. "And," Susan continued, "Jackson said to try this: just turn off your computer for a week and see how productive you'd be. One of these attackers could mess up your computer so you couldn't do anything on it, and it could take a week or more to get it back to normal."

Ellen sat down on the bed. "They can do all of that stuff? Wow, I had no idea." "Neither did I," said Susan. Susan started to feverishly click her mouse and look at her screen. After several minutes Ellen said, "Hey Susan, how do you know if you've been attacked?" Susan suddenly stopped and stared at Ellen. "I don't know."

Table 1-4 Security information terminology

Term	Example in Amanda's Scenario	Example in Information Security
Asset	Car stereo	Employee database
Threat	Steal stereo from car	Steal data
Threat agent	Thief	Attacker, virus, flood
Vulnerability	Hole in fence	Software defect
Exploit	Climb through hole in fence	Send virus to unprotected e-mail server
Risk	Car stereo will be stolen	Information will be stolen

Understanding the Importance of Information Security

Information security is important to businesses and individuals. The main goals of information security are to prevent data theft, thwart identify theft, avoid the legal consequences of not securing information, maintain productivity, and foil cyberterrorism.

Preventing Data Theft Security is often associated with theft prevention: Amanda installs a security system on her car in order to prevent it from being stolen. The same is true with information security: preventing data from being stolen is often cited by businesses as the primary goal of information security. Business data theft involves stealing proprietary business information such as research for a new drug or a list of customers that competitors are eager to acquire.

The theft of data is one of the largest causes of financial loss due to an attack. According to a recent FBI Computer Crime and Security Survey, the loss due to the theft of confidential data for 494 respondents exceeded $10 million. The actual figure of estimated loss could be much higher considering that some businesses might have been reluctant to report losses because of the bad publicity it could generate.

Data theft is not limited to businesses. Individuals are often victims of data thievery. A survey by the Ponemon Institute revealed that 62 percent of respondents have been notified that their confidential data has been lost or stolen. Reported losses from the fraudulent use of online credit card information continue to soar, exceeding $5 billion annually.

Thwarting Identity Theft Identity theft involves using someone's personal information, such as a Social Security number, to establish bank or credit card accounts that are then left unpaid, leaving the victim with the debts and ruining their credit rating. In some instances, thieves have bought cars and even houses by taking out loans in someone else's name.

The costs to individuals who have been victims of identity theft as a result of data breaches have been increasing. A study by Utica College's Center for Identity Management and Information Protection (CIMIP) revealed that the median actual dollar loss for identity theft victims from 2000 through 2006 was $31,356.

At the national, state, and local level, legislation that deals with this growing problem continues to be enacted. For example, the Fair and Accurate Credit Transactions Act of 2003 is a U.S. federal law that addresses identify theft. This law establishes a national system of fraud detection and alerts, and requires credit agencies to identify patterns common to identity theft to prevent its occurrence. Consumers can also receive a free copy of their credit report each year to help recognize more quickly when their identity has been stolen. However, industry experts agree that the best defense against identity theft is to prevent private data from being stolen.

Avoiding Legal Consequences In recent years a number of federal and state laws have been enacted to protect the privacy of electronic data. Businesses that fail to protect data may face serious penalties. Some of these laws include the following:

- *The Health Insurance Portability and Accountability Act of 1996 (HIPAA)*—Under the **Health Insurance Portability and Accountability Act (HIPAA)**, healthcare enterprises must guard protected health information and implement policies and procedures to safeguard it, whether it be in paper or electronic format. Those who wrongfully disclose individually identifiable health information with the intent to sell it can be fined up to $250,000 and spend 10 years in prison.

- *The Sarbanes-Oxley Act of 2002 (Sarbox)*—As a reaction to a rash of corporate fraud, the **Sarbanes-Oxley Act (Sarbox)** is an attempt to fight corporate corruption. Sarbox covers the corporate officers, auditors, and attorneys of publicly traded companies. Stringent reporting requirements and internal controls on electronic financial reporting systems are required. Corporate officers who willfully and knowingly certify a false financial report can be fined up to $5 million and serve 20 years in prison.

- *The Gramm-Leach-Bliley Act (GLBA)*—Like HIPAA, the **Gramm-Leach-Bliley Act (GLBA)** protects private data. GLBA requires banks and financial institutions to alert customers of their policies and practices in disclosing customer information. All electronic and paper containing personally identifiable financial information must be protected. The penalty for noncompliance for a class of individuals is up to $500,000.

- *USA Patriot Act (2001)*—Passed shortly after the terrorist attack of September 11, 2001, the **USA Patriot Act** is designed to broaden the surveillance of law enforcement agencies so they can detect and suppress terrorism. Businesses, organizations, and even colleges must provide information, including records and documents, to law enforcement agencies under the authority of a valid court order, subpoena, or other authorized agency. There are a variety of penalties for violating this Act.

- *The California Database Security Breach Act (2003)*—The **California Database Security Breach Act** was the first state law that covers any state agency, person, or company that does business in California. It requires businesses to inform California residents within 48 hours if a breach of personal information has or is believed to have occurred. It defines personal information as a name with a Social Security number, driver's license number, state ID card, account number, credit card number, or debit card number and required security access codes. Since this act was passed by California in 2003, 40 other states now have similar laws.

California has extended its data breach notification law to include incidents involving electronic medical and health insurance information.

- *Children's Online Privacy Protection Act of 1998 (COPPA)*—In November 1998, the U.S. Congress passed the **Children's Online Privacy Protection Act (COPPA)** and directed the Federal Trade Commission to establish rules for its implementation.

COPPA requires operators of online services or Web sites designed for children under the age of 13 to obtain parental consent prior to the collection, use, disclosure, or display of a child's personal information. COPPA also prohibits sites from limiting children's participation in an activity unless they disclose more personal information than is reasonably necessary to participate.

Although these laws pertain to the U.S., other nations are enacting their own legislation to protect electronic data.

The penalties for violating these laws can be severe. Businesses and individuals must make every effort to keep electronic data secure from hostile outside forces to ensure compliance with these laws and avoid serious legal consequences.

Maintaining Productivity Cleaning up after an attack diverts resources such as time and money away from normal activities. Employees cannot be productive and complete important tasks during an attack and its aftermath because computers and networks cannot function properly. Table 1-5 provides an estimate of the lost wages and productivity during an attack and cleanup.

Table 1-5 Cost of attacks

Number Total Employees	Average Hourly Salary	Number of Employees to Combat Attack	Hours Required to Stop Attack and Clean Up	Total Lost Salaries	Total Lost Hours of Productivity
100	$25	1	48	$4,066	81
250	$25	3	72	$17,050	300
500	$30	5	80	$28,333	483
1000	$30	10	96	$220,000	1,293

The most expensive single malicious attack was the 2000 Love Bug, which cost an estimated $8.7 billion.

Unsolicited e-mail messages are often considered to be more a nuisance than a security breach. However, because many computer attacks can be launched through e-mail messages, these messages are considered a security risk. According to the research group Postini, over two-thirds of daily e-mail messages are unsolicited and could be carrying a malicious payload. It is estimated that U.S. businesses forfeit $9 billion each year in lost productivity as employees spend time trying to restrict spam and deleting it from their e-mail accounts.

Foiling Cyberterrorism An area of growing concern among many defense experts is surprise attacks by terrorist groups using computer technology and the Internet. These attacks could cripple a nation's electronic and commercial infrastructure. Such an attack is known as **cyberterrorism**. Utility companies, telecommunications, and financial services are considered prime targets of cyberterrorists because they can significantly disrupt business and personal activities by destroying a few targets. For example, disabling an electrical power plant could cripple businesses, homes, transportation services, and communications over a wide area.

The U.S. federal government has expressed concern about the growing threat of cyberterrorism. The National Research Council referred to the growing reliance on vulnerable information systems as the "Information Security Problem." Presidential Decision Directive 63 cited the need to protect critical cyber-based systems essential to the minimum operations of the economy and government. The National Strategy to Secure Cyberspace named "A National Cyberspace Security Awareness and Training Program" as its number-three priority.

One of the challenges in combating cyberterrorism is that many prime targets are not owned and managed by the federal government. For example, almost 85 percent of the nation's most critical computer networks and infrastructures are owned by private companies. Because these networks are not centrally controlled, it is difficult to coordinate and maintain security.

Security in Your World

Susan set her drink down on the table and listened to her friends while they ate lunch in the cafeteria. The school had recently been the victim of another hoax in which students and faculty had received an e-mail asking them to enter their username and password for verification. Because so many users had submitted their passwords the school decided to prevent anyone from logging on until new security software was installed. Susan's music class was cancelled because they could not use the computers in the lab.

"Teenagers," said Ava, one of Susan's friends. "They're the ones who do these things. They've got too much free time on their hands and all they do is play games and write these programs. They ought to be locked up for it!"

"I don't know," said Li. "My younger brother's really smart about computers but I don't think he could do that. I wonder if the companies that sell security write these attack programs so that people will have to buy their stuff."

Bryan said, "I read somewhere that it's really international terrorists who are doing it. They can't attack us directly so they're now after our computers."

Just then Professor Helba walked by their table. "Who do you think does this?" Susan asked him. He smiled and said, "Teachers. They do it to cancel classes."

Who Are the Attackers?

The types of people behind computer attacks are generally divided into several categories. These include hackers, script kiddies, spies, employees, cybercriminals, and cyberterrorists.

Hackers

Although the term **hacker** is commonly used, computer experts and others debate its definition. Some use "hacker" in a generic sense to identify anyone who illegally breaks into or attempts to break into a computer system. Used in this way "hacker" is synonymous with "attacker." Others use the term more narrowly to mean a person who uses advanced computer skills to attack computers only to expose security flaws. Although breaking into another person's computer system is illegal, some hackers believe it is ethical as long as they do not commit theft, vandalism, or breach any confidentiality. These hackers (who like to call themselves "White Hats") claim that their motive is to improve security by seeking out security holes so that they can be fixed.

However, security vulnerabilities can be exposed in ways other than attacking another computer without the owner's consent, and most security professionals would not refer to themselves as hackers. The general use of the term hacker to refer to someone who attacks computers is the more widely accepted usage of this word.

Script Kiddies

Script kiddies want to break into computers to create damage. However, whereas hackers have an advanced knowledge of computers and networks, script kiddies are unskilled users. Script kiddies do their work by downloading automated hacking software (scripts) from Web sites and using it to break into computers.

While script kiddies lack the technical skills of hackers, they are sometimes considered more dangerous. Script kiddies tend to be computer users who have almost unlimited amounts of leisure time, which they can use to attack systems. Their success in using automated software scripts tends to fuel their desire to break into more computers and cause even more harm. Because script kiddies do not understand the technology behind what they are doing, they often indiscriminately target a wide range of computers, causing problems for a large audience.

Spies

A computer **spy** is a person who has been hired to break into a computer and steal information. Spies do not randomly search for unsecured computers to attack as script kiddies and hackers do. Rather, spies are hired to attack a specific computer or system that contains sensitive information. Their goal is to break into that computer or system and take the information without drawing any attention to their actions.

Employees

One of the largest information security threats to a business actually comes from an unlikely source: its employees. Why would employees break into their company's computer? Sometimes an employee might want to show the company a weakness in their security. On other occasions, disgruntled employees may be intent on retaliating against the company. Some employees may be motivated by money. A competitor might approach an employee and offer money in exchange for stealing information. In some instances, employees have even been blackmailed into stealing from their employer. In addition, carelessness by employees, who have left laptop computers in airports or who have failed to password protect sensitive data, has also resulted in information being stolen.

Cybercriminals

There is a new breed of computer attackers known as **cybercriminals**. Cybercriminals are a loose-knit network of attackers, identity thieves, and financial fraudsters. These cybercriminals are described as being more highly motivated, less risk-averse, better funded, and more tenacious than hackers.

Many security experts believe that cybercriminals belong to organized gangs of young and mostly Eastern European attackers. Reasons why this area may be responsible for the large number of cybercriminals are summarized in Table 1-6.

Table 1-6 Eastern European promotion of cybercriminals

Characteristic	Explanation
Strong technical universities	Since the demise of the Soviet Union in the early 1990s a number of large universities have left teaching communist ideology and instead turned to teaching technology.
Low incomes	With the transition from communism to a free market system, individuals in the former Soviet Union have suffered from the loss of an economy supported by the state, and incomes remain relatively low.
Unstable legal system	Several Eastern European nations continue to struggle with making and enforcing new laws. For example, Russia currently does not have any antispamming laws.
Tense political relations	Some new nations do not yet have strong ties to other foreign countries. This sometimes complicates efforts to obtain cooperation with local law enforcement.

Cybercriminals often meet in online "underground" forums that have names like *DarkMarket.org* and *theftservices.com*. The purpose of these meetings is to trade information and coordinate attacks around the world.

Instead of attacking a computer to "show off" their technology skills (like hackers), cybercriminals have a more focused goal that can be summed up in a single word: *money*. This difference makes the new attackers more dangerous and their attacks more threatening. Targeted attacks against financial networks, unauthorized access to information, and the theft of personal information is sometimes known as **cybercrime**.

Financial cybercrime is often divided into two categories. The first uses stolen credit card data, online financial account information such as PayPal accounts or Social Security numbers. Once this information has been obtained it is usually posted on a cybercrime Web site for sale to other cybercriminals. Typically this data is advertised to cybercriminals in ways that are not unlike normal ads. In one instance cybercriminals who "register today" received a "bonus" choice of "one Citibank account with online access with 3K on board" or "25 credit cards with PINs for online carding."

Cybercrime Web sites actually function like an online dating service. After selecting the cybercriminal with whom you want to do business, you click on the person's name and are then added to his or her chat room, in which bargaining for the stolen data can be conducted in private.

After the cards have been purchased from the cybercrime Web site they are used to withdraw cash from automated teller machines (ATMs) or to purchase merchandise online. This merchandise is sent to Americans whose homes serve as drop-off points. The Americans then send the goods overseas (called re-shipping) before either the credit card owner or the online merchant is aware that a stolen credit card number was used. Once the merchandise is received it is sold on the black market.

Cybercriminals looking for re-shippers actually take out advertisements in newspapers that mimic ads from online job sites. One such ad proclaimed, "We have a promotional job offer for you!!" for a "shipping-receiving position" that appeared to come from Monster.com. It states that "starting salary is $70-$80 per processed shipment. Health and life benefits after 90 days."

The second category involves sending millions of spam e-mails to peddle counterfeit drugs, pirated software, fake watches, and pornography. Federal law enforcement officials estimate that these spam operations can gross more than $30 million a year.

Cybercrime, both trafficking in stolen credit card numbers and financial information as well as spam, has reached epidemic proportions according to many security experts. The U.S. Federal Trade Commission, which says identity theft is its top complaint, created an Identity Theft Task Force in 2006.

Cyberterrorists

Many security experts fear that terrorists will turn their attacks to the network and computer infrastructure to cause panic among citizens. Known as **cyberterrorists**, their motivation may be defined as ideology, or attacking for the sake of their principles or beliefs. A report distributed by the Institute for Security Technology Studies at Dartmouth College lists three goals of a cyberattack:

- To deface electronic information (such as Web sites) and spread misinformation and propaganda
- To deny service to legitimate computer users
- To commit unauthorized intrusions into systems and networks that result in critical infrastructure outages and corruption of vital data

Cyberterrorists are sometimes considered the attackers that should be feared the most, for it is almost impossible to predict when or where an attack may occur. Unlike hackers who continuously probe systems or create attacks, cyberterrorists can be inactive for several years and then suddenly strike a network in a new way. Their targets may include a small group of computers or networks that can affect the largest number of users, such as the computers that control the electrical power grid of a state or region. An isolated attack could cause a power blackout that would affect tens of millions of people.

Attacks and Defenses

Although there are a wide variety of attacks that can be launched against a computer or network, the same basic steps are used in most attacks. Protecting computers against these steps in an attack calls for five fundamental security principles.

Steps of an Attack

There are a variety of types of attacks. One way to categorize these attacks is by the five steps that make up an attack, as seen in Figure 1-5. The steps are:

1. *Probe for information*—The first step in an attack is to probe the system for any information that can be used to attack it. This type of "reconnaissance" is essential to provide information, such as the type of hardware that is used, the version of software, and even personal information about the users, that can then be used in the next step.

2. *Penetrate any defenses*—Once a potential system has been identified and information about it has been gathered, the next step is to launch the attack to penetrate the defenses. These attacks come in a variety of forms, such as manipulating or breaking a password.

3. *Modify security settings*—Modifying the security settings is the next step after the system has been penetrated. This allows the attacker to re-enter the compromised system more easily.

4. *Circulate to other systems*—Once the network or system has been compromised, the attacker then uses it as a base to attack other networks and computers. The same tools that are used to probe for information are then directed toward other systems.

5. *Paralyze networks and devices*—If the attacker chooses, he or she may also work to maliciously damage the infected computer or network. This may include deleting or modifying files, stealing valuable data, crashing the computer, or performing denial of service attacks.

Defenses Against Attacks

Although multiple defenses may be necessary to withstand an attack, these defenses should be based on five fundamental security principles: protecting systems by layering, limiting, diversity, obscurity, and simplicity. This section examines each of these principles, which provide a foundation for building a secure system.

Layering The Hope diamond is a massive (45 carat) stone that by some estimates is worth one-quarter of a billion dollars. How are precious stones like the Hope diamond protected from theft? They are not openly displayed in public with a single security guard standing at the door. Instead, they are enclosed in protective cases that are bullet-proof, smash-proof, and resistant to almost any outside force. The cases are located in special rooms with massive walls and sensors that can detect slight movements or vibrations. The doors to the rooms are monitored around the clock by remote security cameras, and the video images from each camera are recorded on tape. The rooms are in buildings surrounded by roaming guards and fences. In short, precious stones are protected by *layers* of security. If one layer is penetrated—such as the thief getting into the building—several more layers must still be breached, and each layer is often more difficult or complicated than the previous. A layered approach has the advantage of creating a barrier of multiple defenses that can be coordinated to thwart a variety of attacks.

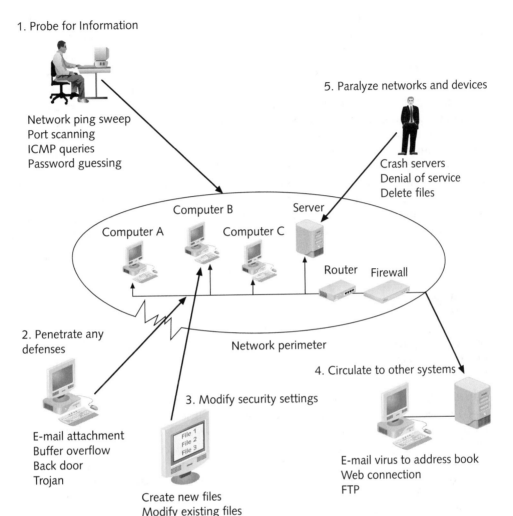

1. Probe for Information

Network ping sweep
Port scanning
ICMP queries
Password guessing

5. Paralyze networks and devices

Crash servers
Denial of service
Delete files

Computer B   Server

Computer A   Computer C

Router   Firewall

2. Penetrate any
defenses

Network perimeter

4. Circulate to other systems

E-mail attachment
Buffer overflow
Back door
Trojan

3. Modify security settings

File 1
File 2
File 3

E-mail virus to address book
Web connection
FTP

Create new files
Modify existing files
Install new services
Register trap door
Weaken existing security

Figure 1-5 Steps of an attack

Course Technology/Cengage Learning

NOTE

The Hope diamond has not always had multiple layers of security. In 1958, this priceless diamond was placed in a plain brown paper wrapper and sent by registered first-class U.S. mail to the Smithsonian Institution! The envelope in which it was sent is on display at the Smithsonian along with the diamond itself.

Information security likewise must be created in layers. One defense mechanism may be relatively easy for an attacker to circumvent. Instead, a security system must have layers, making it unlikely that an attacker has the tools and skills to break through *all* the layers of defenses. A layered approach can also be useful in resisting a variety of attacks. Layered security provides the most comprehensive protection.

Limiting Consider again protecting a precious diamond. Although a diamond may be on display for the general public to view, permitting anyone to touch the stone increases the chances that it will be stolen. Only approved personnel should be authorized to handle the diamond. Limiting who can access the diamond reduces the threat against it.

The same is true with information security. Limiting access to information reduces the threat against it. Only those who must use data should have access to it. In addition, the amount of access granted to someone should be limited to what that person needs to know. For example, access to the human resource database for an organization should be limited to only approved employees, such as a department manager. An entry-level computer technician might back up the data every day, but he should not be able to view the data, such as the salaries of the vice presidents, because he has no job-related need to do so.

What level of access should users have? The best answer is the *least amount necessary* to do their jobs, and no more.

TIP

Some ways to limit access are technology-based (such as assigning file permissions so that a user can only read but not modify a file), while others are procedural (prohibiting an employee from removing a sensitive document from the premises). The key is that access must be restricted to the bare minimum.

Diversity Diversity is closely related to layering. Just as it is important to protect data with layers of security, it is important that the layers be different (diverse) so that if attackers penetrate one layer, they cannot use the same techniques to break through all other layers. A jewel thief, for instance, might be able to foil the security camera by dressing in black clothes but should not be able to use the same technique to trick the motion detection system.

Using diverse layers of defense means that breaching one security layer does not compromise the whole system. Diversity may be achieved in several ways. For example, some organizations use security products provided by different vendors. An attacker who can circumvent a Brand A device would have more difficulty trying to break through both Brand A and Brand B devices because they are different.

Obscurity Suppose a thief plans to steal a precious diamond during a shift change of the security guards. When the thief observes the guards, however, she finds that the guards do not change shifts at the same time each night. On Monday they rotate shifts at 7:15 PM, while on Tuesday they rotate at 6:50 PM, and the following Monday at 6:25 PM. The thief cannot find out the times of these changes because they are kept secret. The thief, not knowing when a change takes place, cannot detect a clear pattern of times. Because the shift changes are confusing and not well known, an attack becomes more difficult. This technique is sometimes called "security by obscurity." Obscuring what goes on inside a system or organization and avoiding clear patterns of behavior make attacks from the outside much more difficult.

An example of obscurity would be not revealing the type of computer, operating system, software, and network connection a computer uses. An attacker who knows that information can more easily determine the weaknesses of the system to attack it. However, if this information is hidden, it takes much more effort to acquire the information and, in many instances, an attacker will then move on to another computer in which the information is easily available. Obscuring information can be an important way to protect information.

Simplicity Because attacks can come from a variety of sources and in many ways, information security is by its very nature complex. The more complex something becomes, the more difficult it is to understand. A security guard who does not understand how motion detectors interact with infrared trip lights may not know what to do when one system alarm shows an intruder but the other does not. In addition, complex systems allow many opportunities for something to go wrong. In short, complex systems can be a thief's ally.

The same is true with information security. Complex security systems can be hard to understand, troubleshoot, and feel secure about. As much as possible, a secure system should be simple for those on the inside to understand and use. Complex security schemes are often compromised to make them easier for trusted users to work with—but this can also make it easier for the attackers. In short, keeping a system simple from the inside but complex on the outside can sometimes be difficult but reaps a major benefit.

Building a Comprehensive Security Strategy

Defending against attacks through the fundamental security principles of layering, limiting, diversity, obscurity, and simplicity is a theoretical model for building a secure system. Yet how are all these principles put into practice? That is, what would a practical, comprehensive security strategy look like? There are four key elements to creating a practical security strategy: block attacks, update defenses, minimize losses, and send secure information. These elements are by no means new; these tactics go back to the days of medieval castles in Europe and probably much earlier. Understanding these key elements as they were used during the Middle Ages helps bring them in focus in developing practical security today.

Block Attacks The word *castle* comes from a Latin word meaning *fortress*, and most castles served in this capacity. One of a castle's primary functions was to protect the king's family and citizens of the countryside in the event of an attack from a hostile enemy. A castle was designed to block enemy attacks in two distinct ways. First, a castle was surrounded by a deep moat that was filled with water, which prevented the enemy from getting close to the castle. In addition, many castles had a high protective stone wall between the moat and the outer walls of the castle. The purpose of the moat and protective wall was to create a *security perimeter* around the castle: any attacker would have to get through the strong perimeter to get to the castle.

The moat along with the high protective stone wall formed layers as well as diversity of security.

Effective information security follows this same model of blocking attacks by having a strong security perimeter. Usually this security perimeter is part of the computer network to which a personal computer is attached. If attacks are blocked by the network security perimeter, the attacker will be unable to reach the personal computer on which the data is stored.

Security devices can be added to a computer network that will continually analyze traffic coming into the network from the outside (such as e-mail or Web pages) and block unauthorized or malicious traffic.

In addition to perimeter security, most castles provided *local security* as well. If an arrow shot by an attacker travels over the moat and outer wall, those inside the castle would be vulnerable to these attacks even if there was a strong security perimeter. The solution is to provide each defender with a personal shield to hold to deflect the arrows.

This analogy also applies to information security. As important as a strong network security perimeter is to blocking attacks, some attacks will slip through the defense. It is vital to also have local security on all of the personal computers as well to defend against any attack that breaches the perimeter.

A recent local security technique is for the network to automatically check the security settings of each personal computer on the network. Computers that lack the proper local security hardware or software are immediately disconnected from the network until their configurations have been corrected.

Update Defenses Imagine a castle in which each defender had been given a personal leather shield to protect against arrows shot over the wall. The defenders may be feeling that they have adequate protection against the attacker's arrows. Yet what if suddenly the arrows came over the wall with their tips on fire? If the defenders had never seen flaming arrows before, they would be at a loss regarding how to prevent their leather shields from catching on fire when struck with one of these arrows. This "new technology" of flaming arrows could prove to be disastrous if the defenders had no means to change their type of shields.

Today's information security attackers are equally if not more inventive than attackers 1,000 years ago. New types of online attacks appear on a regular basis. It is essential that users today be resourceful in continually updating defenses to protect their information. This involves updating defensive hardware and software as well as applying operating system patches on a regular basis.

Minimize Losses As a flaming arrow sails over the castle wall, it might strike a bale of hay and set it ablaze. If the defenders were not prepared with a bucket of water to douse the flames, then the entire castle could burn up. Being prepared to minimize losses was essential in defending a castle.

Likewise, in information security it is important to realize that some attacks will get through security perimeters and local defenses. It is important that action be taken in advance in order to minimize losses. This may involve keeping backup copies of important data stored in a safe place. Or, for an organization it may mean having an entire business recovery policy that details what to do in the event of a successful attack.

Send Secure Information A castle that is under siege for an extended period of time may require outside help from an ally. So how can these friendly distant forces receive the cry for help? In some instances a messenger might be sent out from the castle on horseback to break through the enemy lines to reach the supporters. To have any chance of delivering the message, the messenger would need a swift horse and layers of protective body armor.

A parallel can be drawn in today's world of information security. As users send e-mail and other information out over the Internet, it is important that it be protected and kept secure. This might involve "scrambling" the data so that unauthorized eyes cannot read it. In other instances it might require establishing a secure electronic link between the sender and receiver that would prevent an attacker from being able to reach the information. In any case, information security is more than just being on the defensive; it often involves taking proactive steps to thwart attackers.

Chapter Summary

- Attacks against information security have grown exponentially in recent years, despite the fact that billions of dollars are spent annually on security defenses. Computer systems based on Microsoft Windows and Apple Macintosh operating systems, as well as other types of operating systems, are all vulnerable to attacks.

- There are several reasons why it is difficult to defend against today's attacks. These include the speed of the attacks, greater sophistication of attacks, increased simplicity of attack tools, faster detection of vulnerabilities by attackers, delays in patching hardware and software products, distributed attacks coming from multiple sources, and user confusion.

- Information security may be defined as that which protects the integrity, confidentiality, and availability of information on the devices that store, manipulate, and transmit the information through products, people, and procedures. As with many advanced subjects, information security has its own set of terminology.

- The main goals of information security are to prevent data theft, thwart identity theft, avoid the legal consequences of not securing information, maintain productivity, and foil cyberterrorism.

- Several types of people are typically behind computer attacks. The term hacker generally refers to someone who attacks computers. Script kiddies do their work by downloading automated hacking software (scripts) from Web sites and then using it to break into computers. A computer spy is a person who has been hired to break into a computer and steal information. One of the largest information security threats to a business actually comes from its employees. A new breed of computer attackers is known as cybercriminals, who are a loose-knit network of attackers, identity thieves, and financial fraudsters. Cyberterrorists turn their attacks to the network and computer infrastructure to cause panic among citizens for the sake of their principles or beliefs.

- There are five general steps that make up an attack: probe for information, penetrate any defenses, modify security settings, circulate to other systems, and paralyze networks and devices. Although multiple defenses may be necessary to withstand the steps of an attack, these defenses should be based on five fundamental security principles: layering, limiting, diversity, obscurity, and simplicity.

- A practical, comprehensive security strategy involves four key elements. The first is to block attacks by having a strong security perimeter, both on the network and on the personal computer as well. Another strategy is to regularly update defenses to protect against the latest attacks. Also, it is important to minimize losses for any attacks that may be successful. Finally, sending secure information to prevent attackers from accessing it is another key element.

Key Terms

asset   An entity that has value.

availability   Ensures that data is accessible to authorized users.

California Database Security Breach Act   A state act that requires disclosure to California residents if a breach of personal information has or is believed to have occurred.

Children's Online Privacy Protection Act (COPPA)   A U.S. federal act that requires operators of online services or Web sites directed at children under the age of 13 to obtain parental consent prior to the collection, use, disclosure, or display of a child's personal information.

confidentiality   Ensures that only authorized parties can view the information.

cybercrime   Targeted attacks against financial networks, unauthorized access to information, and the theft of personal information.

cybercriminals   A loose-knit network of attackers, identity thieves, and financial fraudsters that are more highly motivated, less risk-averse, better funded, and more tenacious than hackers.

cyberterrorism   Attacks launched by cyberterrorists that could cripple a nation's electronic and commercial infrastructure.

cyberterrorist   An attacker motivated by ideology to attack computers or infrastructure networks.

exploit   To take advantage of a vulnerability.

Gramm-Leach-Bliley Act (GLBA)   A U.S. federal act that requires private data to be protected by banks and other financial institutions.

hacker   (1) Anyone who illegally breaks into or attempts to break into a computer system; (2) A person who uses advanced computer skills to attack computers but not with malicious intent.

Health Insurance Portability and Accountability Act (HIPAA)   A U.S. federal act that requires healthcare enterprises to guard protected health information.

identity theft   Using someone's personal information, such as a Social Security number, to establish bank or credit card accounts that are then left unpaid, leaving the victim with the debts and ruining their credit rating.

information security   The tasks of guarding information that is in a digital format. More specifically, that which protects the integrity, confidentiality, and availability of information on the devices that store, manipulate, and transmit the information through products, people, and procedures.

integrity   Ensures that the information is correct and no unauthorized person or malicious software has altered that data.

malware   Malicious software.

risk   The likelihood that a threat agent will exploit a vulnerability.

Sarbanes-Oxley Act (Sarbox)   A U.S. federal act that enforces reporting requirements and internal controls on electronic financial reporting systems.

script kiddie   An unskilled user who downloads automated attack software to attack computers.

spy   A person who has been hired to break into a computer and steal information.

threat   An event or action that may defeat the security measures in place and result in a loss.

threat agent   A person or thing that has the power to carry out a threat.

USA Patriot Act   A U.S. federal act that broadens the surveillance of law enforcement agencies to enhance the detection and suppression of terrorism.

vulnerability   A weakness that allows a threat agent to bypass security.

zero day attack   An attack that occurs when an attacker discovers and exploits a previously unknown flaw, providing "zero days" of warning.

Review Questions

1. Each of the following is a reason why it is difficult to defend against today's attackers except _____.

   a.   speed of attacks

   b.   greater sophistication of attacks

   c.   complexity of attack tools

   d.   delays in patching hardware and software products

2. A(n) _____ attack takes advantage of vulnerabilities that have not been previously revealed.

   a.   Unrecognized Attack Vector (UAV)

   b.   resource

   c.   suspense

   d.   zero day

3. Information security is defined as _____.

   a.   the tasks of guarding information in a digital format

   b.   protecting networks but not personal computers

   c.   monitoring user resources

   d.   regulating access to Internet resources

4. _____ ensures that data is accessible to authorized users.

   a.   Availability

   b.   Integrity

   c.   Confidentiality

   d.   ICA

5. Each of the following is a successive layer in which information security is achieved except _____.

   a. risk

   b. people

   c. procedures

   d. products

6. A(n) _____ is a person or thing that has the power to carry out a threat.

   a. vulnerability

   b. threat agent

   c. exploit

   d. risk factor

7. An example of a(n) _____ is the likelihood of the theft of a computer.

   a. exploit

   b. vulnerability

   c. asset

   d. risk

8. Each of the following is a goal of information security except to _____.

   a. prevent data theft

   b. decrease user productivity

   c. avoid legal consequences

   d. foil cyberterrorism

9. Using someone else's personal information, such as a Social Security number, to establish bank or credit card accounts that are then left unpaid is known as _____.

   a. accountability theft

   b. personal impersonation attacks (PIA)

   c. debit fraud

   d. identity theft

10. The _____ requires banks and financial institutions to alert customers of their policies and practices in disclosing customer information.

    a. Health Insurance Portability and Accountability Act (HIPAA)

    b. Sarbanes-Oxley Act (Sarbox)

    c. Gramm-Leach-Bliley Act (GLBA)

    d. Hospital Protection and Insurance Association Agreement (HPIAA)

11. Utility companies, telecommunications, and financial services are considered prime targets of _____ because attackers can significantly disrupt business and personal activities by destroying a few targets.

    a. cyberterrorists

    b. kiddie scripters

    c. computer spies

    d. blue hat hackers (BHH)

12. A hacker who claims to be motivated by improving security by uncovering vulnerabilities is called a(n) _____.

    a. Black hat attacker

    b. White hat attacker

    c. Cowboy attacker

    d. Resource attacker

13. Which of the following have the least amount of technical skills?

    a. hackers

    b. script kiddies

    c. spies

    d. cyberterrorists

14. _____ are described as being more highly motivated, less risk-averse, better funded, and more tenacious than average attackers.

    a. Script kiddies

    b. Cybercriminals

    c. Black hat hackers

    d. Spies

15. After an attacker probed a computer or network for information she would next _____.

    a. modify security settings

    b. penetrate any defenses

    c. paralyze networks and devices

    d. circulate to other systems

16. Purchasing security products from different vendors in the hopes that security breaches of one vendor's product would not compromise the whole system is an example of _____.

    a. obscurity

    b. layering

    c. limiting

    d. diversity

17. _____ involves creating a barrier of multiple defenses that can be coordinated to thwart a variety of attacks.
    a. Layering
    b. Limiting
    c. Diversity
    d. Obscurity

18. _____ attacks come from multiple sources instead of a single source.
    a. Distributed
    b. Isolated
    c. Script resource malware (SRM)
    d. Form resource

19. The motivation of _____ is ideology, or attacking for the sake of principles or beliefs.
    a. cybercriminals
    b. cyberterrorists
    c. spies
    d. script kiddies

20. Each of the following is a characteristic of cybercriminals except _____.
    a. low motivation
    b. less risk-averse
    c. better funded
    d. more tenacious

Hands-on Projects

HANDS-ON PROJECTS

Project 1-1: Scan for Malware Using the Microsoft Windows Malicious Software Removal Tool

Microsoft Windows updates are installed on your computer and an updated version of the Microsoft Windows Malicious Software Removal Tool is installed and runs in the background. It checks computers for infections by specific malware and helps remove any infection found. This tool can also be downloaded and run at any time. In this project you will download and run the Microsoft Windows Malicious Software Removal Tool.

1. Open your Web browser and enter the Web address **www.microsoft.com/security/malwareremove/default.mspx**.

The location of content on the Internet such as this program may change without warning. If you are no longer able to access the program through the above Web address then use a search engine like Google (www.google.com) and search for "Microsoft Windows Malicious Software Removal Tool".

2. Click **Microsoft Download Center**.

3. Click **Download**.

4. Click **Save** and save the program to the desired location on your local computer.

5. When the download completes click **Run** and follow the default installation instructions, including accepting the end user license agreement.

6. When the Microsoft Windows Malicious Software Removal Tool dialog box appears, click **Next**.

7. Select **Quick scan** if necessary.

8. Click **Next**.

9. Depending on your computer this scan may take several minutes. Analyze the results of the scan to determine if there is any malicious software found in your computer.

10. Click **View detailed results of the scan**. After reviewing the results, click **OK**.

11. If any malicious software was found on your computer run the scan again and select **Full scan**.

12. Close all windows.

Project 1-2: Inspect for Insecure Versions of Applications Using Secunia Online Software Inspector

It is critical that security updates be applied in order that computer systems remain secure. Unpatched application software programs are increasingly becoming the target of attackers. Although Microsoft has developed a process through which users of its software are notified of security updates each month, most other software vendors do not have this feature and many applications are unpatched.

One solution is to use an online software scanner that will compare all applications on your computer with a list of known patches from software vendors. The online software scanner can alert you to any applications that are not properly patched. In this project you will use Secunia's Online Software Inspector to identify any applications that need to be patched.

1. Open your Web browser and enter **secunia.com/vulnerability_scanning/online/**.

The location of content on the Internet such as this program may change without warning. If you are no longer able to access the program through the above Web address then use a search engine like Google (www.google.com) and search for "Secunia Online Software Inspector".

2. Read through the summary of the features of Software Inspector.

3. Click **Start scanner.**

4. Click **Start.**

5. Check the box **Enable thorough system inspection.** This will allow Software Inspector to search for applications that are not stored in their default locations.

6. Click **Start.**

7. Software Inspector will begin its scan. Depending on the number of applications that are on your computer, the scan may take several minutes to complete, although it will begin displaying information as it completes applications.

8. When Software Inspector has finished it will display a dialog box stating that the scan is complete. Click **OK.**

9. A list of the applications that have been scanned will be displayed, as seen in Figure 1-6. Click on the + next to the application name to display further information.

10. Click the links to access the updates to secure these applications.

11. Close all windows.

Project 1-3: Scan for Malware Using Symantec Security Scan

Several online security scanners are available to identify security issues. In this project you will use the Symantec Security Check.

1. Open your Web browser and enter the Web address **security.symantec.com** and click **Continue to Symantec Security Check.**

The location of content on the Internet such as this program may change without warning. If you are no longer able to access the program through the above Web address then use a search engine like Google (www.google.com) and search for "Symantec Security Scan".

2. Click **Start** under **Security Scan.**

3. When the End-User License Agreement appears click **I accept.**

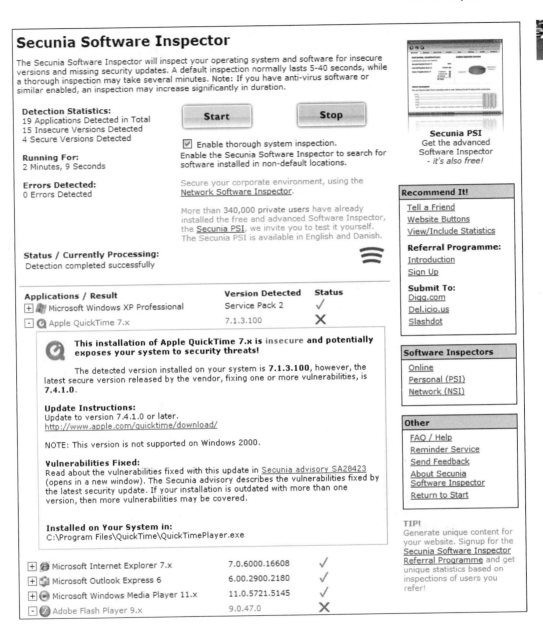

Figure 1-6 Results of Software Inspector

Course Technology/Cengage Learning

4. Click **Next**.

5. If a message appears in a yellow bar at the top of the browser regarding requiring an ActiveX control click on the bar.

6. Click **Install ActiveX Control**.

7. Click **Install**.

8. If the message "This website wants to run the following add-on: Symantec Security Check Utilities" appears in a yellow bar at the top of the browser click on the bar, click **Run ActiveX Control**, and click **Run**.

9. A message will appear that indicates the Symantec Security Scan is examining your computer.

10. When the scan completes a summary will appear indicating items that are "At Risk!", "Possible Risk!" and "Safe". Click on the **Show Details** link to view the detail of each category.

11. Do you consider this information to be useful? Would you recommend it to a friend? Why or why not?

12. Close all windows.

Project 1-4: Automatically Receive Security Information

To keep your computer secure, it is important to know the latest security threats. Instead of making constant visits to security Web sites and looking for information, this process can be automated and the information delivered to you. RSS (Really Simple Syndication) is format for automatically retrieving content from a Web page and delivering it to your browser. From within the browser, you can then quickly scan, sort, and scroll through headline and article summaries in one pane while viewing the corresponding Web page in the other pane. RSS feeds are available for financial information, news headlines, and security alerts. Today all Web browsers have built-in RSS readers. An alternative to subscribing using the Web browser is to use an online RSS aggregator, which are Web sites that allow you to subscribe to view RSS content through a Web site. In this project you will use the Google Reader aggregator.

1. Open a Web browser and enter the Web address **www.google.com/reader**.

 The location of content on the Internet may change without warning. If you are no longer able to access the site through the above Web address then use a search engine like Google (www.google.com) and search for "Google Reader".

2. If you already have a Google account, log in. If you do not have an account click on "**Create an account**" and create a Google account.

3. Open a new window in your Web browser (for example, in Internet Explorer press **Ctrl + t**).

4. Enter the URL **securityincite.com**, which is a blog about the information security business.

5. Under Get the Blog Via RSS, click the **Google** icon.

6. Click **Add to Google Reader**.

7. You are now subscribed to this RSS feed.

8. Click **Sign out** and exit Google.

9. Log back in to Google. You will see your security blog RSS feeds that you can read.

10. Log out of Google.

11. Close all windows.

Project 1-5: Use Google Reconnaissance

Just as Google can be used to locate almost anything stored on Web servers, it can also be used by attackers in order to uncover unprotected information or information that can be used in an attack. This is sometimes called "Google reconnaissance." In this project you will perform Google reconnaissance.

The purpose of this project is to provide examples of the type of information that attackers can gather using search engines. Any information that is gained through these searches should never be used in an unethical fashion to attack systems or expose data.

1. Open your Web browser and enter the URL **www.google.com**.

2. Click **Advanced Search** to display the Advanced Search screen, as seen in Figure 1-7.

3. First you will search for any Microsoft Excel spreadsheet that contains the words *login:* and *password=*. Under Find web pages that have ... in the text box "all these words:" enter **"login:*"** **"password=*"**.

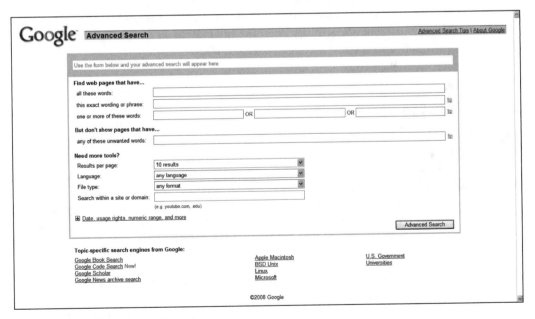

Figure 1-7 Google Advanced Search screen

Course Technology/Cengage Learning

The asterisk (*) stands for a "wildcard," which means that a document that contains login:ryan.roberts, login:jhunt, or login:Glenda_hughes will all be found.

4. In the File type: line click the down arrow and select **Microsoft Excel (.xls)**.

5. Click **Advanced Search**. The pages of results will be displayed. Open selected documents and view their contents. Note that some of the results are only blank spreadsheets that had headings "Login:" and "Password=". However, other documents actually contain user login names and passwords. Return back to the Google Advanced Search page.

6. This time you will look for a text file that contains a list of passwords in cleartext. Under File type: change it back to **any format**. In the "all these words:" textbox, enter **"index.of passlist"**.

7. Click **Advanced Search**. The pages of results will be displayed. Open selected documents and view their contents. Are you surprised how easy it is to find passwords listed on the Internet? Return to the Google Advanced Search page.

8. Google and other search engines are aware of these attempts by attackers to use their search engines for malicious means. Because of that, the search engines now will filter and deny requests for specific types of searches. For example, one type of search that attackers used was to look for a range of credit card numbers that might be available. In the "all these words:" textbox, enter **visa 4356000000000000..4356999999999999** and then click **Advanced Search**. Note how Google denies this request.

9. Close your Web browser.

Case Projects

Case Project 1-1: The Current State of Security

What are the most recent attacks on computer security that you face this month? The security vendor SANS publishes a monthly newsletter *Ouch* that lists the risks that users face at **www.sans.org/newsletters/ouch/**. Download and read the current month and the previous month's newsletters and read through them. What are the new attacks this month? How dangerous are these new attacks? What new defenses are being proposed? Write a one-page paper on your research.

Case Project 1-2: Security MP3 Podcasts

A number of security vendors and security researchers now post weekly MP3 podcasts on security topics. Using a search engine like Google, locate three different MP3 podcasts about computer security. Download them to your MP3 player or computer and listen to them. Then, write a summary of what was discussed and a critique of the podcasts. Were they beneficial to you? Would you recommend them to someone else? Write a one-page paper on your research.

Case Project 1-3: State Computer Security Acts

The California Database Security Breach Act was the first state information security law that covers any state agency, person, or company that does business in California. It requires businesses to inform California residents within 48 hours if a breach of personal information has or is believed to have occurred. Since its passage in 2003, 40 states have passed similar laws. How do these state laws compare? Use the Internet to locate a copy of your state's security act (or, if your state has not yet passed such an act then select another state) and compare it to the original California act (or, if you live in California select another state's act). What are its strengths? What are its weaknesses? How many times has it been invoked in the last 12 months because of a security breach? Would you have any recommendations to modify it? Write a one-page paper on your research.

Case Project 1-4: Information Security Terminology in Your World

The scenario of Amanda purchasing a new stereo for her car was used in this chapter to introduce the six key terms used in information security: asset, threat, threat agent, vulnerability, exploit, and risk. Create your own one paragraph scenario using a situation with which you are familiar. Also, create a table similar to Table 1-4 that lists these terms and how they are used in your scenario.

Case Project 1-5: Attack Experiences

Based on your own personal experiences or those of someone you know (you may have to interview other students or a friend), write a paragraph regarding a computer attack that occurred. When did it happen? What was the attack? What type of damage did it inflict? How was the computer "fixed" after the attack? What could have prevented it?

Case Project 1-6: Helping Others with Security

As Jackson explained to Susan about security in the Security in Your World boxes in this chapter, what could he have done to help her with her concerns? Make a list of the different options that Jackson could have presented to Susan that would have given her more information about security. Are there short classes at a local college in your area that cover security from a user's perspective? Do computer stores have workshops on making computers more secure? Are there any magazines that explore home security that are easy to read and understand? What about Web sites that contain important information? Create a list of several different options for the area in which you live or go to school.

Case Project 1-7: Winstead Computer Consultants

Winstead Computer Consultants (WCC) is a local information technology company that specializes in security. WCC often hires outside experts to assist them with projects. A company that rents caps and gowns for graduates to wear at commencement exercises, Independent Attire, was the victim of a security attack that caused their computers and network to be unavailable for several days. Independent Attire has contacted WCC for help.

WCC has contracted with you to create a presentation about computer security. The presentation should cover what computer security is, why it is important, and the basic steps in an attack and defense. Create a PowerPoint presentation of at least eight slides that covers this information. Because the audience does not have a strong technical background, your presentation should be general in its tone.

chapter 2

Desktop Security

After completing this chapter you should be able to do the following:

- Describe the different types of software and hardware attacks
- List types of desktop defenses
- Explain how to recover from an attack

Security in Your World

"Something funny happened at work today," Alexis said to his roommate, Gerald. Alexis works at the home center store in the department that sells doors and windows. "A man came in and said that he wanted to buy the best deadbolt lock to install on the front door of his new house. I showed to him a model that will stop a tank, but it's really expensive. He grabbed it right up, said 'Thanks,' and put it in his shopping cart."

Alexis continued. "I then noticed in his cart that he had a new garage door opener but it was one of those cheap models. I asked him if he was going to install that too, and he said yes. I pointed out to him that a thief could easily duplicate the access code on that model of opener and open the door in just a few seconds. His eyes got real big! I then showed him another garage door model that has over 3 billion codes so it's almost impossible to duplicate a code. It's funny that he was going to spend all that money on an expensive deadbolt door lock but leave the garage door unprotected!"

Gerald closed his book. "I know just what you mean. In fact, we were talking about that in our computer class today." Alexis laughed and said, "You were talking about garage door openers in a computer class?" Gerald smiled and said, "Well, not exactly. We were talking about computer security and about how people wrongly think that their computer is fully protected when they only have one kind of defensive software installed. The instructor said that it's like having a front door made out of armor but all the windows are wide open."

Alexis sat down at his computer. "You mean there's more than one kind of software that I need to protect my computer? I have antivirus software installed. Isn't that enough?" Gerald walked over to Alexis's computer. "No, it's not. Antivirus software only stops one kind of bad stuff from infecting your computer. There are a whole lot of other things that you have to defend against, too."

Alexis looked up from his computer. "What kind of other things?"

Protecting your desktop computer has become a serious challenge, even for the most advanced computer users. This is because many different types of attacks can be launched against a personal computer, and each type of attack might have thousands of different variations. Because attackers create and modify their attacks regularly, users must be constantly vigilant to protect their desktop computers.

Another challenge in protecting a desktop computer is that no one single type of software can protect a computer from all the different types of attacks. Different types of "defensive" software must be properly installed and regularly updated—sometimes even daily—in order to keep a computer secure. The challenge of knowing what to install, how to install it, and how to keep it regularly updated often baffles computer users and leaves the door wide open for attackers.

In this chapter, we will examine desktop computer security. We will start by looking at the types of desktop computer attacks that occur today. Next, we will discuss what defenses must be in place to keep desktop information secure. Because it's not possible to guarantee that defenses will be successful, we will conclude by looking at how to recover from an attack.

Attacks on Desktop Computers

Although there are a variety of attacks that target desktop computers, most of the attacks fall into two categories. These categories are malicious software attacks and attacks on hardware.

Desktop computers refer to all types of personal computers, including computers that sit on a user's desk, portable laptop computers, and lightweight netbook computers. Attacks and defenses for powerful file server computers that support multiple users across computer networks may be different.

Malicious Software Attacks

Malware is a general term that refers to a wide variety of damaging or annoying attack software that enters a computer system without the owner's knowledge or consent. One way to classify malware is by its primary objective. Two of the primary objectives of malware are to infect a computer system with destructive software or to conceal a malicious action.

Infecting Malware The two types of malware that have the primary objective of infecting a computer system are viruses and worms. These are also some of the earliest types of malware to impact personal computer systems.

Viruses A computer **virus** is a malicious program that, like its biological counterpart, needs a "carrier" in order to survive. Computer viruses actually require two carriers. The first carrier is a document or program. A virus secretly attaches itself to one of these legitimate carriers and then executes its malicious payload when that document is opened or program is launched. Although a virus might do something as simple as display an annoying message, such as that seen in Figure 2-1, most viruses are much more harmful. Viruses have performed the following functions:

- Caused a computer to crash repeatedly
- Erased files from a hard drive
- Installed hidden programs, such as stolen software, which is then secretly distributed from the computer
- Made multiple copies of itself and consumed all of the free space in a hard drive
- Reduced security settings and allowed intruders to remotely access the computer
- Reformatted the hard disk drive

It is estimated that there are over eight million computer viruses in existence.

The second carrier that a virus needs is a user. Most viruses cannot spread to other computers by themselves; instead, viruses rely on the actions of users to spread the virus to another

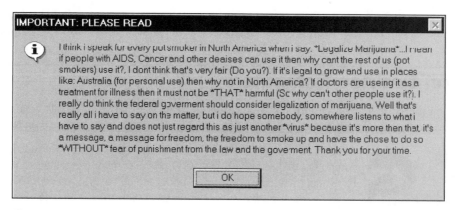

Figure 2-1 Annoying virus message

Course Technology/Cengage Learning

computer. For example, a user may send an infected file as an e-mail attachment, or give a USB flash drive with the infected file to another user, or download an infected file from the Internet, and once the virus reaches that computer it begins to infect it. The virus then spreads to other computers and files whenever the infected files are exchanged. There are several types of computer viruses. These include:

- A **file infector virus** typically infects program executable files (files with a Windows .EXE or .COM file extension). When the program is launched the virus is activated.

 A file infector virus can actually infect about 70 different types of files on a Microsoft Windows computer.

- A **resident virus** is loaded into random access memory (RAM) each time the computer is turned on and stays there. A resident virus can interrupt almost any function executed by the computer operating system and alter it for its own malicious purposes. For example, a resident virus may corrupt a document or program that is opened, copied, or renamed through RAM.

- A **boot virus** infects the **Master Boot Record** (MBR) of a hard disk drive. The MBR contains the program necessary for the computer to start up and a description of how the hard drive is organized (the **partition table**). Instead of damaging individual files, a boot virus is intended to harm the hard disk drive itself.

- A **companion virus** adds a program to the operating system that is a malicious copycat version to a legitimate program. For example, a companion virus might add the malicious program NOTEPAD.COM as a companion to the authentic Microsoft program NOTEPAD.EXE. If the user were to attempt to launch the program from the command prompt by typing "NOTEPAD" (without the three character file extension), Windows would execute the malicious NOTEPAD.COM instead of the authentic NOTEPAD.EXE because of how Windows handles programs.

Because Windows programs are most commonly run by clicking an icon instead of typing the name of the program, companion viruses are not as common as they once were.

- A **macro virus** is written in a script known as a macro. A **macro** is a series of commands and instructions that can be grouped together as a single command. Macros often are used to automate a complex set of tasks or a repeated series of tasks. Macros can be written by using a macro language, such as Visual Basic for Applications (VBA), and are stored within the user document (such as in an Excel .XLSX worksheet). A macro virus takes advantage of the "trust" relationship between the application (Excel) and the operating system (Microsoft Windows). Once the user document is opened, the macro virus instructions execute and infect the computer.

Be cautious about opening any e-mail attachment because doing so could launch a macro virus. If you are not expecting a document with an attachment or you do not know the sender it is best not to open the attachment without first contacting the sender.

In order to avoid detection, some viruses can alter how they appear. These are known as **metamorphic viruses**. A **polymorphic virus** not only changes how it appears but it also encrypts its contents differently each time, making it even more difficult to detect.

Worms The second type of infecting malware is a worm. A **worm** is a program designed to take advantage of a vulnerability in an application or an operating system in order to enter a system. Once the worm has exploited the vulnerability on one system, it deposits its payload and immediately searches for another computer that has the same vulnerability.

A worm uses a network to send copies of itself to other devices connected to the network.

Although often confused with viruses, worms are different. A virus must attach itself to a program or document and is spread by traveling with the carrier. A worm, however, can travel by itself. A second difference is that a virus needs the user to perform an action such as starting a program or opening an e-mail attachment to start the infection, while a worm does not require any user action to begin its execution.

Some early worms were benign and designed simply to spread quickly and not corrupt the systems they infected. These worms slowed down the network through which they were transmitted by replicating so quickly that they consumed all network resources. Today worms can leave behind a payload on the systems they infect and cause harm. Actions that worms have performed include deleting files on the computer or allowing the computer to be remote-controlled by an attacker.

One of the first wide-scale worm attacks occurred in 1988. This worm exploited a misconfiguration in a program that allowed commands e-mailed to a remote system to be executed on that system and it also carried a payload that contained a program that attempted to determine user passwords. Almost 6,000 computers, or 10 percent of the devices connected to the Internet at that time, were affected. The worm was attributed to Robert T. Morris, Jr., who was later convicted of federal crimes in connection with this incident.

Concealing Malware Several types of malware have the primary objective of hiding their presence from the user, as opposed to infecting and damaging the system like a virus or worm. Concealing malware includes Trojan horses, rootkits, logic bombs, and zombies and botnets.

Trojan Horses According to ancient legend, the Greeks won the Trojan War by hiding soldiers in a large hollow wooden horse that was presented as a gift to the city of Troy. Once the horse was wheeled into the fortified city, the soldiers crept out of the horse during the night and attacked the unsuspecting defenders. A computer **Trojan horse** (or just **Trojan**) is a program advertised as performing one activity but actually does something else (or it may perform both the advertised and malicious activities). For example, a user may download what is advertised as a free calendar program, yet when it is launched, in addition to installing a calendar it scans the system for credit card numbers and passwords, connects through the network to a remote system, and then transmits that information. Trojan horse programs are typically executable programs that contain hidden code that attacks the computer system.

Unlike a virus that infects a system without the user's knowledge or consent, a Trojan horse program may be installed on the computer system with the user's full knowledge. The Trojan horse just conceals its malicious payload.

One technique used by Trojan horses is to make the program appear as though it is not even an executable program but only contains data or information. For example, the file FREE-COUPONS.DOCX.EXE at first glance may appear to be only a non-executable Microsoft Word document (because it appears as if its file extension is .DOCX), yet is an executable program (because its actual file extension is .EXE) that steals the user's password. Because Microsoft Windows by default does not show common file extensions, the program will only appear as FREE-COUPONS.DOCX.

It is recommended that all file extensions should be displayed. To set this option in Microsoft Windows, open Windows Explorer, click Tools and then Folder Options, and then the View tab. Uncheck the option "Hide extensions for known file types."

Rootkits A rootkit is a set of software tools used by an intruder to break into a computer, obtain special privileges to perform unauthorized functions, and then hide all traces of its existence. In almost all cases, the rootkit's goal is not to damage a computer directly like a virus does; instead, its function is to hide the presence of other types of malicious software, such as Trojan horses, viruses, or worms. Rootkits even go to great lengths to ensure that they are not detected and removed. For example, every time a computer runs one of the rootkit's commands, the rootkit also checks to see that other system commands on that computer are still compromised and reinfects them if necessary.

A rootkit generally limits itself to the computer on which it is installed and does not by itself seek to spread to other computers.

Rootkits function by replacing operating system commands with modified versions that are specifically designed to ignore malicious activity so it can escape detection. For example, on a computer the antivirus software may be instructed to scan all files in a specific directory, and in order to do this the antivirus software will receive from the operating system a list of those files. A rootkit will replace the operating system's ability to retrieve a list of files with its own modified version that ignores specific malicious files. The antivirus software assumes that the computer will willingly carry out those instructions and retrieve all files; it does not know that the computer is displaying only files that the rootkit has approved. The operating system does not know that it is being compromised and is carrying out what it thinks are valid commands. The fundamental problem with a rootkit is that *users can no longer trust their computer*. A rootkit may actually be in charge and hide information.

Detecting a rootkit can be difficult. Although there are programs available that can check for a rootkit, these programs might not always detect its presence, because the rootkit could hide itself from these detection programs as well. Removing a rootkit from an infected computer is also difficult. This is because the rootkit itself must be erased and the portions of the operating system programs and files that were altered must be replaced with the original files. It is unlikely that the corrupted operating system programs can be removed without causing the computer to become unstable. Ultimately, the only safe and foolproof way to handle a rootkit infection is to reformat the hard drive and reinstall the operating system and programs.

One way to detect a rootkit is to reboot the computer not from the hard drive but from clean alternative media, such as a rescue CD-ROM or a dedicated USB flash drive, and then run a rootkit detection program. This may work because a rootkit that is not running cannot hide its presence.

Logic Bombs   A **logic bomb** is a computer program or a part of a program that lies dormant until it is triggered by a specific logical event, such as a certain date reached on the system calendar or a person's rank in an organization dropped below a previous level. Once triggered, the program can perform any number of malicious activities. For example, a logic bomb might be planted in a company's payroll system by an employee. The program could be designed so that if the employee's name was removed from the payroll (meaning he quit or was fired), after three months the logic bomb would corrupt the entire computerized accounting system.

Logic bombs have often been used to ensure payment for software. If a payment is not made by the due date, the logic bomb activates and prevents the software from being used again. In some instances, the logic bomb even erased the software and the accompanying files from the computer.

Some of the most famous logic bombs are listed in Table 2-1.

Table 2-1 Famous logic bombs

Description	Reason for Attack	Results
A logic bomb was planted in a financial services computer network that caused 1,000 computers to delete critical data.	A disgruntled employee had counted on this causing the company's stock price to drop and he would earn money when the stock dropped.	The logic bomb detonated yet the employee was caught and sentenced to 8 years in prison and ordered to pay $3.1 million in restitution.
A logic bomb at a defense contractor was designed to delete important rocket project data.	The employee's plan was to be hired as a highly paid consultant to fix the problem.	The logic bomb was discovered and disabled before it triggered. The employee was charged with computer tampering and attempted fraud and was fined $5,000.
A logic bomb at a health services firm was set to go off on the employee's birthday.	None was given.	The employee was sentenced to 30 months in a federal prison and paid $81,200 in restitution to the company.

Logic bombs are extremely difficult to detect before they are triggered. This is because logic bombs are often embedded in large computer programs, some containing tens of thousands of lines of code. An attacker can easily insert three or four lines of computer code into a long program without anyone detecting the insertion.

Zombies and Botnets One of the more common types of malware today that is carried by Trojan horses, worms, and viruses is a program that will allow the infected computer to be placed under the remote control of an attacker. This infected "robot" computer is known as a **zombie**. When hundreds, thousands, or even tens of thousands of zombie computers are manipulated under remote control, this creates a **botnet** (the attacker controlling the botnet is called a **bot herder**).

Attackers use **Internet Relay Chat (IRC)** to remotely control the zombies. IRC is an open communication protocol that is used for real-time "chatting" with other IRC users over the Internet. It is mainly designed for group or one-to-many communication in discussion forums called **channels**. Users access IRC networks by connecting a local IRC client to a remote IRC server, and multiple IRC servers can connect to other IRC servers to create large IRC networks.

Often an attacker will hide an IRC server installation on an educational or corporate site, where high-speed connections can support a large number of other bots.

Once a computer is infected it is joined to a specific IRC channel on an IRC server and awaits instructions, allowing an attacker to remotely control the zombie. Once under the control of a bot herder, botnets can be used for many different malicious purposes, which are summarized in Table 2-2.

The number of zombies and botnets is staggering. One botnet controlled by a European bot herder contained 1.5 million zombies, and botnets of 10,000 zombies are not uncommon. Some security experts estimate that up to 25 percent of all computers on the Internet, or over 125 million computers, are zombies.

Table 2-2 Uses of botnets

Type of Attack	Description
Spreading malware	Botnets can be used to spread malware and create new zombies and botnets. Zombies have the ability to download and execute a file sent by the attacker.
Attacking IRC networks	Botnets are often used for attacks against IRC networks. The bot herder orders each botnet to connect a large number of zombies to the victim IRC network, which is flooded by service requests and then cannot function.
Manipulating online polls	Because each zombie has a unique address, each "vote" by a zombie will have the same credibility as a vote cast by a real person. Online games can be manipulated in a similar way.
Denying services	Botnets can flood a Web server with thousands of requests and overwhelm it to the point that it cannot respond to legitimate requests.

Hardware Attacks

Just as attacks can be directed at software operating systems and applications through malware, attacks can also be directed to hardware. Hardware that often is the target of attacks includes the BIOS, USB devices, cell phones, and the physical theft of laptop computers and information.

BIOS All personal computers have a chip that contains the **Basic Input/Output System (BIOS)**. The BIOS is a coded program embedded on the processor chip that recognizes and controls different devices on the computer system. The BIOS program is executed when the computer system is first turned on and provides low-level access to the hard disk, video, and keyboard.

On older computer systems the BIOS was a **Read Only Memory (ROM)** chip and could not be reprogrammed. Today's computer systems have a **PROM (Programmable Read Only Memory)** chip in which the contents can be rewritten to provide new functionality. The process for rewriting the contents, known as **flashing** the BIOS, in the past required creating either a bootable floppy disk or CD-ROM that contains a small operating system, a flash loader program, and the new BIOS upgrade. Today many manufacturers offer software to flash the BIOS that functions from within the Windows environment, just like running a regular program.

Because it can be flashed, the BIOS has been the object of attacks. One virus overwrites the contents the BIOS and the first part of the hard disk drive, rendering the computer completely dead. Because the computer cannot boot without the BIOS, the BIOS chip has to be replaced. Another attack does not cripple the BIOS but instead uses it to store malicious code. Research has shown that an attacker could infect a computer with a virus and then flash the BIOS to install a rootkit on the BIOS. Because it is stored on the BIOS and not the hard drive, the rootkit could survive a complete hard drive reinstallation or even a change in the operating system.

TIP

To prevent an attacker from flashing the BIOS, it is recommended that the BIOS be set to not allow flashing. Disabling BIOS flashing can be done through the BIOS setting usually named *Write Protect BIOS*.

USB Devices *USB devices* is a generic term for a wide variety of external devices that can be attached through the USB (universal serial bus) connector and are typically small, lightweight, removable, and contain rewritable storage. USB flash drives have replaced floppy disks as a storage and transport medium because they are smaller, faster, can hold more data, and have no moving parts. Two of the most common types of USB **removable storage** devices, or devices that can store data from a computer and then be disconnected, are USB flash memory and MP3 players.

Despite their many advantages, USB devices can also introduce serious security risks. First, USB devices are primary targets of attacks to spread malware. A user may bring an infected document into an organization on a USB device from home or a public computer and spread malware to other users. Also, USB devices allow spies or disgruntled employees to copy and steal sensitive corporate data. In addition, data stored on USB devices can be lost or fall into the wrong hands. Because most USB devices have no security features, a user who misplaces her device may find that its important data is forever lost.

Attackers in London installed a malware Trojan horse on USB flash drives and then left the devices scattered in a parking garage. Unsuspecting users who found the infected drives inserted them into their own computers, which were immediately infected with malware that stole the users' login credentials.

To reduce the risk introduced by USB devices, some organizations have a written policy that prohibits such a device from being connected to any computer belonging to the organization. Another approach is to restrict their use through technology. These techniques include:

- *Disable the USB in hardware*—It is possible to disable through the BIOS the ability of the computer to recognize a USB device.

- *Disable the USB through the operating system*—Files can be removed in the operating system that will prevent the USB device from being recognized.

- *Use third-party software*—There are several software solutions that can control USB device permissions.

Cell Phones   Cellular telephones (**cell phones**) are portable communication devices that are rapidly replacing wired telephones. Almost all cell phones today have the ability to send and receive text messages and connect to the Internet. Attackers try to take advantage of these services in order to launch the following attacks:

- *Lure users to malicious Web sites*—Attackers can send text messages to cell phones that appear to be from a legitimate entity and convince the user to visit a malicious site by claiming that there is a problem with an account. Once that site is accessed, the user may be lured into providing personal information or downloading a malicious file.

- *Infect a cell phone*—An attacker can infect a cell phone with malicious software that will damage the phone or allow the attacker to use the cellular service.

- *Launch attacks on other cell phones*—Attackers who can gain control of a cell phone can use it to attack other phones.

- *Access account information*—Cell phones are increasingly being used to perform transactions such as paying for parking or conducting larger financial transactions. An attacker who can gain access to a phone that is used for these types of transactions may be able to discover and use account information.

- *Abuse the cell phone service*—Some cell phone plans charge for the number of text messages that can be sent and received. An attacker can send spam cell phone text messages resulting in the user being charged additional fees.

Physical Theft Whereas attackers can attempt to break into a computer to steal data, sometimes it is easier to just steal the computer itself. Portable laptop computers are particularly vulnerable to theft. By one estimate 12,000 laptops are lost or stolen just in airports each week, or one every 50 seconds.

Often attackers do not even need to look for an unclaimed laptop or break into a home to steal a computer. Because of the difficulty in disposing of older computers, many organizations and individuals recycle older computers by giving them to schools, charities, or selling them online. However, information that should have been deleted from hard drives often is still available on recycled computers. This is because with many operating systems, such as Microsoft Windows, simply deleting a file (and even emptying the Recycle Bin folder) does not necessarily make the information irretrievable. For example, when a word processing document is created, Windows enters information into a table including the name of the file and its location on the hard drive. When that file is deleted, only the name is removed from the table; as more files are saved, the disk space that was used by the first file can be reclaimed and used for other files. Thus deleting a file means that the filename is removed from the table but the information itself remains on the hard drive until it is overwritten by new files. This means that data can be retrieved from a hard drive by an attacker even after its file has been deleted.

Two users purchased 158 recycled computers or hard drives at second-hand computer stores and through online auctions. Of the 129 drives that functioned, 69 contained recoverable files and 49 contained "significant personal information," such as medical correspondence, love letters, and 5,000 credit card numbers. One computer contained an entire year's worth of transactions with account numbers from a cash machine.

Security in Your World

Alexis was so involved with his computer that he did not realize that Gerald had walked into the room. "Alexis, let's go grab some lunch," said Gerald. Alexis looked up and said. "I'm glad that you're back," he said. "After all that stuff you told me about viruses and worms and everything else, I'm worried that I need to try to block them from getting in my computer. I found something on the Internet that said it would guarantee that I would never be attacked but it costs $300 plus an annual renewal fee of $75. Is that what I should buy?"

"Well," said Gerald, "I would be a little skeptical about something that guarantees you'll never be attacked. And $300 sounds a little pricey to me. I think that you can protect your computer for a whole lot less than that. Your computer comes with many security features—all you have to do is to turn them on. Would you like me to show you how?"

Alexis stood up. "If you'll do that, I'll buy your lunch!"

Desktop Defenses

There are several different defenses that should be used to ward off attackers. These defenses include managing patches, installing antivirus software, using buffer overflow protection, protecting against theft, and creating data backups.

Managing Patches

To address the vulnerabilities in operating systems and application programs that are uncovered after the software has been released, software vendors usually deploy a program that is designed to "patch" the vulnerability. A security **patch** is a general software security update intended to cover vulnerabilities that have been discovered after the program was released.

Modern operating systems, such as Apple Mac OS and Microsoft Windows, have the ability to perform automatic patch updates to their software. The desktop system interacts with the vendor's online update service and can automatically download and install patches or alert the user to their presence, depending upon the configuration option that is chosen. The automatic update configuration options for most operating systems are similar to those for Windows, as seen in Figure 2-2. These options include:

- *Install updates automatically*—This option checks the Microsoft Web site every day at a user-designated time and, if there are any patches, automatically downloads and installs them.

- *Download updates but let me choose whether to install them*—The Download option automatically downloads the patches but does not install them, allowing the user to review and choose which patches to install.

- *Check for updates but let me choose whether to download and install them*—This option alerts the user that patches are available but does not download or install them. The user must go to the Microsoft Web site to review and install the patches.

- *Never check for updates*—This option disables automatic updates.

Microsoft releases its patches on the second Tuesday of each month, called "Patch Tuesday," unless the patch addresses a particularly serious vulnerability, and it is then released immediately.

Although operating systems have an integrated ability to perform automatic updates, applications such as word processors or graphics programs usually lack this capability, yet may have vulnerabilities that need to be patched. Recently operating system vendors have enhanced their automatic update capabilities to include updates from other vendors.

Antivirus Software

One of the oldest software security applications is **antivirus (AV)** software. This software can scan a computer's hard drive for infections as well as monitor computer activity and examine all new documents, such as e-mail attachments, that might contain a virus. If a virus is detected, options generally include cleaning the file of the virus, quarantining the infected file, or deleting the file. Figure 2-3 shows some of the settings of an AV program.

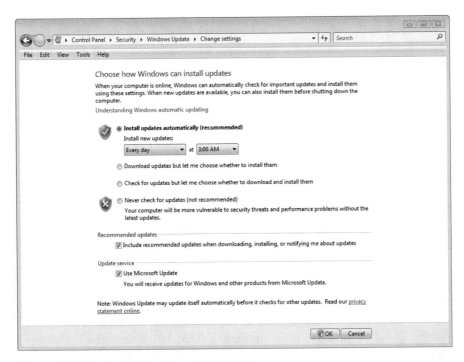

Figure 2-2 Windows automatic update options

Course Technology/Cengage Learning

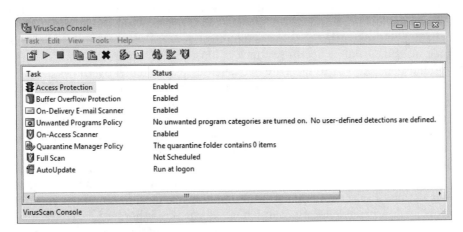

Figure 2-3 AV program settings

Course Technology/Cengage Learning

The drawback of AV software is that it must be continuously updated to recognize new viruses. Most AV software identifies malware on a computer by matching it to a known pattern or "signature" of the malware. Thus AV software on a computer must have its **signature files** regularly updated by downloads from the Internet.

The flood of potential malware each month has increased to the point that the traditional signature-based method of detecting viruses and other malware may be reaching the breaking point. One antivirus software vendor receives over 200,000 submissions of potential malware each month. At this rate the antivirus vendor would have to update and distribute its signature files every 10 minutes to keep users fully protected.

Antivirus software should be configured to constantly monitor for viruses and automatically check for updated signature files. In addition, the entire hard drive should be scanned for viruses on a regular basis.

Not all AV software is the same. Free AV software that is available for download through the Internet may only look for viruses in standard files. Most commercial AV software will also look for Trojans, worms, and macro viruses in standard files as well as in compressed (.ZIP) files.

Buffer Overflow Protection

A **buffer overflow** occurs when a computer process attempts to store data in RAM beyond the boundaries of a fixed-length storage buffer. This extra data overflows into the adjacent memory locations and under certain conditions may cause the computer to stop functioning. Attackers also use a buffer overflow in order to compromise a computer. The storage buffer typically contains the memory location of the software program that was being executed when another function interrupted the process: that is, the storage buffer contains the "return address" of the program to which the computer's processor should return once the new process has finished. An attacker could overflow the buffer with a new "return address" and point to another area in the data memory area that contains the attacker's malware code instead. A buffer overflow attack is illustrated in Figure 2-4.

For Windows-based systems there are two defenses against buffer overflows. **Data Execution Prevention (DEP)** is a Windows feature that prevents attackers from using buffer overflow to execute malware. An attacker who launches a buffer overflow attack to change the "return address" to point to his malware code stored in the data area of memory would be defeated because DEP will not allow code in the memory area to be executed. DEP can be enabled for Windows programs or for all other application programs as well, as seen in Figure 2-5.

Another Windows defense mechanism that makes it harder for malicious code to exploit system functions is **Address Space Layout Randomization (ASLR)**. Whenever a Windows computer is turned on or rebooted, ASLR randomly assigns executable operating system code to one of 256 possible locations in RAM. This makes it harder for an attacker to locate and take advantage of any functionality inside these executables. Because ASLR moves the function entry points around in memory so they are in unpredictable locations, an attacker only has a .39 percent (1 out of 256) chance of guessing the correct location.

Normal process

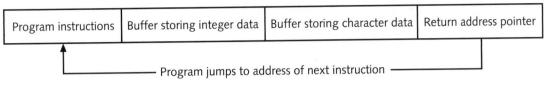

Program jumps to address of next instruction

Buffer overflow

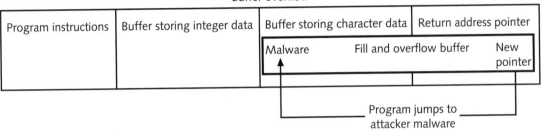

Program jumps to
attacker malware

Figure 2-4 Buffer overflow attack

Course Technology/Cengage Learning

Protecting Against Theft

One of the most effective means of protecting a portable laptop computer against theft is by securing it to a desk or another object. This can be done with a **device lock**, which consists of a steel cable and a lock. One end of the cable locks into a laptop's security slot, usually located on the back left or back right side of the laptop. The security slot allows a laptop device lock to attach and lock onto the computer case, as shown in Figure 2-6. The other end of the device lock is secured to a desk or chair. Device locks are economical, simple and quick to install.

Another approach for protecting against theft is similar to that used to protect automobiles. A special transmitter, hidden in a vehicle, can help police quickly track and recover a stolen car because the transmitter sends out a signal that indicates its location. In a similar fashion, a software tracking system is available for laptop computers. Instead of hiding a transmitter in a laptop, this software can report information that may help identify its location when the stolen laptop is connected to a network.

One of the drawbacks of software tracking is that the tracking company could trace the location of any laptop—whether it was stolen or not—without the owner's permission. Now there are free and open source systems for tracking the location of a laptop that do not depend upon a proprietary central service that you have to trust. When the software is installed on a laptop, no one besides the owner (or an agent of the owner's choosing) can track a laptop. The software can even take a picture of the thief through the laptop's built-in camera.

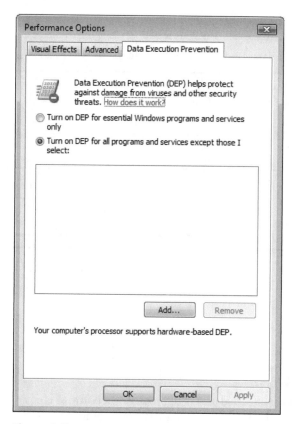

Figure 2-5 DEP options

Course Technology/Cengage Learning

Figure 2-6 Device lock

Course Technology/Cengage Learning

Creating Data Backups

One of the best defenses against attacks is to create **data backups** on a regular basis. Creating a data backup is copying data from a computer's hard drive onto other digital media and then storing it in a secure location.

Data backups not only protect data against computer attacks; they also can protect against hardware malfunctions, user error, software corruption, and natural disasters.

Data backups for large organizations are essential in order to protect the organization's data. Sophisticated hardware and software can back up data on a regular schedule or even on a continual basis so that any loss of data—whether due to a malicious virus that wipes out a hard drive or a user who accidentally erases an important spreadsheet—can be quickly restored. These backups are transparent to the user.

For personal computer users, creating data backups is likewise critical, yet most users consider it too inconvenient to regularly back up their data. Today there are several solutions to make creating backups easier. Recent versions of all operating systems can perform automated backups, and third-party software is also available that provides additional functionality.

There are four basic questions that should be answered when creating a personal backup strategy. These include what information should be backed up, how often should it be backed up, what media should be used, and where the backup should be stored.

What Information to Back Up There are two different approaches to determining the information that should be backed up:

1. *Back up only user files*—This approach only backs up user-created files that cannot be easily or quickly recreated. Programs installed on the computer, such as a word processor, are not backed up because the program can easily be reinstalled from the original installation disc or from the Internet. However, personal documents that were created using the program, such as the manuscript for a book created using a word processor, should be backed up, along with digital photos, personal financial information, and other information that cannot be easily replaced. The advantage to this approach is that backups can be performed more quickly because only a smaller set of data is being saved; the disadvantage is that it may be easy to overlook an important file that should be backed up.

2. *Back up all files*—Instead of only backing up user files, this approach backs up everything stored on the computer, including the operating system and all application programs. Although this ensures that all data is captured, performing a full backup can be time-consuming. As an option, once a full backup is performed then only those files that have changed are subsequently backed up. This can be achieved through the use of the **archive bit**. Software can internally designate which files have already been backed up by setting an archive bit in the properties of the file: a file with the archive bit cleared (set to *0*) indicates that the file has been backed up, yet any time the contents of that file are changed, the archive bit is set (to *1*), meaning that this modified file now needs

to be backed up. Figure 2-7 illustrates the use of an archive bit. Once a full backup is taken, then a **differential backup** (copies all files changed since the last full backup) or an **incremental backup** (copies all files changed since the last full or incremental backup) can be made. A **copy backup** only copies selected files to a new location and does not reset the archive bit. These backups are summarized in Table 2-3.

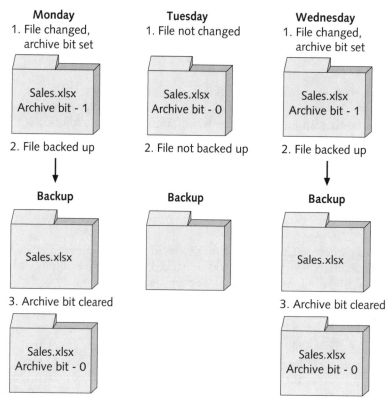

Figure 2-7 Archive bit

Course Technology/Cengage Learning

Table 2-3 Types of data backups

Type of Backup	Description	How Used	Archive Bit After Backup
Full backup	Copies all files	Part of regular backup schedule	Cleared
Differential backup	Copies all files since last full backup	Part of regular backup schedule	Not cleared
Incremental backup	Copies all files changed since last full or incremental backup	Part of regular backup schedule	Cleared
Copy backup	Copies selected files	Copies files to a new location	Not cleared

Frequency of Backups The ideal approach is to back up a document every time it changes. However, for a user to perform this task manually would be impractical. Backup software can be used to create a regular backup schedule, such as once a day or once a week.

If it is critical that information be constantly protected, a technology known as **RAID (Redundant Array of Independent Drives)** can be implemented. RAID uses multiple hard disk drives for increased reliability. There are several RAID configurations (called *levels*). One of the most common levels for personal computer users is RAID Level 1. RAID Level 1 uses **disk mirroring**. Disk mirroring involves connecting multiple hard disk drives in the computer and writing data to both hard drives. By "mirroring" the action on the primary drive, the other drives become exact duplicates. In case the primary drive fails, the other drives take over with no loss of data. This is shown in Figure 2-8.

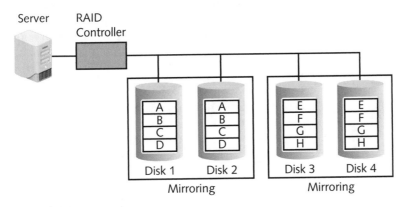

Figure 2-8 RAID Level 1

Course Technology/Cengage Learning

Backup Storage Media Temporary storage media, such as floppy disks or Universal Serial Bus (USB) flash drives, should not be used for long-term storage. Instead, the following alternatives should be considered:

- *Portable USB hard drives*—These devices connect to the USB port of a computer and provide backup capabilities that are fast, portable, and can store large amounts of data.

- *Network Attached Storage (NAS)*—A **network attached storage** (**NAS**) device is similar to a portable USB hard drive except it has additional "intelligence" that allows all devices connected to the computer network to access it (instead of moving it from computer to computer). NAS devices are increasing in popularity among home network users.

- *Internet services*—Fee-based Internet services are available that allow users to back up documents over the Internet to a centralized backup server. Some of these services provide "transparent access" to the backups in that they look like another hard drive attached to a desktop computer.

- *Disc storage*—Compact Disc–Recordable (CD-R) or Digital Versatile Disc (DVD) storage is compact, stable, and inexpensive. The disadvantage to disc storage is that it requires the user to be present during the backup process to continually "feed" discs into the drive if multiple discs are required.

Location of Backup Storage One of the challenges with creating backups is to protect against not only virus attacks but also against hardware malfunctions, user error, software corruption, and natural disasters. Often users protect against one element but not others. For example, a user might perform a backup to a portable USB hard drive that is located in the same room as the desktop computer. Although this backup may protect against a virus attack that corrupts the data or a hard drive failure, it may not protect against a lightning strike or fire.

It is recommended that users consider protecting against all types of potential disasters when developing a backup strategy.

In order to protect against a broad range of disasters, backups ideally should be stored in a location away from the device that contains the information. This protects the data if a fire, flood, or storm destroys the computer. If it is not possible to store the backups in another location, then they should be clearly labeled and stored in another room of the house or apartment.

Another option, known as remote online storage, is to back up over the Internet to a remote site. This process can be automated so that whenever a file changes or a new file is added it is marked for backup at the next backup point (the interval can be set from 10 minutes to two hours). The disadvantage is that the backups and restorations can be slow, depending upon your connection speed.

Security in Your World

"That should do it!" proclaimed Alexis proudly as he and Gerald finished installing antivirus software and patching his Windows operating system. "Attackers, give me your best shot! You won't get to my computer now!"

Gerald leaned back in his chair. "Well, I'm not sure that I would go that far. Chances are that an attacker might still get through and infect your computer."

Alexis looked surprised. "How?" he asked. "We just finished installing some of the latest software out there."

"I know," said Gerald. "But remember that these attackers never sleep. Right now they are working on attacks that take advantage of security holes in this software that we don't even know are there."

"So what should I do?" asked Alexis.

"My instructor says that you should take the approach that it's not a matter of *if* you will be attacked but rather *when*. That means you have to be prepared for when that attack gets through," said Gerald. "Here, let me show you what you can do to be ready."

Recovering from an Attack

MINIMIZE LOSSES

In spite of the best defenses, sooner or later an attack may be successful. Just as a homeowner cannot be absolutely certain that her house will never be broken into even if she has installed strong door locks, the same is true with computer security: the best defense is to "hope for the best but prepare for the worst."

Because there are so many different types of attacks, it is difficult to prescribe precisely what actions to take to recover from an attack. These are the basic steps to perform in the event of a successful virus attack:

1. *Disconnect*—The first action to be taken is to physically disconnect the computer from the network. This will prevent the computer from infecting other computers and will also prevent any further damage to the computer from attackers.

2. *Identify*—The next step is to determine exactly what infection has taken place on the computer. If the AV software installed did not stop the infection, it could be a result of the signature files being out of date, the AV software being turned off or malfunctioning, or the AV software unable to detect that particular virus. First run a scan of the entire computer's hard drive with the AV software to identify the infection. If that is not successful it may be necessary to reconnect to the network and use an online scanner to examine the computer (most AV vendors have free online scanners available at their Web site that do not require installation).

3. *Disinfect*—Once the attack has been identified the malware needs to be removed from the system. The AV software should be set to "Disinfect" or "Quarantine" any malware that it finds. There are also malicious software removal tools available online to purge a system of malware.

4. *Recheck*—Once the malware has been removed the computer should be scanned again for any signs of malware. It is recommended that a different brand of AV software be used for this recheck. Because running multiple versions of different AV software is not recommended, an online scanner from a different AV vendor can be used to scan the computer.

5. *Reinstall*—If the malware continues to be identified and cannot be purged then it may be necessary to wipe the hard drive clean of all programs and reinstall using the latest backup.

6. *Analyze*—The final step is to determine why the attack was successful. Were the virus definition files not being updated properly? Were all patches faithfully installed? Were any suspicious e-mail attachments opened? Are all downloaded files being scanned? A thorough examination of the desktop security practices for the computer can help prevent a successful attack from occurring again.

Chapter Summary

- Malicious software (malware) is software that enters a computer system without the owner's knowledge or consent and includes a wide variety of damaging or annoying software. Malware's primary objectives include infecting computers and hiding the presence of the malware.

- Infecting malware includes computer viruses and worms. A computer virus secretly attaches itself to a legitimate "carrier" and then executes when its carrier document is opened or program is launched. Once a virus infects a computer it activates its malicious payload. A worm is a program that is designed to take advantage of a vulnerability in an application or an operating system in order to enter a system. Once the worm has exploited the vulnerability on one system, it immediately searches for another computer that has the same vulnerability.

- Concealing malware includes Trojan horses (Trojans), rootkits, logic bombs, and zombies and botnets. A Trojan is a program advertised as performing one activity but actually does something else, either in addition to the advertised activity or as a substitute for it. A rootkit is a set of software tools used by an intruder to break into a computer, obtain special privileges to perform unauthorized functions, and then hide all traces of its existence. A logic bomb is a computer program or a part of a program that lies dormant until it is triggered by a specific logical event, such as a certain date reached on the system calendar. Programs that will allow the infected computer to be placed under the remote control of an attacker are commonplace. This infected computer is known as a zombie, and when many of these zombie computers are under the control of an attacker, this creates a botnet.

- Hardware is also the target of attackers. All personal computers have a chip that contains the Basic Input/Output System (BIOS), which is a coded program embedded on the chip that recognizes and controls different devices on the computer system. Today's BIOS chips can have their contents rewritten, and attackers use this capability to install malware on the BIOS. A USB device is a generic term for a wide variety of external devices that can be attached through the universal serial bus connector and are small, lightweight, removable, and contain rewritable storage. USB devices can be used to spread malware or steal sensitive data. Almost all cell phones today have the ability to send and receive text messages and connect to the Internet, and attackers try to take advantage of these services in order to launch attacks. Finally, data theft is a serious problem. A laptop computer can be stolen by attackers or a hard drive that is not properly erased can expose sensitive data to attackers.

- There are several tactics for defending desktop systems. A security patch is a general software security update to address vulnerabilities uncovered after the program was released. It is important that patches be installed as they are released from the software vendor. Antivirus (AV) software can scan a computer's hard drive for infections and also monitor all activity to determine if a virus is present. Buffer overflow protection prevents attackers from using a buffer overflow to infect a computer.
Device locks and software tracking systems can be used to prevent the theft of a laptop computer or identify its location. Creating a data backup is copying data from a computer's hard drive onto other digital media and then storing it in a secure location, and is one of the most important defenses against attacks.

- Despite the best defenses, an attack against a computer may be successful. There are basic steps which should be followed to disinfect a computer and restore it to its original state.

Key Terms

Address Space Layout Randomization (ASLR)   A Windows feature that randomly assigns executable operating system code to one of 256 possible locations in RAM.

antivirus (AV)   Software that can scan a computer's hard drive for infections as well as monitor computer activity and scan all new documents that might contain a virus.

archive bit   A file setting that indicates whether a file has been backed up.

Basic Input/Output System (BIOS)   A coded program embedded on a processor chip that recognizes and controls different devices on the computer system.

boot virus   A virus that infects the Master Boot Record (MBR) of a hard disk drive.

bot herder   An attacker who controls several botnets.

botnet   A group of zombie computers that are under the control of an attacker.

buffer overflow   An error that occurs when a computer process attempts to store data in RAM beyond the boundaries of a fixed-length storage buffer.

cellular telephones (cell phones)   Portable communications devices that function in a manner unlike wired telephones.

channels   Internet Relay Chat (IRC) discussion forums.

companion virus   A virus that adds a program to the operating system that is a copycat "companion" to a legitimate program.

copy backup   A backup that only copies selected files to a new location and does not reset the archive bit.

data backup   The process of copying data from a computer's hard drive onto other digital media and then storing it in a secure location.

Data Execution Prevention (DEP)   A Windows feature that prevents attackers from using buffer overflow to execute malware.

device lock   A steel cable and a lock used to secure a laptop computer against theft.

differential backup   A backup that copies all files changed since the last full backup.

disk mirroring   A RAID technology for copying data to two disks simultaneously.

file infector virus   A virus that infects program executable files with an .EXE or .COM file extension.

flashing   The process for rewriting the contents of the BIOS.

incremental backup   A backup that copies all files changed since the last full or incremental backup.

Internet Relay Chat (IRC)   An open communication protocol that is used for real-time "chatting" with other IRC users over the Internet. Also used to remotely control zombie computers in a botnet.

logic bomb   A computer program or a part of a program that lies dormant until it is triggered by a specific logical event.

macro   A series of commands and instructions that can be grouped together as a single command.

macro virus   A virus written in a scripting language.

Master Boot Record (MBR)   An area on a hard disk drive that contains the program necessary for the computer to start up and a description of how the hard drive is organized.

metamorphic virus   A virus that alters how it appears in order to avoid detection.

network attached storage (NAS)   A device with additional "intelligence" that allows all devices connected to the computer network to access it for storage.

partition table   A table on the hard drive that describes how the hard drive is organized.

patch   A general software security update intended to cover vulnerabilities that have been discovered after the program was released.

polymorphic virus   A virus that changes how it appears and also encrypts its contents differently each time.

PROM (Programmable Read Only Memory)   A chip in which the contents can be rewritten to provide new functionality.

Read Only Memory (ROM)   A chip that cannot be reprogrammed.

Redundant Array of Independent Drives (RAID)   A technology for using multiple hard disk drives for increased reliability.

removable storage   Devices, such as USB flash drives, that can store data from a computer and then be disconnected.

resident virus   A virus that is loaded into random access memory and can interrupt almost any function executed by the computer operating system and alter it.

rootkit   A set of software tools used by an intruder to break into a computer, obtain special privileges to perform unauthorized functions, and then hide all traces of its existence.

signature files   Files that contain the pattern of a virus that AV software uses to identify malware.

Trojan horse (Trojan)   A program advertised as performing one activity but actually does something else, or it may perform both the advertised and malicious activities.

virus   A program that secretly attaches itself to a document or program and then executes when that document is open or program is launched.

worm   A program that is designed to take advantage of a vulnerability in an application or an operating system in order to enter a system.

zombie   Computer under the control of an attacker.

Review Questions

1. A _____ is a program that secretly attaches itself to a carrier such as a document or program and then executes when that document is opened or program is launched.
   a. virus
   b. worm
   c. rootkit
   d. Trojan

2. A virus can spread to another computer by each of the following except _____.
   a. an infected file as an e-mail attachment
   b. an infected file on a USB flash drive
   c. downloading an infected file from the Internet
   d. rebooting the computer

3. Which of the following is not a type of computer virus?

   a. file infector virus

   b. remote virus

   c. resident virus

   d. boot virus

4. A computer program that pretends to install a calendar program but actually erases files is known as a _____.

   a. worm

   b. rootkit

   c. logic bomb

   d. Trojan

5. A difference between a worm and a virus is that:

   a. Worms run faster than viruses.

   b. Viruses expand the Master Boot Record.

   c. A virus must be attached to a carrier.

   d. A worm cannot harm a computer like a virus can.

6. The primary goal of a rootkit is to:

   a. hide its presence

   b. reformat the hard drive

   c. replicate to other computers

   d. start a botnet

7. A _____ is a computer program or a part of a program that lies dormant until it is triggered by a specific logical event.

   a. logic bomb

   b. trigger

   c. worm

   d. virus

8. When thousands of zombie computers are manipulated under remote control this creates a _____.

   a. botnet

   b. zombie-net

   c. Trojan network

   d. herd

9. Each of the following is a technique to restrict the use of a USB device except:

 a. Disable the USB in hardware.

 b. Use third-party software to disable the USB.

 c. Flash the ROM BIOS.

 d. Disable the USB through the operating system.

10. A(n) _____ is a general software security update intended to cover vulnerabilities that have been discovered after the program was released.

 a. key

 b. resource

 c. update release program (URP)

 d. patch

11. Attackers use _____ to remotely control zombies.

 a. Google

 b. e-mail

 c. spam

 d. Internet Relay Chat (IRC)

12. On modern computer systems the BIOS is stored on a _____ chip.

 a. Silver flash

 b. Basic Output/Input

 c. Programmable Read Only Memory (PROM)

 d. Read Only Memory (ROM)

13. Each of the following is an advantage of a USB device except:

 a. large size

 b. contains rewritable storage

 c. lightweight

 d. removable

14. Each of the following is an option of antivirus (AV) software once it discovers a virus except:

 a. Clean the virus from the file.

 b. Quarantine the infected file.

 c. Send an e-mail to attacker that the virus has been exposed.

 d. Delete the file that contains the virus.

15. Each of the following is an attack that can be used against cell phones except:

 a. Lure users to malicious Web sites.

 b. Infect the cell phone with malware.

 c. Attack other cell phone users.

 d. Turn off the cell phone.

16. Attackers use a _____ to insert a new "return address" and point to another area in the data memory area that contains the attacker's malware code.

   a. buffer overflow

   b. RAM segmentation

   c. storage register

   d. migration attack

17. Each of the following should be considered when creating a data backup strategy except:

   a. What information should be backed up?

   b. How often should it be backed up?

   c. What media should be used?

   d. Is it necessary to perform a backup?

18. RAID Level 1 uses disk mirroring which involves:

   a. reading data from the hard drive twice

   b. writing data to multiple hard drives

   c. flashing the BIOS

   d. decreased reliability

19. Each of the following is a storage media for backups except:

   a. USB flash drives

   b. portable USB hard drives

   c. Network attached storage (NAS)

   d. Internet services

20. An attacker who controls multiple zombies in a botnet is known as a _____.

   a. bot herder

   b. zombie shepherd

   c. rogue IRC

   d. cyber-robot

Hands-on Projects

Project 2-1: Scan for Rootkits Using RootkitRevealer

In this project you download and install Microsoft's RootkitRevealer tool to help detect the presence of a rootkit. You should have administrative rights on your computer in order to run this program.

1. Open your Web browser and enter the URL **www.microsoft.com/technet/ sysinternals/Security/RootkitRevealer.mspx**.

The location of content on the Internet such as this program may change without warning. If you are no longer able to access the program through the above URL then use a search engine like Google (www.google.com) and search for "RootkitRevealer".

2. Scroll to the bottom of the page and click on **Download RootkitRevealer (231 KB)**. When the File Download dialog box appears, download the file to your desktop or another location designated by your instructor.

3. When the download is complete, click **Open** to open the compressed (.ZIP) file.

If you receive a warning that a Web site wants to open Web content using the program, click **Allow**.

4. Click **Extract all files** to launch the Extraction Wizard. Follow the steps in the wizard to extract all files to your desktop or another location designated by your instructor.

5. Navigate to the location where the files were extracted and start the program by double-clicking on **RootkitRevealer.exe**. If you receive an Open File - Security Warning dialog box click **Run**. Click **Agree** to the Rootkit Revealer License Agreements. The RootkitRevealer screen appears.

6. Click **File** and then **Scan** to begin a scan of the computer for a rootkit.

7. When completed, RootkitRevealer will display discrepancies between the Windows registry keys (which are not always visible to specific types of scans) and other parts of the registry. Any discrepancies that are found do not necessarily indicate that a rootkit was detected.

8. Close RootkitRevealer and all windows.

Project 2-2: Block a USB Drive

One of the methods for blocking a USB drive is to use third-party software that can control USB device permissions. In this project you download and install a software-based USB write blocker to prevent data from being written to a USB device.

1. Open your Web browser and enter the URL **irongeek.com/i.php?page= security/thumbscrew-software-usb-write-blocker**.

The location of content on the Internet such as this program may change without warning. If you are no longer able to access the program through the above URL then use a search engine like Google (www.google.com) and search for "Irongeek Thumbscrew".

2. Click **Download Thumbscrew**.

3. When the File Download dialog box appears click **Save** and follow the instructions to Save this file in a location such as your Desktop or a folder designated by your instructor. When the file finishes downloading click **Open** and extract the files in a location such as your Desktop or a folder designated by your instructor. Navigate to that location and double-click on **thumbscrew.exe** and follow the default installation procedures.

4. After installation, notice that a new icon appears in the system tray in the lower right corner of the screen.

5. Insert a USB flash drive into the computer.

6. Navigate to a document on the computer.

7. Right click on the document and select **Send To**.

8. Click the appropriate **Removable Disk** icon of the USB flash drive to copy the file to the flash drive. If necessary point to the Thumbscrew icon and click **Make USB Writeable**.

9. Now make the USB flash drive write protected so it cannot be written to. Click on the icon in the system tray.

10. Click **Make USB Read Only**. Notice that a red circle now appears over the icon to indicate that the flash drive is write protected.

11. Navigate to a document on the computer.

12. Right-click the document and select **Send To**.

13. Click the appropriate **Removable Disk** icon of the USB flash drive to copy the file to the flash drive. What happens?

14. Close all windows.

Project 2-3: Configure Data Execution Prevention (DEP)

Data Execution Prevention (DEP) can provide protection from buffer overflow attacks. In this project you determine if your system can run DEP and if it can to configure DEP using Microsoft Windows.

1. The first step is to determine if the computer supports DEP. Use your Web browser to go to **www.grc.com/securable**. Click **Download now**.

The location of content on the Internet such as this program may change without warning. If you are no longer able to access the program through the above URL then use a search engine like Google (www.google.com) and search for "Securable".

2. When the File Download dialog box appears, click **Save** and download the file to your desktop or another location designated by your instructor.

3. When the download is complete click **Run**.

4. Securable will launch and display the results, as seen in Figure 2-9. If it reports that **Hardware D.E.P.** is "No" then that computer's processor does not support NX. Close the Securable application.

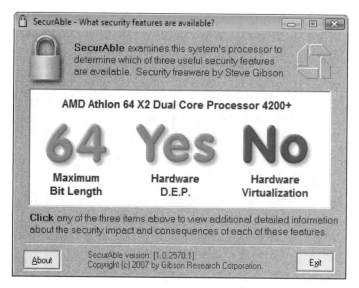

Figure 2-9   SecurAble results

Course Technology/Cengage Learning

5. The next step is to check the DEP settings. Click **Start** and **Control Panel**.

6. For Microsoft Windows Vista click **System and Maintenance** and then click **System** and then click **Advanced system settings** and finally click the **Advanced** tab. For Microsoft Windows XP click **Performance and Maintenance** and then click **System** and finally click the **Advanced** tab.

7. Click **Settings** under **Performance** and then click the **Data Execution Prevention** tab.

8. If the configuration is set to **Turn on DEP for essential Windows programs and services only** then click **Turn on DEP for all Windows programs and services except those I select**. This will provide full protection to all programs.

9. If an application does not function properly it may be necessary to make an exception for that application and not have DEP protect it. If this is necessary click the **Add** button and search for the program. Click on the program to add it to the exception list.

10. Close all windows and applications and then restart your computer to invoke DEP protection.

Project 2-4: Test AV Software

Antivirus software is important, yet free AV products may not offer the best protection. In this project you download a virus test file to determine how your AV software reacts. The file downloaded is not a virus but is designed to appear to an antivirus scanner as if it were a virus. You need to have antivirus software installed on your computer to perform this project.

1. Open your Web browser and enter the URL **www.eicar.org/anti_virus_test_file.htm**.

The location of content on the Internet such as this program may change without warning. If you are no longer able to access the program through the above URL then use a search engine like Google (www.google.com) and search for "EICAR AntiVirus Test File".

2. Read the "Anti-Virus or Anti-Malware test file" information carefully. The file you will download is not a virus but is designed to appear to an antivirus scanner as if it were a virus.

3. Click the file **eicar.com,** which contains a fake virus. A dialog box opens that asks if you want to download the file. Wait to see what happens. What does your antivirus software do? Close your antivirus message and click **Cancel** to stop the download procedure.

4. Now click **eicar_com.zip.** This file contains a fake virus inside a compressed (ZIP) file. What happened?

5. If your antivirus software did not prevent you from accessing the eicar_com.zip file, when the File Download dialog box appears click **Save** and download the file to your desktop or another location designated by your instructor.

6. When the download is complete, click **Close,** if necessary.

7. Right-click the **Start** button and then click **Explore.**

8. In Windows Explorer navigate to the folder that contains the eicar_com.zip file.

9. Right-click the file **eicar_com.zip** and then click **Scan for viruses** on the shortcut menu (your menu command might be slightly different). What happened now?

10. Return to the Web site and this time click **eicarcom2.zip.** This file has a double-compressed ZIP file with a fake virus. What happened?

11. If your antivirus software did not prevent you from accessing the eicarcom2.zip file, when the File Download dialog box appears click **Save** and download the file to your desktop or another location designated by your instructor.

12. When the download is complete, click **Close,** if necessary.

13. Return to Windows Explorer.

14. In Windows Explorer navigate to the folder that contains the eicarcom2.zip file.

15. Right-click the file **eicarcom2.zip** and then click **Scan for viruses** on the shortcut menu (your menu command might be slightly different). What happened now?

16. Erase both files from your hard drive.

17. Close all windows.

Project 2-5: Perform a Baseline Security Audit

Before creating a configuration baseline it is important to know what security configurations are set on a system. In this project you perform an audit using the Microsoft Baseline Security Analyzer (MBSA).

1. Open your Web browser and enter the URL **http://www.microsoft.com/ technet/security/tools/mbsahome.mspx.**

The location of content on the Internet such as this program may change without warning. If you are no longer able to access the program through the above URL then use a search engine like Google (www.google.com) and search for "Microsoft Baseline Security Analyzer".

2. Click on the latest version of MBSA and download the program to your computer.

3. When the file finishes downloading click **Run** and follow the default installation procedures.

4. Double-click the **Microsoft Baseline Security Analyzer** icon on the desktop.

5. Click **Scan a computer.**

6. Accept the default settings for the scan by clicking **Start Scan.**

7. When the scan is complete, a report appears. Items with a green check indicate that the item passed the scan. An item with a yellow check or red check means it has located a vulnerability and should be attended to. Scroll down to any item that has a yellow or red check and click **What was scanned.** Close that window when completed.

8. Click **How to correct this.**

9. Close all windows.

Case Projects

Case Project 2-1: Virus Attacks

Although viruses seldom receive the kind of attention that they have in the past, they still pose a deadly threat to users. Use the Internet to search for the latest information regarding current viruses. You may want to visit security vendor sites, like Symantec or McAfee, or security research sites such as SANS to find the latest information. What are the latest attacks? What type of damage can they do? What platforms are the most vulnerable? Write a one-page paper on your research.

Case Project 2-2: Operating System Patches

Select the operating system of your choice and research the patches that have been available over the past three months. How many were there? What was the severity of the threats? What vulnerabilities did they address? Were there any known problems with these patches (did they cause other problems)?

Case Project 2-3: Cell Phone Attacks

In many countries cell phones are used for much more than voice communication. In Japan and other nations cell phones are routinely used to buy merchandise and conduct financial transactions. As cell phone usage expands, what types of protections are available to protect cell phones from attackers? Use the Internet to research cell phone use in some non-U.S. nations and the protections that are in place. Are these adequate? Should they be extended? What would you suggest to protect cell phones? Should the cell phone provider be responsible for blocking attacks, or should it be the user's responsibility? Do you have any recommendations? Write a one-page paper on your research.

Case Project 2-4: AV Software Comparison

Select two brands of antivirus software. What features do they have that are different from other vendors' products? What are their strengths? What are their weaknesses? How much does it cost to be able to update the signature files? How expensive is each compared to competing products? Would you recommend these products to others? Write a one-page summary of your findings.

Case Project 2-5: Backup Software Comparison

Select two brands of backup software and compare their features, advantages, costs, etc. Would you recommend these products to others? Write a one-page summary of your findings.

Case Project 2-6: Winstead Computer Consultants

Winstead Computer Consultants (WCC) is a local information technology company that specializes in security. WCC has hired you to assist them with a project. A community college in the area has asked for someone to come speak to a computer class about security, particularly what a student should do to protect his or her computer.

Create a PowerPoint presentation of eight or more slides that covers this information. Because the audience does not have a strong technical background, your presentation should be general in its tone.

chapter **3**

Internet Security

After completing this chapter you should be able to do the following:

- Explain how the World Wide Web and e-mail work
- List the different types of Internet attacks
- Explain the defenses used to repel Internet attacks

Security in Your World

"This is really frustrating!" said Quy as he pushed the mouse away. Katrina looked up from her computer. "What's the matter?" she asked. "I get so aggravated at this," he said. "I'm trying to download a file from this Web site but I keep getting a message that it is blocked and I can't download it." Quy and Katrina were sitting in one of the student computer labs located in the school's library. "The school just doesn't want us to download music anymore so they blocked everything from downloading. And this isn't even an MP3 file. I'm so mad!"

"I don't think this is anything like blocking music downloads. See, look here. It's the security settings on the Web browser that's blocking it," said Katrina. "What do you mean?" asked Quy. "Well, these security settings won't let a file be downloaded without your permission," said Katrina. "That way the computers won't get infected with anything bad from the Internet."

"But I can't get those files that I need," complained Quy. "What am I supposed to do?" Katrina slid her chair over to Quy's computer. "All you have to do is click right here and then click OK to download the file. See?"

"Oh, I didn't know that," said Quy. "Well, they don't need to block everything. They're just paranoid about security. After all, I'm just surfing the Web. That's what I do in my dorm room and my computer's never been infected."

"I'm afraid not," replied Katrina. "You're doing more than just surfing. Remember, you just tried to download a file. And even if you're only surfing or reading your e-mail through a Web browser that doesn't mean that you are safe. You still have to set your security on your Web browser and even install security programs to keep the bad stuff out."

Quy looked over at Katrina. "What bad stuff?"

The impact of the Internet upon our world has been nothing short of astonishing. With more than 1.5 billion users worldwide connected to the Internet and the number of users and Web sites growing at an exponential rate, the Internet has had a revolutionary impact on how we learn, interact, and communicate with each other. Some even claim that the Internet is creating a collective force of unprecedented power. For the first time in human history, mass participation and cooperation across space and time is possible, empowering individuals and groups all over the globe.

What is equally remarkable is the speed at which the Internet has become a core tool of our society. Since the 'Net' entered the consumer computer world in the early 1990s, it has permeated nearly all parts of our lives. Whereas other technological advances have taken years to be accepted (for example, almost 30 years passed before the telephone was widely used), the Internet has changed our world in just a fraction of that amount of time.

For all of the benefits that the Internet has provided, it also has become the primary pathway for attackers to reach our computers. One recent study revealed that a computer connected to the Internet is probed by an attacker on average once every 39 seconds. An unprotected computer that is connected to the Internet can be infected in just a matter of minutes. And the number of Internet-based attacks continues to dramatically increase each year.

In this chapter, we will examine some of the attacks on personal computers that come through the Internet and what can be done to minimize those risks. First, we'll explore how the Internet works and then identify the types of attacks that can occur. Then, we'll examine the defenses that can be set up to make using this valuable tool a more enjoyable, safe, and productive experience.

How the Internet Works

The **Internet** is a worldwide set of interconnected computers, servers, and networks. The Internet is not owned or regulated by any organization or government entity. Instead, computers and networks that are operated by industry, governments, schools, and individuals all loosely cooperate to make the Internet a global information resource. Understanding how some of the basic Internet tools work helps to provide the foundation for establishing Internet security. The two main Internet tools that are used today are the World Wide Web and e-mail, and it is through these tools that the majority of Internet attacks occur.

The World Wide Web

The **World Wide Web (WWW)**, better known as the Web, is composed of Internet server computers that provide online information in a specific format. The format is based on the **Hypertext Markup Language (HTML)**. HTML allows Web authors to combine text, graphic images, audio, video, and **hyperlinks** (which allow users to jump from one area on the Web to another with a click of the mouse button) into a single document. Instructions written in HTML code specify how a local computer's Web **browser** should display the words, pictures, and other elements on a user's screen, as shown in Figure 3-1.

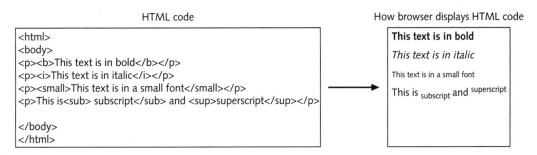

Figure 3-1 How a browser displays HTML code

Course Technology/Cengage Learning

TIP

The HTML code for a Web page can be displayed in a browser. Using Microsoft Internet Explorer, click View on the menu bar and then click Source.

Web servers distribute HTML documents based on a set of standards, or **protocols,** known as the **Hypertext Transport Protocol (HTTP).** HTTP is a subset of a larger set of standards for Internet transmission known as the **Transmission Control Protocol/Internet Protocol (TCP/IP).**

NOTE

The word *protocol* comes from two Greek words for *first* and *glue,* and originally referred to the first sheet glued onto a manuscript on which the table of contents was written. The term later evolved to mean an "official account of a diplomatic document" and was used in France to refer to a formula of diplomatic etiquette.

Most Internet transmissions are based on port numbers. A **port number** identifies the program or service that is being requested. For example, a Web browser computer that sends a request to a remote Web server would specify port 80, which is the standard port for HTTP transmissions. The Web server knows by the port number that the request is for an HTML document and responds by sending the entire HTML document (again using HTTP), which is stored on the user's local computer. The Web browser then displays the document. This process is illustrated in Figure 3-2.

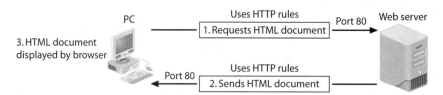

Figure 3-2   HTML document sent to browser

Course Technology/Cengage Learning

The local computer does not view the HTML document on the Web server; rather, the entire document is transferred and then stored on the local computer before the browser displays it. This transfer-and-store process creates opportunities for sending different types of malicious code to the user's computer, and makes Web browsing a potentially risky security experience.

E-Mail

Since developer Ray Tomlinson sent the first e-mail message in 1971, e-mail has become an essential part of everyday life. The Radicati Group estimates the number of e-mail messages sent each day to be over 210 billion, or more than 2 million every second. E-mail has become the primary communication tool for businesses.

E-mail systems use two TCP/IP protocols to send and receive messages: the **Simple Mail Transfer Protocol (SMTP)** handles outgoing mail, while the **Post Office Protocol (POP,** more commonly known as **POP3** for the current version) is responsible for incoming mail. The SMTP server listens on port number 25 while POP3 listens on port 110, as seen in Figure 3-3.

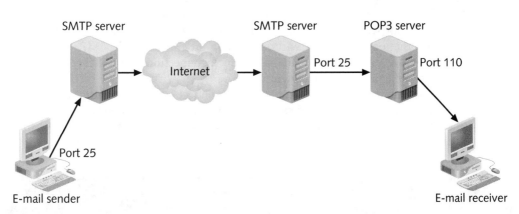

Figure 3-3 E-mail transport

Course Technology/Cengage Learning

An example of how e-mail works is as follows:

1. The sender (*sender@source.com*) uses a stand-alone e-mail client such as Microsoft Outlook to compose and address the message to the receiver (*receiver@destination.com*) and then transmits the message by clicking the Send button in Outlook.

2. Outlook connects to the SMTP server at *mail.source.com* using port 25 and passes the message.

3. The SMTP server divides the "To" address into two parts: the recipient name (*receiver*) and the domain name (*destination.com*). If the domain name of the receiver is the same as the sender, the SMTP server hands the message to the local POP3 server for *source.com* using a program called the delivery agent.

4. The SMTP server at *source.com* connects through the Internet with the SMTP server at *destination.com* using port 25 and passes the e-mail message.

5. The SMTP server at *destination.com* recognizes that the domain name for the message is *destination.com*, so it hands the message via the delivery agent to the POP3 server for *destination.com*, which in turn puts the message in receiver's mailbox.

 If the SMTP server at *source.com* cannot connect with the SMTP server at *destination.com*, the message goes into a waiting queue at *source.com*, which periodically tries to resend the message, normally about every 15 minutes. After 4 hours, it sends an e-mail message to the sender indicating a problem. After 5 days, most servers stop attempting to send the message.

POP3 is a basic protocol that allows users to retrieve messages sent to the server by using an e-mail client to connect to the POP3 server and downloading the messages onto the local computer. After the messages are downloaded, they may be erased from the POP3 server. **IMAP (Internet Mail Access Protocol,** or **IMAP4)** is a more advanced mail protocol. With IMAP, the e-mail remains on the e-mail server and is not downloaded to the user's computer. Mail can be organized into folders on the mail server and read from any computer. IMAP users can work with e-mail while offline. This is accomplished by downloading e-mail onto the local computer without erasing the e-mail on the IMAP server. A user can read and reply to e-mail offline. The next time a connection is established, the new messages are sent and any new e-mail is downloaded.

E-mail **attachments** are documents that are connected to an e-mail message, such as word processing documents, spreadsheets, or pictures. These attachments are encoded in a special format and sent as a single transmission along with the e-mail message itself. When the receiving computer receives the attachment it converts it back to its original format.

Security in Your World

"Look," said Quy, "I don't know as much about security as you do, but I do know that just surfing the Web or reading my e-mail isn't going to infect my computer." Katrina smiled. "Oh, no? Here, let me show you." She opened up her e-mail account and showed Quy a message from a bank that contained the hyperlink *Click here for more information.* "Quy, would you click there?" she asked. "Sure, said Quy, "If I wanted more information. I click on those all the time."

"Well," said Alexis, "How do you know where that click will take you? Will it go to the bank's actual Web site? What if an attacker had sent me this e-mail, and clicking there took me to his Web site, while I thought I was at the bank's site?" Quy paused. "I see, because the attacker's site could ask for your bank's password and then use it to break into your real account. Am I right?"

"Yes," said Katrina, "Now you're starting to catch on."

"OK. What other things can happen?" asked Quy.

Internet Attacks

There are a variety of different attacks that can be launched through the Internet. These include downloaded browser code, privacy attacks, attacks initiated while surfing to Web sites, and attacks through e-mail.

Downloaded Browser Code

In the early days of the Web, users viewed *static* content (information that does not change) such as text and pictures through a Web browser. As the Internet increased in popularity, the demand rose for content that can change—such as animated images or customized information—based on who is viewing it or even the time of day. Because basic HTML code could not provide these functions, this dynamic content required special computer code to be downloaded into the user's Web browser. However, this code could also be used by attackers. The most common examples of downloaded browser code are JavaScript, Java, and ActiveX.

JavaScript JavaScript is a scripting language that does not create standalone applications. A **scripting language** is similar to a computer programming language that is typically "interpreted" into a language the computer can understand without the need of a special computer program. JavaScript resides inside HTML documents. When a Web site that uses JavaScript is accessed, the HTML document with the JavaScript code is downloaded onto the user's computer and the browser then executes that code using a Java interpreter. Figure 3-4 illustrates how JavaScript works.

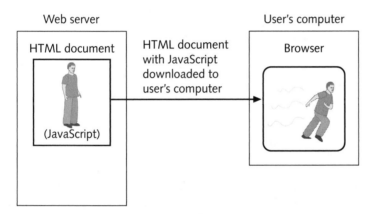

Figure 3-4 JavaScript

Course Technology/Cengage Learning

Because visiting a Web site that automatically downloads code to run on a local computer can be dangerous, several defense mechanisms are intended to prevent JavaScript programs from causing serious harm. First, JavaScript does not support certain capabilities: JavaScript running on a local computer cannot read, write, create, delete, or list the files on that computer. In addition, JavaScript has no networking capabilities, so that it cannot establish a direct connection to any other computers on the network. This prevents a JavaScript program from using a local computer to launch attacks on other network computers.

However, there are other security concerns with JavaScript. JavaScript programs can capture and send user information without the user's knowledge or authorization. For example, a malicious JavaScript program could capture and send the user's e-mail address to a source or even send a malicious e-mail from the user's e-mail account.

Java Unlike JavaScript, **Java** is a complete programming language that can be used to create standalone applications. Java can also be used to create a special type of smaller application called a **Java applet.** Whereas JavaScript is embedded in an HTML document, a Java applet is a separate program. Java applets are stored on the Web server and then downloaded onto the user's computer along with the HTML code, as seen in Figure 3-5. Java applets can perform interactive animations, immediate calculations, or other simple tasks very quickly because the user's request does not have to be sent to the Web server for processing and then returned with the answer; all of the processing is done on the local computer by the Java applet.

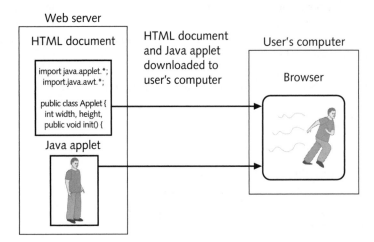

Figure 3-5 Java applet

Course Technology/Cengage Learning

A defense against a hostile Java applet is a **sandbox**. Downloaded Java applets are intended to run within a security sandbox, which is like a fence that surrounds the program and keeps it away from private data and other resources on a local computer. Unfortunately, breakdowns in the Java sandbox have occurred, allowing hostile Java applets to access data and passwords stored on the hard drive.

Two types of Java applets are defined by their relation to sandboxes. An **unsigned Java applet** is a program that does not come from a trusted source. A **signed Java applet** has information that proves the program is from a trusted source and has not been altered. Unsigned Java applets by default run in the sandbox and are restricted regarding what they can do, while signed Java applets are not restricted. Unsigned Java applets that attempt to do something outside of the sandbox automatically generate a warning message to the user. For example, an attacker may display a fake dialog box using a Java applet to attempt to obtain a password from a user. Figure 3-6 shows an older version of Java that displays a message at the bottom of the dialog box (*Warning: Applet Window*) intended to alert the user that this is an unsigned Java applet. Figure 3-7 illustrates the warning with newer versions of Java, which include an exclamation mark in a yellow triangle and a flashing border around the dialog box.

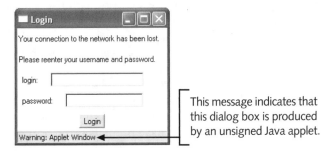

This message indicates that this dialog box is produced by an unsigned Java applet.

Figure 3-6 Older unsigned Java applet warning

Course Technology/Cengage Learning

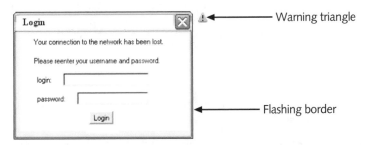

Warning triangle

Flashing border

Figure 3-7 Updated unsigned Java applet warning

Course Technology/Cengage Learning

Most users are unaware of what the unsigned Java applet warnings are and provide the password to the attacker.

ActiveX ActiveX is not a scripting or programming language but a set of rules for how applications under the Windows operating system should share information. **ActiveX controls** (also called add-ons) represent a specific way of implementing ActiveX and are sometimes called ActiveX applications. ActiveX controls can be invoked from Web pages through the use of a scripting language or directly by an HTML command.

An ActiveX control is similar to a Java applet in that it can perform many of the same functions. Unlike Java applets, however, ActiveX controls do not run in a sandbox, but have full access to the underlying Windows operating system. Anything a user can do on a computer, an ActiveX control can do, such as deleting files or reformatting a hard drive.

ActiveX controls are like miniature applications that can be run through the Web browser. They allow a Web site to interact directly with Windows and to perform functions that would not be possible using standard HTML code or scripting techniques.

To control this risk, Microsoft developed a registration system so that browsers can identify and authenticate an ActiveX control before downloading it. ActiveX controls can be signed or unsigned. A signed control provides a high degree of verification that the control was produced by the signer and has not been modified. However, signing does not guarantee the trustworthiness of the signer but only provides assurance that the control originated from the signer.

ActiveX poses a number of security concerns. First, the user's decision to allow installation of an ActiveX control is based on the *source* of the ActiveX control and not on the ActiveX control itself. The person who signed the control may not have properly assessed the control's safety and left open security vulnerabilities. Also, a control is registered only once per computer. If a computer is shared by multiple users, any user can download a control, making it available to all users on the machine. This means that a malicious ActiveX control can affect all users of that computer. And, nearly all ActiveX control security mechanisms are set in the Web browser such as Internet Explorer (IE). However, ActiveX controls do not rely exclusively on the Web browser, but can be installed and executed independently. Third-party applications that use ActiveX technology may not provide the security mechanisms available in Internet Explorer.

Privacy Attacks

Another type of attack is designed to invade a user's privacy. The two most common types of privacy attacks are using cookies and adware.

Cookies HTTP makes it impossible for a Web site to track whether a user has previously visited that site. Any information that was entered on a previous visit, such as site preferences or the contents of an electronic shopping cart, is not retained so that the Web server can identify repeat customers. Instead of the Web server asking the user for the same information each time she visits that site, the server can instead store that user-specific information in a file on the user's local computer and then retrieve it later. This file is called a **cookie**.

There are two types of cookies. A **first-party cookie** is created from the Web site that a user is currently viewing. For example, when viewing the Web site *www.12345.org*, the cookie *12345-ORG* would be saved on the computer's hard drive. Whenever the user returns to this site, that cookie would be used by *www.12345.org* to see the user's preferences. However, some Web sites attempt to access cookies they did not create. If a user went to *www.98765.org*, that site might attempt to retrieve the cookie *12345-ORG* from the hard drive. The cookie is now known as a **third-party cookie** because it was not created by the Web site that attempts to access the cookie.

Cookies by themselves are not dangerous. A cookie cannot contain a virus or steal personal information stored on a hard drive. It only contains information that can be used by a Web server. However, a third-party cookie can pose a privacy risk. Cookies can be used to track the browsing or buying habits of a user. When multiple Web sites are serviced by a single marketing organization, cookies can be used to track browsing habits on all the client's sites. The marketing organization can track browsing habits from page to page within all the client sites and know which pages are being viewed, how often they are viewed, and the Internet address of the computer. This information can be used to infer what items the user may be interested in, and to target advertising to the user.

Adware Adware is software that delivers advertising content in a manner that is unexpected and unwanted by the user. Adware typically displays advertising banners, opens new Web browser windows while the user is accessing the Internet, or displays popup ads. A **popup** is a small Web browser window that appears over the Web site that is being viewed. Most popup windows are created by advertisers and launch as soon as a new Web site is visited.

Users resist adware because:

- Adware may display objectionable content, such as gambling sites or pornography.
- Frequent popup ads can interfere with a user's productivity.
- Popup ads can slow a computer or even cause crashes and the loss of data.
- Unwanted advertisements can be a nuisance.

Adware can be a privacy risk. Many adware programs perform a tracking function, which monitors and tracks a user's online activities and then sends a log of these activities to third parties without the user's authorization or knowledge. For example, a user who visits online automobile sites to view specific types of cars can be tracked by adware and classified as someone interested in buying a new car. Based on the order of the sites visited and the types of Web sites, the adware can also determine whether the surfers' behavior suggests they are close to making a purchase or are also looking at competitors' cars. This information is gathered by adware and then sold to automobile advertisers, who send the users more ads about their cars.

Attacks while Surfing

It is often thought that as long as the user is only "passively" surfing the Web and not actively interacting with a Web site by providing information or downloading software, that the user is safe from attacks. Unfortunately, that may not always be the case. Attacks on users can occur while pointing the browser to a site or just viewing a site. Two of the most common attacks while surfing are redirecting Web traffic and drive-by downloads.

Redirecting Web Traffic It is not uncommon for a user to make a mistake when typing a Web address into a browser. Table 3-1 lists some of the typical mistakes when attempting to enter the address *www.course.com*.

Table 3-1 Typical errors in entering Web addresses

Type of Mistake	Example
Misspell the address	*www.corse.com*
Omit a dot	*wwwcourse.com*
Omit a word	*www.course*
Incorrect punctuation	*www-course.com*

Usually these mistakes result in the Web browser not being able to access the site and instead an error message is displayed. However, attackers can exploit a misaddressed Web name by registering the names of similar-sounding Web sites, such as *www.corse.com, www.courrse. com, www.cuorse.com* and *www.course.org*. When users attempt to enter *www.course.com* but make typing errors they are instead directed to the attacker's Web site. Because this site may be designed to look similar to the genuine site, users can be tricked into entering personal information that is then stolen.

Redirecting Web traffic is not limited to attackers. Several well-known Internet service providers (ISPs) automatically funnel misspelled addresses into their own Web site that contains a search feature.

Drive-by Downloads Most Internet users know that in order to avoid being infected while surfing they should not download any suspicious software or even click the *Yes* button if a popup window appears. Yet what if just *viewing* at a Web page could cause the computer to become infected? And what if that Web page was on a well-known and reputable Web site, such as a bank or a retailer? That is what is occurring today. **Drive-by downloads** are making even casual Web surfing open to attacks.

Drive-by downloads are considered especially dangerous because traditional defenses cannot prevent these infections from occurring and the Web sites themselves are generally reputable.

Attackers first identify a well-known Web site and then attempt to inject content by exploiting it through vulnerable scripting applications. These vulnerabilities permit the attacker to gain direct access to the Web server's underlying operating system and then inject new content into the compromised Web site. To avoid visual detection, the attackers often will craft a **zero pixel IFrame**. IFrame (short for *inline frame*) is an HTML element that allows for one HTML document to be embedded inside the main document. A zero pixel IFrame is virtually invisible to the naked eye.

When unsuspecting users visit an infected Web site, their browsers download through an IFrame the initial exploit script (usually written in JavaScript) that targets a vulnerability in the user's browser. If the script can run successfully on the user's computer, it will instruct the browser to connect to the attacker's own Web server to download malware, which is then automatically installed and executed on the user's computer. Often the malware will turn the user's computer into a zombie and connect it to a botnet. Unlike a traditional download that asks for the user's permission to perform an action, a drive-by download can be initiated by simply visiting a Web site.

CNET.com, ABC News' homepage, and Walmart.com have all at one time or another been infected with drive-by download malware.

Drive-by downloading is spreading at an alarming pace. An analysis by Google over a 10-month period revealed that over 3 million Web sites were infected and distributed drive-by downloads. The security firm Sophos recently reported more than 6,000 new drive-by-infected Web pages each day, or about one every 14 seconds.

E-Mail Attacks

One of the more common means of distributing attacks is through e-mail. These include sending spam, malicious attachments, and embedded hyperlinks.

Spam   The amount of **spam**, or unsolicited e-mail, that goes through the Internet continues to escalate. Cisco Systems estimates that 90 percent of all e-mails sent can be defined as spam, or 200 spam e-mails per day for every Internet user in the world. Spam has an even greater impact on organizations. According to the security firm Sophos, 97 percent of all business e-mail is spam. Spam significantly reduces productivity as employees spend more than half an hour each day deleting spam messages. Nucleus Research reports that spam e-mail, on average, costs U.S. organizations $874 per person annually in lost productivity.

The reason why users receive so many spam messages that advertise drugs, cheap mortgage rates, and watches for sale is because sending spam is a lucrative business. It costs spammers very little to send millions of spam e-mail messages. In the past spammers would purchase a list of valid e-mail addresses ($100 for 10 million addresses) and rent a motel room with a high-speed Internet connection ($85 per day) as a base for launching attacks. Today, however, almost all spam is sent from compromised zombie computers that have been linked into a botnet. A spammer who does not own his own botnet can lease time from other attackers ($40 per hour) to use a botnet of up to 100,000 infected computers to launch a spam attack.

The Russian-owned network McColo was widely believed to be the hosting command and control center for five major botnets. When McColo was disconnected from the Internet at 1:23 PM on November 11, 2008, all of their botnets stopped functioning and spam volumes worldwide immediately fell by 75 percent.

Even if spammers receive only a very small percentage of responses, they still make a large profit. For example, if a spammer sent spam to six million users for a product with a sale price of $50 that cost only $5 to make, and if only 0.001 percent of the recipients responded and bought the product (a typical response rate), the spammer would make over $270,000 in profit.

Text-based spam messages that include words such as *Viagra* or *investments* can easily be trapped by special **spam filters** that look for these words and block the e-mail. Because of the increased use of these filters, spammers have turned to another approach for sending out their spam. Known as **image spam**, it uses graphical images of text in order to circumvent text-based filters. These spam messages often include nonsense text so that it appears the e-mail message is legitimate (an e-mail with no text can prompt the spam filter to block it). Figure 3-8 shows an example of an image spam.

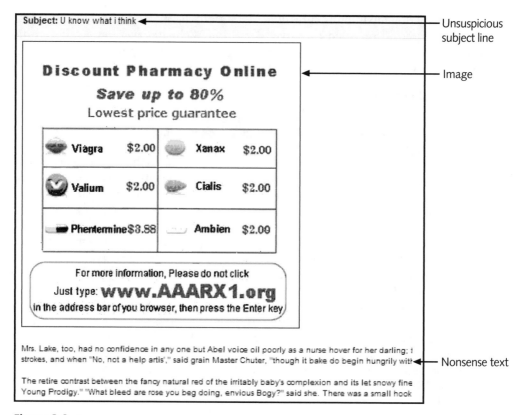

Figure 3-8 Image spam

Course Technology/Cengage Learning

In addition to sending a single graphical image, spammers also use other techniques. These include:

- **GIF layering** is an image spam that is divided into multiple images, much like a biology textbook that has transparent plastic overlays of the different parts of the human body. Each piece of the message is divided and then layered to create a complete and legible message, so that one spam e-mail could be made up of a dozen layered GIF images, as illustrated in Figure 3-9.

- **Word splitting** involves separating words so that they can still be read by the human eye. Word splitting is illustrated in Figure 3-10.

- **Geometric variance** uses "speckling" and different colors so that no two spam e-mails appear to be the same. Geometric variance is seen in Figure 3-11.

Image spam cannot be filtered based on the content of the message because it appears as an image instead of text. To detect image spam, one approach is to examine the context (along with the content) of the message and create a profile, asking questions such as who sent the message, what is known about the sender, where does the user go if she responds to this e-mail, what is the nature of the message content, and how is the message technically constructed. For example, an e-mail that originates from a specific Internet

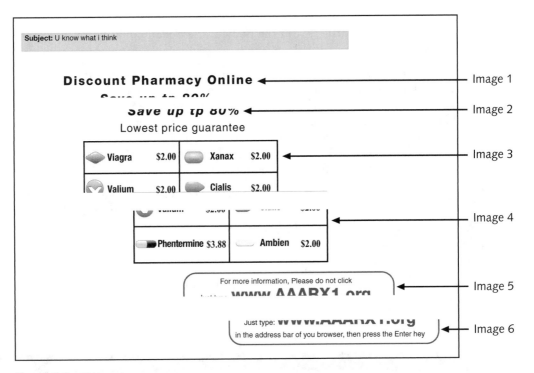

Subject: U know what i think

Discount Pharmacy Online ◄———————————— Image 1

Save up tp 80% ◄———————————— Image 2

Lowest price guarantee

Viagra	$2.00	Xanax	$2.00	◄——— Image 3

| Valium | $2.00 | Cialis | $2.00 |

◄——— Image 4

| Phentermine $3.88 | Ambien $2.00 |

For more information, Please do not click
www AAARX1 org ◄——— Image 5

Just type: **WWW.AAARX1.org**
in the address bar of you browser, then press the Enter hey ◄——— Image 6

Figure 3-9 GIF layering

Course Technology/Cengage Learning

Discount Pharmacy Online

Save up to 80%

Figure 3-10 Word splitting

Course Technology/Cengage Learning

Investors A
Continues m
Thursday!

Th Investor ALER
S   for New Film!
Pr
     The Motion Pi
Ir Symbol: MPRG
Co Price: $0.22

     MPRG secures
     from the Co-A

Figure 3-11 Geometric variance

Course Technology/Cengage Learning

address, contains a certain header pattern, has an embedded image of a specific size-range and type, and contains little text in the body of the e-mail could be an indication that the message is spam.

Malicious Attachments Another common means of distributing attacks is through e-mail attachments, or files that are sent with an e-mail message. E-mail-distributed viruses typically trick the recipient into opening an attachment and infecting their computers. After infecting a computer, many viruses replicate by sending themselves in an e-mail message to all of the contacts in an e-mail address book. The unsuspecting recipients, seeing that an e-mail and attachment arrived from a "friend," typically with a provocative subject line, open the attachment and infect their computers.

 If a file attached to an e-mail message contains a virus, the virus is launched when the file attachment is opened. This is usually done by double-clicking the attachment icon.

In recent years the number of attacks distributed through e-mails has started to decline. Table 3-2 shows the average rate of e-mails with infected attachments as reported by the security firm Sophos.

Table 3-2 E-mails with infected attachments

Year	Average number of infected attachments
2005	1 in 44
2006	1 in 337
2007	1 in 909
2008	1 in 714

Embedded Hyperlinks E-mail messages can contain **embedded hyperlinks,** as seen in Figure 3-12. Clicking on the link (*log in to Online Account Services*) will open the Web browser and take the user to a specific Web site. E-mail messages with embedded hyperlinks are commonly used by banks or financial institutions as a shortcut for the user to access the login page of their Web site to enter their username and password. Instead of opening a browser and typing in a lengthy Web address, the user can simply click the embedded hyper-link and be taken directly to the login page.

However, attackers can take advantage of embedded hyperlinks to trick users to be directed to the attacker's Web site instead. This "trickery" can be easily accomplished be-cause an embedded hyperlink can display only words and not the actual address of the Web site. For example, an attacker could create an embedded hyperlink that appears legitimate to the reader (*log in to Online Account Services*) yet the address to which the user is directed by clicking can be to the attacker's site. Even an embedded hyperlink that appears to be a legitimate Web address (*www.capitalone.com*) can be crafted so that it goes to a different

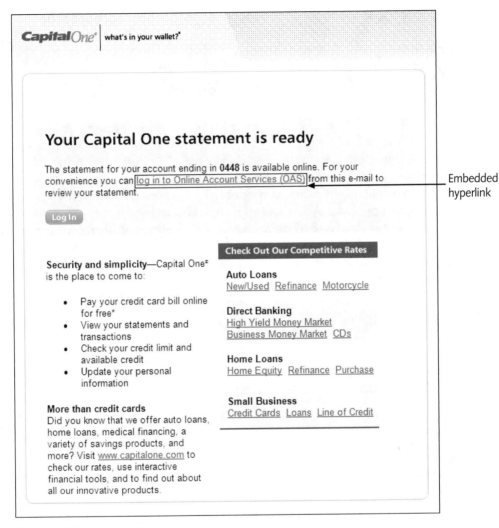

Figure 3-12 Embedded hyperlink

Course Technology/Cengage Learning

Web site (*www.attackers-dungeon.net*). The attacker's "look-alike" Web site asks the user to enter a username and password, which the attacker can use to break into the user's actual account. In short, users who click embedded hyperlinks do not know where they are being taken.

 One organization distributed an e-mail from the IT security department that specifically warned users not to click on embedded hyperlinks because of the danger associated with them. However, at the bottom of the e-mail it said, "For more information click on this link"!

Security in Your World

"Katrina," said Quy, "If you were trying to scare me you've done a pretty good job!" Katrina had just finished explaining to Quy several of the types of attacks that can occur through the Internet. "But what do I do now? Should I just hope that attackers won't find me since there are so many other Internet users out there?"

"Trying to get lost in the crowd probably isn't a very good defense," said Katrina. "There are some programs you can install that can help you stay secure, and you can also configure your browser to help, too. But one of the most important things is to use common sense. Just like my mother used to tell me not to drive around at night with my car doors unlocked, there are some basic common sense computer security things you can do to protect yourself."

"I feel like I'm surfing the Internet with my doors unlocked!" said Quy. "Can you show me what to do?"

Internet Defenses

There are several defenses that can be used to deflect Internet attacks. These defenses include using security application programs, configuring browser settings, and using general good practices.

Defenses Through Applications

There are three primary security applications that can be used to defend against Internet-based attacks. These defenses are popup blockers, spam filtering applications, and the security settings in e-mail programs.

Popup Blockers A **popup blocker** can be a separate program or a feature incorporated within a browser. As a separate program, a popup blocker may be part of a larger "suite" of security applications. A browser popup blocker allows the user to limit or block most popups. Users can select the level of blocking, ranging from blocking all popups to allowing specific popups. When a popup is detected an alert can be displayed in the browser such as, *Popup blocked; to see this popup or additional options click here*. The configuration settings for a typical browser popup blocker are seen in Figure 3-13.

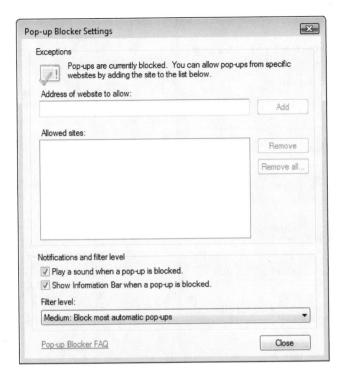

Figure 3-13 Popup blocker settings

Course Technology/Cengage Learning

Spam Filters Beyond being annoying and disruptive, spam can also pose a serious security risk. Spammers can distribute viruses as attachments through their spam e-mail messages. Spam filtering applications can be implemented on both the user's local computer as well as at the corporate or the Internet Service Provider level. An **Internet Service Provider (ISP)** is a business from which users purchase Internet access.

The reason why most users receive only a small amount of spam in their local e-mail inbox is that 90 percent of spam is blocked at the corporate or ISP level.

Filtering spam on the local computer can often be accomplished by using the local e-mail client. Most e-mail clients, such as Microsoft Outlook, can be configured to filter spam, as seen in Figure 3-14. Typically the e-mail client contains several features to block spam, such as:

- *Level of spam e-mail protection*—Users can select a level of protection that is the most appropriate for them. The highest level of protection will only accept e-mail messages from a preapproved list of senders.

- *Blocked senders*—A list of senders can be entered for which the user does not want to receive any e-mail, also known as a **blacklist**. Any message received from one of the

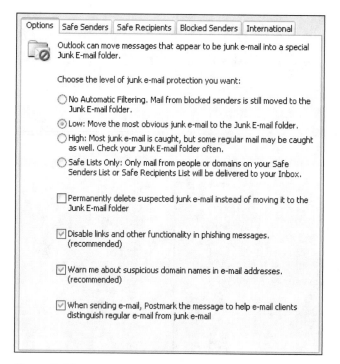

Figure 3-14 Spam filter settings

Course Technology/Cengage Learning

senders is sent to the junk e-mail folder. Several databases of blacklists are available on the Internet that include known spammers and others who distribute malicious content, and some sites allow users to download the lists and automatically add them to their e-mail server.

- *Allowed senders*—A list of senders can be entered for which the user will accept e-mail, also known as a **whitelist**.

- *Blocked top level domain list*—E-mail from entire countries or regions can also be blocked and treated as spam, as seen in Figure 3-15.

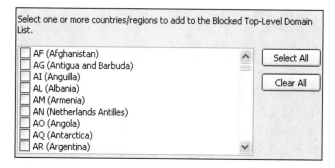

Figure 3-15 Blocking e-mail from countries to avoid spam

Course Technology/Cengage Learning

Microsoft Outlook automatically blocks 84 different types of file attachments known as Level 1 attachments that may contain viruses or worms.

If the local e-mail client application does not provide spam filtering, an alternative is to install separate filtering software that works with the e-mail client software. Sophisticated e-mail filters can use a technique known as **Bayesian filtering**. The user divides e-mail messages that have been received into two piles, spam and not-spam. The filter then analyzes every word in each e-mail and determines how frequently a word occurs in the spam pile compared to the not-spam pile. A word such as "the" would occur equally in both piles and be given a neutral 50 percent ranking. A word such as "report" may occur frequently in non-spam messages and would receive a 99 percent probability of being a non-spam word, while a word like "sex" may receive a 100 probability of being a spam word. Whenever e-mail arrives, the filter looks for the 15 words with the highest probabilities to calculate the message's overall spam probability rating. Although Bayesian filters are not perfect, they generally trap a much higher percentage of spam than other techniques.

Filtering spam at the corporate or ISP level requires the organization to install its own corporate spam filter. This filter works with the receiving e-mail server, which is typically based on the SMTP protocol for sending e-mail SMTP, and POP3 protocol for retrieving e-mail. The more common approach for installing a corporate spam filter is to install the spam filter to work with the SMTP server. The spam filter and SMTP server can run together on the same computer or on separate computers. The filter (instead of the SMTP server) is configured to listen on port 25 for all incoming e-mail messages and then passes the non-spam e-mail to the SMTP server that is listening on another port (such as port 26). This configuration prevents the SMTP server from notifying the spammer that it was unable to deliver the message. Installing the spam filter with the SMTP server is seen in Figure 3-16.

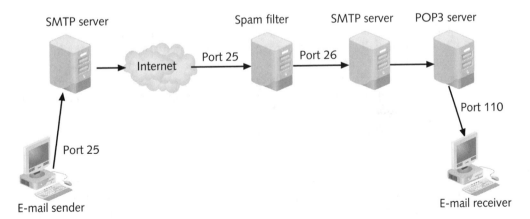

Figure 3-16 Spam filter on SMTP server

Course Technology/Cengage Learning

Although the spam filter can be installed on the POP3 server, this would mean that all spam must first pass through the SMTP server and be delivered to the user's mailbox. This can result in increased costs for storage, transmission, backup, and deletion.

E-mail Security Settings In addition to spam filters on the local e-mail client, there are typically security settings that can be configured through the e-mail client application. These include:

- *Read messages using a reading pane*—Most e-mail clients contain a **reading pane** that allows the user to read an e-mail message without actually opening it. Received e-mail messages can be viewed safely in the reading pane because malicious scripts and attachments are not activated or opened automatically in the reading pane.

Although malicious attachments may be blocked by using the e-mail reading pane, messages and attachments from unknown or unsolicited senders should always be treated with caution.

- *Block external content*—E-mail clients can be configured to block external content, such as hyperlinks to pictures or sounds, in HTML e-mail messages that are received. When a user opens an e-mail message or it is even displayed in the reading pane, the computer downloads the external content so that the picture can be displayed or the sound played. Spammers often send out spam to a wide range of e-mail addresses, not knowing which e-mail addresses exist or are accurate. In order to determine which e-mail addresses are valid and actually exist, a spammer can note which e-mail accounts downloaded the external content and then add those e-mail accounts to their spam list. Typical configuration settings for blocking external content are seen in Figure 3-17.

- *Preview attachments*—When an attachment is received with an e-mail message, some e-mail clients will permit the user to view the contents of the attachment without saving and then opening it. This helps to protect the user from malicious code that may be embedded in the attachment because scripts and ActiveX controls are disabled during attachment preview. To preview an attached file created in a specific application that application must be installed on the computer. For example, to preview a Microsoft Word attachment, Word must be installed on the client computer.

- *Use an e-mail postmark*—Occasionally it may be necessary to send a legitimate e-mail message that could look like spam and the recipient's spam filter could reject it. Some e-mail clients, like Microsoft Outlook, have an e-mail postmark feature. When the user sends a message with "spamlike" characteristics, the e-mail client solves a computationally costly puzzle and then puts that information about the puzzle and solution into two fields in the e-mail message's header. The recipient of the message does not see this information, but if she is using a compatible e-mail client it can use the contents of the message to determine that the message is valid and not spam.

You can control whether Outlook automatically downloads and displays pictures when you open an HTML e-mail message.

Blocking pictures in e-mail messages can help protect your privacy. Pictures in HTML e-mail can require Outlook to download the pictures from a server. Communicating to an external server in this way can verify to the sender that your e-mail address is valid, possibly making you the target of more junk mailings.

☑ Don't download pictures automatically in HTML e-mail messages or RSS items
    ☑ Permit downloads in e-mail messages from senders and to recipients defined in the Safe Senders and Safe Recipients Lists used by the Junk E-mail filter
    ☑ Permit downloads from Web sites in this security zone: Trusted Zone
    ☑ Permit downloads in RSS items
    ☑ Permit downloads in SharePoint Discussion Boards
    ☑ Warn me before downloading content when editing, forwarding, or replying to e-mail

Trusted Publishers

Add-ins

Privacy Options

E-mail Security

Attachment Handling

Automatic Download

Macro Security

Programmatic Access

Figure 3-17 Block external content

Course Technology/Cengage Learning

Although the sender of a message using the e-mail postmark probably will not notice the slight delay on an individual message when the puzzle is being computed, a spammer who tried to add an e-mail postmark to all of his spam would significantly slow down his computer, thus making postmarking impractical for spammers.

Defenses Through Browser Settings

Another line of defense against Internet attack is properly configuring the security settings on the Web browser. Modern Web browsers are highly customizable and allow the user to tailor the settings based on personal preferences. Beyond basic settings such as the color and the size of displayed characters, browsers also allow the user to customize security and privacy settings.

Microsoft Internet Explorer (IE) is a typical Web browser that can be configured for security. This configuration of IE browser settings is performed through selecting security options to be turned on or off. IE Web browser defenses can be divided into three categories: advanced security settings, security zones, and restricting cookies.

Besides IE, other popular Web browsers include Firefox, Safari, Opera, and Chrome. Each of the browsers has settings similar to those illustrated in IE.

Advanced Security Settings Web browsers offer a wide range of configuration settings. For example, IE has over 60 configuration settings, many related to security. Figure 3-18 illustrates some of the basic security settings, several of which are described in the following list.

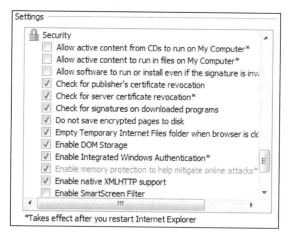

Figure 3-18 IE security settings

Course Technology/Cengage Learning

- *Do not save encrypted pages to disk*—When a Web site is viewed, the actual HTML documents are sent from the Web server to the local computer and saved on the hard drive in an area known as Temporary Internet Files for the browser to display. A secure Web site may transmit sensitive information in a special encrypted form that prevents attackers from seeing the information while in transit. However, after the HTML document is saved on the hard drive, an attacker who could gain access to the computer may be able to view it. This option prevents sensitive encrypted Web pages from being permanently saved on the hard drive.

- *Empty Temporary Internet Files folder when browser is closed*—To speed up processing, a Web browser first checks the hard drive on which the HTML documents are stored when they are received from the Web server. If the requested document is already stored, a Web browser only has to redisplay it and not request it again from the Web server. However, the stored information could be used by an attacker. This browser security option empties this folder whenever the browser is closed.

- *Warn if changing between secure and not secure mode*—Many Web sites use the standard HTTP protocol for sending data through the Internet. However, this protocol is not secure and an attacker could view the contents of the transmission. However, an enhanced version of HTTP encrypts the data sent between the Web browser and the Web server so that it cannot be viewed by others. By turning on this option the IE Web browser will alert the user with a warning message when the Web server changes from secure to not secure mode.

Other advanced security settings restrict downloaded browser code. For example, a setting that relates to Java applets and ActiveX can disable, enable, or prompt the user before the code runs. However, disabling code may result in Web pages not being displayed properly.

Security Zones One of the drawbacks of the security configuration settings in Web browsers is that the same settings should not be applied to all Web sites. For example, a school's Web site may require specific browser settings to access an online exam, yet this more secure setting may not be necessary for other sites.

Web browsers provide the ability to use Web zones. This allows the user to set customized security for these zones and then assign specific Web sites to a zone. For example, IE divides the Internet into four security zones, each of which can have a predefined (Low, Medium-low, Medium or High) or customized security level, as shown in Figure 3-19. Table 3-3 lists the different Web zones.

Figure 3-19 IE security zones

Course Technology/Cengage Learning

Table 3-3 IE Web security zones

Zone	Description	Default security level
Internet	This zone contains all of the Web sites that have not been placed in any other zone.	Medium-High
Local intranet	Web pages from an organization's internal Web site can be added to this zone.	Medium-Low
Trusted sites	Web sites that are trusted not to pose any harm to a computer can be placed here.	Low
Restricted sites	A Web site that is considered to be potentially harmful can be placed in the Restricted Sites zone.	High

Web sites can be assigned to one of these four zones. When that site is accessed, the security level for that zone is automatically invoked. This makes it easier to set browser viewing security levels for different Web sites.

When a Web site that has been placed in one of the security zones is viewed, an icon representing that zone is displayed on the right side of the status bar in Internet Explorer.

Restricting Cookies Restricting how cookies are created and used can also be done through configuring the Web browser. In IE this is accomplished through adjusting privacy settings. Privacy levels can be established for each of the four security zones (Internet, local, trusted sites, and restricted sites). The privacy levels for restricting cookies are:

- Block all cookies
- High
- Medium High
- Medium
- Low
- Accept All Cookies

Each privacy level can also be custom configured by the user.

E-mail Defenses Through Good Practices

Using common-sense procedures to protecting against harmful e-mail is also helpful. For example, when a user receives an e-mail with an attachment, the following questions may be considered:

- Is the e-mail from someone that I know?
- Have I received e-mail from this sender before?
- Was I expecting an attachment from this sender?

- Does e-mail from the sender with the contents as described in the Subject line and the name of the attachment make sense? For example, would a college professor send an e-mail message with the Subject line "Dude, Check This Out!" that contains the attachment *AnnaKournikovaPicture.jpg.vbs*?

Other good e-mail procedures include:

- Never click on an embedded hyperlink in an e-mail message.
- Be aware that e-mail is a common method for infecting computers and treat it cautiously.
- Never automatically open an unexpected attachment, even if it is sent from a known source.
- Use reading panes and preview attachments.
- Never answer an e-mail request for personal information; pick up the phone and call the company that requested it, using the number found in the telephone book and not in the e-mail message.

Internet Defense Summary

Although the Internet provides a virtually unlimited amount of information and instant communication, caution must often be used when accessing it. Table 3-4 lists several of the defenses that can be used to deflect Internet attacks.

Table 3-4 Internet defense summary

Attack	Defense	Comments
Downloaded browser code (JavaScript, Java, and ActiveX) performs malicious action	Disable from running in Web browser through browser settings	Some Web pages may not function properly if browser code is disabled
Third-party cookies used to track browsing	Restrict cookies in Web browser through browser settings	Time-consuming to keep up with cookies generated from different sites
Redirected Web traffic through misspellings	Double-check typed address before submitting	Difficult to see misspellings in long addresses
Attacks through e-mail through spam or infected attachments	Use spam filters, reading panes, and preview attachments	Can easily be set through e-mail client
Embedded hyperlinks sends to attacker's Web site	Do not click on embedded hyperlinks	These hyperlinks can mask the actual destination
Drive-by downloads infect computer	Set up browser security zones	Takes time to manage multiple sites

A good general defense against Internet attacks is to keep a current backup. Backups are covered in Chapter 2.

Chapter Summary

- The Internet is composed of server computers that provide online information in the Hypertext Markup Language (HTML) format, which allows Web authors to combine text, graphic images, audio, video, and hyperlinks. Instructions written in HTML code indicate to a local computer's Web browser how it should be displayed. Web servers distribute HTML documents based on a set of protocols known as the Hypertext Transport Protocol (HTTP). E-mail has become the standard means of written communication, particularly for businesses. E-mail attachments are documents that are connected to an e-mail message, such as word processing documents, spreadsheets, or pictures.

- One form of Internet-based attack takes advantage of downloaded browser code. The dynamic content required for Web pages requires special computer code to be downloaded into the user's Web browser in order to display it. JavaScript is a scripting language that resides inside HTML documents. When a Web site that uses JavaScript is accessed, the HTML document with the JavaScript code is downloaded onto the user's computer and the browser then executes that code using a Java interpreter. Attackers can use JavaScript programs to capture and send user information without the user's knowledge or authorization. Java is a complete programming language that can be used to create a special type of smaller application called a Java applet.

- Whereas JavaScript is embedded in an HTML document, a Java applet is a separate program. An unsigned Java applet is a program that does not come from a trusted source, whereas a signed Java applet has information that proves the program is from a trusted source and has not been altered. Unsigned Java applets that attempt to do something outside of the sandbox automatically generate a warning message to the user. However, most users are unaware of these warning messages. ActiveX is a set of rules for how applications should share information. ActiveX controls have full access to the underlying Windows operating system. Anything a user can do on a computer, an ActiveX control can do. ActiveX poses a number of security concerns.

- A Web server can insert user-specific information in a file on the user's local computer known as a cookie for later retrieval. Cookies by themselves are not dangerous. A cookie cannot contain a virus nor steal personal information stored on a hard drive. It only contains information that can be used by a Web server. However, a certain type of cookie can pose a privacy risk. Adware is a software program that delivers advertising content in a manner that is unexpected and unwanted by the user. Adware can be a privacy risk. Many adware programs perform a tracking function, which monitors and tracks a user's online activities and then sends a log of these activities to third parties without the user's authorization or knowledge.

- It is not uncommon for a user to make a mistake when typing a Web address into a browser. However, attackers can exploit a misaddressed Web name by registering the names of similar-sounding Web sites and stealing a user's information. Drive-by downloads can be used to infect a user's computer just by viewing a Web page.

- E-mail attacks are often used by attackers to distribute malware. Spam, or unsolicited e-mail, is both annoying and dangerous. Another common means of distributing attacks is through e-mail attachments, or files that are sent with an e-mail message.

Attackers also take advantage of embedded hyperlinks to trick users to be directed to the attacker's Web site instead. This is because an embedded hyperlink can display only words and not the actual address of the Web site.

- There are three primary security applications used to defend against Internet-based attacks: popup blockers, spam filtering applications, and the security settings in e-mail programs. In addition, there are security settings that can be configured through the e-mail client application to stop spam and reduce the risk of infections. Another line of defense against Internet attack is properly configuring the security settings on the Web browser, because browser settings allow the user to customize security and privacy. Specifically Web browsers provide the ability to use Web zones, which allows the user to set customized security for these zones and then assign specific Web sites to a zone. Many e-mail attacks can be defeated by simply using common sense and good practices.

Key Terms

ActiveX   A set of technologies developed by Microsoft for creating special features in an HTML document, also called add-ons.

ActiveX controls   A specific way of implementing ActiveX.

adware   A software program that delivers advertising content in a manner that is unexpected and unwanted by the user.

attachments   Documents that are connected to an e-mail message.

Bayesian filtering   A sophisticated e-mail filtering technique.

blacklist   A list of senders for which the user does not want to receive any e-mail.

browser   A program that displays HTML documents.

cookie   A computer file that contains user-specific information.

drive-by downloads   Infections that occur by only passively viewing a Web page.

embedded hyperlinks   A hyperlink typically contained in an e-mail message or other document.

first-party cookie   A cookie created from the Web site that a user is currently viewing.

geometric variance   Spam that uses "speckling" and different colors so that no two spam e-mails appear to be the same.

GIF layering   Image spam that is divided into multiple images.

hyperlinks   A notation in an HTML document that allows the user to jump from one area to another.

Hypertext Markup Language (HTML)   A language that allows text, graphic images, audio, video, and hyperlinks to be combined into a single document.

Hypertext Transport Protocol (HTTP)   A set of standards for transmitting HTML documents.

image spam   Spam that uses graphical images of text in order to circumvent text-based filters.

IMAP (Internet Mail Access Protocol, or IMAP4)   An advanced e-mail protocol.

Internet   A worldwide, interconnected set of computers, servers, and networks.

Internet Service Provider (ISP)   A business from which users purchase Internet access.

Java A complete programming language that can be used to create standalone applications.

Java applet A separate program for creating special features in an HTML document.

JavaScript A programming language for creating special features in an HTML document.

popup A small Web browser window that appears over the Web site that is being viewed.

popup blocker A separate program or a feature incorporated within a browser that limits or blocks most popups.

port numbers A number that identifies what program or service is being requested.

Post Office Protocol (POP or POP3) A protocol that handles incoming e-mail.

protocol A set of standards.

reading pane A feature in an e-mail client that allows the user to read an e-mail message without opening it.

sandbox A restrictive area that surrounds a program and keeps it away from private data and other resources on a local computer.

scripting language A language that is similar to a computer programming language that is "interpreted" into a language the computer can understand without the need of a special computer program.

signed Java applet A Java applet with a digital signature that proves the program is from a trusted source and has not been altered.

Simple Mail Transfer Protocol (SMTP) A protocol that handles outgoing e-mail.

spam Unsolicited e-mail.

spam filters Special filters that look for evidence of e-mail spam.

third-party cookie A cookie that is not created by the Web site that attempts to access the cookie.

Transmission Control Protocol/Internet Protocol (TCP/IP) A set of standards for Internet transmissions.

unsigned Java applet A Java applet that does not come from a trusted source.

whitelist A list of senders from whom a user wants to receive e-mail messages.

word splitting Separating words in a spam message so that they can still be read by the human eye.

World Wide Web (WWW) A system of Internet server computers that provide online information in a specific format.

zero pixel IFrame An HTML element used in drive-by downloads that allows malicious code to be embedded in an HTML document.

Review Questions

1. The _____ is a worldwide, interconnected set of computers, servers, and networks.

   a. Intranet

   b. Internet

   c. HTTP net

   d. HTML Web

2. _____ is used to combine text, graphic images, audio, and video into a single document.

    a. Transmission Control Protocol/Internet Protocol (TCP/IP)

    b. Hypertext Markup Language (HTML)

    c. Hypertext Transport Protocol (HTTP)

    d. Hyperlink Scripting Language (HSL)

3. The _____ protocol handles outgoing mail.

    a. Simple Mail Transfer Protocol (SMTP)

    b. Post Office Protocol (POP3)

    c. IMAPI-3

    d. Transmission Hypertext Mail System (THMS)

4. Each of the following is a programming tool that can be used to create downloaded browser code except _____.

    a. ActiveX

    b. Java applet

    c. JavaScript

    d. Windows Net Language (WNL)

5. A cookie that was not created by the Web site that attempts to access it is called a _____.

    a. first-party cookie

    b. second-party cookie

    c. third-party cookie

    d. fourth-party cookie

6. _____ resides inside an HTML document.

    a. ActiveX

    b. JavaScript

    c. Java

    d. Virtual machine

7. A Java applet _____ is a barrier that surrounds the applet to keep it away from resources on the local computer.

    a. fence

    b. playpen

    c. sandbox

    d. container

8. A _____ is a list of pre-approved e-mail addresses from which the user will accept mail.

   a. botnet

   b. blacklist

   c. whitelist

   d. cleanlist

9. A _____ is a program that does not come from a trusted source.

   a. unsigned Java applet

   b. JavaScript applet

   c. ActiveX Controller Entity

   d. signed JavaScript application

10. ActiveX controls _____.

    a. run in a sandbox

    b. have full access to the underlying Windows operating system

    c. can only be signed

    d. have been replaced by JavaX

11. A cookie _____.

    a. can contain a virus

    b. acts like a worm

    c. may pose a privacy risk

    d. places a small file on the Web server computer

12. A drive-by download _____.

    a. can infect a user's computer just by passively viewing a Web site

    b. requires the user to be running older versions of Internet Explorer

    c. only infects attacker's Web servers

    d. is the primary means used to spread worms

13. Almost all spam today is sent from _____.

    a. compromised zombie computers that have been linked into a botnet

    b. China

    c. spammers using college campus computers

    d. ActiveX controls

14. _____ involves separating words so that they can still be read by the human eye.

    a. Geometric variance

    b. Word splitting

    c. GIF layering

    d. Image filtering

15. Each of the following is true regarding embedded hyperlinks except _____.

    a. they are often found in e-mail messages

    b. they may not display the actual destination of the link

    c. are rarely used anymore

    d. require the user to click in order to launch

16. A spam filter _____.

    a. may be used by an Internet Service Provider (ISP) to block messages from ever reaching users

    b. can only be used on a local e-mail client

    c. requires that both a blacklist and a whitelist be created

    d. can only be used on a POP3 server

17. A reading pane allows the user to read an e-mail message _____.

    a. after the attachment has been saved to the hard drive

    b. only one time

    c. without actually opening it

    d. and requires that certain applications to preview the message be first installed

18. Each of the following regarding the Temporary Internet Files folder is true except _____.

    a. it is the location where a Web browser will first check to see if the HTML documents are already stored

    b. is where special encrypted files are saved

    c. should be periodically deleted

    d. should never be deleted

19. Each of the following is an Internet zone in IE except _____.

    a. Internet

    b. Extranet

    c. Trusted sites

    d. Restricted sites

20. Each of the following is a privacy level for restricting cookies in IE except _____.

    a. Accept all cookies

    b. Block all cookies

    c. High

    d. Internet

Hands-on Projects

Project 3-1: Set Web Browser Security Using Advanced Settings

Setting browser security is important to keep a computer secure. In this project, you use the Windows Internet Explorer (IE) Version 8 Web browser.

1. Start Internet Explorer.

2. Click **Tools** on the menu bar, and then click **Internet Options** to display the Internet Options dialog box. Click the **General** tab, if necessary.

3. First remove all of the HTML documents and cookies that are in the cache on the computer. Before erasing the files, look at what is stored in the cache. Under **Browsing history** click the **Settings** button and then click the **View files** button to see all of the files. If necessary, maximize the window that displays the files.

4. Click the **Last Checked** column heading to see how long this information has been on the computer.

5. Next, select a cookie by locating one in the **Name** column (it will be something like *cookie: windows_vista@microsoft.com*). Double-click the name of the cookie to open it. If you receive a Windows warning message, click **Yes**. What information does this cookie provide? Close the cookie file and open several other cookies. Do some cookies contain more information than others?

6. Close the window listing the cookie files to return to the dialog box. Click the **Cancel** button.

7. In the Internet Options dialog box under Browsing history click **Delete**.

8. On the Delete Browsing History dialog box check all of the boxes listed.

9. Uncheck **Preserve Favorites website data**. Click **Delete**. Close the Internet Options dialog box.

10. Check if the IE Pop-up Blocker is enabled. Click **Tools** and point to **Pop-up Blocker**. If the menu says **Turn-On Pop-up Blocker** then it is turned off. Click **Turn On Pop-up Blocker** if necessary to turn it on.

11. Click **Tools** and **Manage Add-ons** to display the Manage Add-ons dialog box as shown in Figure 3-20.

12. Under Add-on Types select **Toolbars and Extensions** if necessary.

13. Under **Show** click **Run without permission**. These are the ActiveX controls that run without asking you for permission. How many controls are listed? Are you surprised at the number?

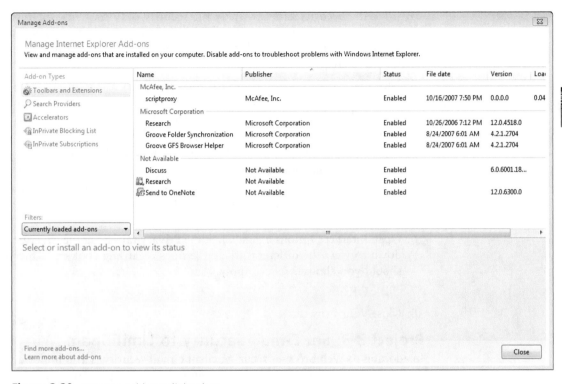

Manage Add-ons						
Manage Internet Explorer Add-ons						
View and manage add-ons that are installed on your computer. Disable add-ons to troubleshoot problems with Windows Internet Explorer.						
Add-on Types	Name	Publisher	Status	File date	Version	Loa
Toolbars and Extensions	McAfee, Inc.					
Search Providers	scriptproxy	McAfee, Inc.	Enabled	10/16/2007 7:50 PM	0.0.0.0	0.04
Accelerators	Microsoft Corporation					
InPrivate Blocking List	Research	Microsoft Corporation	Enabled	10/26/2006 7:12 PM	12.0.4518.0	
InPrivate Subscriptions	Groove Folder Synchronization	Microsoft Corporation	Enabled	8/24/2007 6:01 AM	4.2.1.2704	
	Groove GFS Browser Helper	Microsoft Corporation	Enabled	8/24/2007 6:01 AM	4.2.1.2704	
	Not Available					
	Discuss	Not Available	Enabled		6.0.6001.18...	
	Research	Not Available	Enabled			
	Send to OneNote	Not Available	Enabled		12.0.6300.0	
Filters: Currently loaded add-ons						

Select or install an add-on to view its status

Find more add-ons...
Learn more about add-ons   Close

Figure 3-20 Manage Add-ons dialog box

Course Technology/Cengage Learning

Some add-ons that are *pre-approved* can come from Microsoft, your ISP, computer manufacturer, or network administrator.

14. Close the dialog box.

Project 3-2: Set Web Browser Security Zones

Web browsers provide the ability to use Web zones, which allows the user to set customized security for these zones and then assign specific Web sites to a zone. IE divides the Internet into four security zones, each of which can have a predefined (Low, Medium-low, Medium or High) or a customized security level. Setting browser security is important to keep a computer secure. In this project, you use the Windows Internet Explorer (IE) Version 8 Web browser to set security zones.

1. Start Internet Explorer.

2. Click **Tools** on the menu bar, and then click **Internet Options** to display the Internet Options dialog box. Click the **General** tab, if necessary.

3. Click the **Security** tab to display the security options. Click the **Internet** icon. This is the zone in which all Web sites are placed that are not in another zone. Under **Security level for this zone** move the slider to look at the various settings.

4. Now place a Web site in **Restricted** zone. Click **OK** and return to your Web browser. Go to **www.bad.com** and view the information on that site. Notice that the status bar displays an Internet icon, indicating that this Web site is in the Internet zone. Click your **Home** button.

5. Click **Tools** on the menu bar and then click **Internet Options** to display the Internet Options dialog box again. Click the **Security** tab and then click **Restricted sites**. Click **Sites**, and enter **www.bad.com**, click **Add**, and then click **Close** and **OK**. Now return to that site again. What happens this time? Why?

6. Open Internet Options again. Click the **Privacy** tab. Drag the slider up and down to view the different privacy settings regarding cookies. Which one should you choose? Click **Apply**.

7. Click **OK**.

8. Close your browser.

Project 3-3: Set E-mail Security to Limit Spam

In addition to Web browser security, client e-mail security is also important. In this project, you configure Microsoft Outlook security to restrict spam.

1. Launch Microsoft Outlook 2007.

2. Click **Tools** on the menu bar, and then click **Options**. The Options dialog box opens.

3. Click **Junk E-mail** to display the Junk E-mail dialog box.

4. Click **Safe Lists Only**.

5. Click the **Blocked Senders** tab.

6. Click **Add**. Enter the e-mail address of a partner in the class and click **OK**.

7. Click **Safe Senders**.

8. Check the boxes **Also trust e-mail from my Contacts** and **Automatically add people I e-mail to the Safe Senders list**.

9. Click **Apply** and then **OK**. Close the Options dialog box.

10. Ask your partner to send you an e-mail message. What happens when it arrives? Where does Outlook put the message? Why?

11. Create an e-mail message and send it to a third party who is not in your contacts list. Now look at your Safe Senders list again. Is that person added?

12. Close Microsoft Outlook.

Project 3-4: Set E-mail Security to Restrict Infections

Client e-mail security can also be used to reduce the risk of infections by downloaded content and attachments. In this project, you configure Microsoft Outlook security to use the reading pane and preview attachments.

1. Launch Microsoft Outlook 2007.

2. First turn the reading pane on if necessary. Click **Inbox**. If the reading pane is not displayed click **View** and then **Reading Pane** and click **Right**.

3. Scroll through several messages and notice that they can be read in the reading pane yet any scripts are not started.

4. Open an e-mail document that has an attachment or ask a classmate to send you an e-mail message with an attachment.

5. Single click on the attachment name to open the preview pane.

6. Click **Preview file**. The attachment will open and can be previewed safely.

7. Now double click on the attachment name. What warning message do you receive? If you click **Open** it will launch the application to view the attachment and could allow an infected attachment to harm your computer. A safer option is to click **Save** and allow the computer's antivirus software to scan it. Click **Cancel**.

8. Close all windows.

Case Projects

Case Project 3-1: Your E-mail Security

How secure is your personal e-mail account? Using the information contained in this chapter and other Internet or print sources, create a list of e-mail security settings. Next, rank them in order of importance, with the most important receiving the highest number and the least important the lowest number. Finally, view your personal e-mail settings and give yourself a score. Then apply that same list to a friend or other student and evaluate his or her e-mail security. What suggestions would you make to improve your e-mail security? Write a one-page paper on your results.

Case Project 3-2: Antispamming Laws

The federal government along with several states are now passing or attempting to pass antispamming laws. Research several of these laws and select the strongest points from each one. Then, create your own antispamming law along with penalties for noncompliance. Write a one-page document regarding your new law.

Case Project 3-3: Comparing Browser Security

Besides IE, other popular Web browsers include Firefox, Safari, Opera, and Chrome. Which is the most secure? Using the Internet, research the security features of each of these browsers. Create a table that lists the different security features. In your opinion, is there one browser that is more secure than the rest? Is there a browser that is the least secure? Give reasons for your conclusion.

Case Project 3-4: Using Security Zones

Although security zones can help provide a higher degree of security, most users are unaware of the advantages of zones or find that it takes too much time to use. For three days, use security zones for all of your Web surfing, and place sites that you visit in your zones. Then, write a paper on your experience. Was it easy or hard to use security zones? What difficulties did you encounter? What could be done to encourage the average user to take advantage of zones? Create a one-page summary of your work with security zones.

Case Project 3-5: Adware Arguments

Adware can be considered a privacy risk because it can monitor and track a user's online activities and send a log of these activities to third parties. However, proponents argue that adware serves a useful function by identifying users' spending habits and preferences and providing them with useful information about products and services that they are interested in. What do you think? Write a one-page summary of the pros and cons of adware.

Case Project 3-6: Winstead Computer Consultants

Winstead Computer Consultants (WCC), a local information technology company that specializes in security, has hired you to assist them with a project. Matchett Architects Associates (MAA) provides design services for businesses and consumers. In the past six months MAA has been the victim of two computer attacks, resulting in corrupted blueprints that were being developed for a large project. MAA wants to provide training for its employees about Internet defenses, and WCC has contracted with you to help them.

Create a PowerPoint presentation of eight or more slides that covers the basics of Internet-based attacks and a summary of defenses. Because the audience does not have a strong technical background, your presentation should be general in its tone.

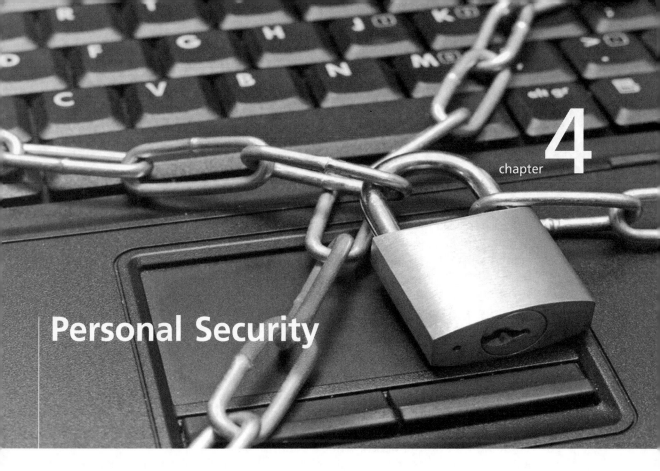

chapter 4

Personal Security

After completing this chapter you should be able to do the following:

- Describe attacks on personal security
- Explain the dangers of identity theft
- List the defenses against personal security attacks
- Define cryptography and explain how it can be used

"Maggie, did you see what I posted on Facebook last night?" asked Lindsay. Maggie and Lindsay attended the same college and met each morning in a coffee shop across from the school. Maggie shrugged and said, "Yeah, I saw it." "What's the matter? You don't look very excited about it," Lindsay said. "Well, I was trying to work up the courage to talk with you about it," said Maggie. "What do you mean?" asked Lindsay.

"Do you think it's a good idea to post a video of yourself on your trip to Florida last spring? I mean, it's not exactly tame," said Maggie. "Oh, Maggie, you're acting just like my mother. What's the matter with posting that video for my friends to see?" asked Lindsay.

"Let me ask you this: what would your boss at the copy center think if he saw it?" asked Maggie. Lindsay paused for a moment. Her boss Shaun had a reputation for being very "strait laced." "Well, I'm sure Shaun wouldn't approve. But he can't fire me for that!" said Lindsay. Maggie set down her latte. "No, he can't fire you for that, but couldn't it affect his opinion of how professional you are? Remember, you want to apply for that open supervisor's position at the end of the month. If he saw that video of you doing that on the beach, what would he think?"

Lindsay shifted in her chair. "But I only put that up there for my friends to see." "Lindsay," said Maggie, "You didn't set it to 'Only my friends'. All of your networks can also see it. Your network probably has hundreds of people, and you have no control over who else joins the network." Lindsay remembered seeing an embarrassing photo of a classmate Byron who had let his network see it instead of only his friends. "And besides," Maggie continued, "Is it really a good idea to post the dates that you'll be gone to Florida again this spring? Isn't that just the sort of information that a thief would like to know when you're away from your apartment that week?"

Lindsay opened her purse and took out her cell phone. "Maggie, you're right. I'm going to change that right now. You obviously have thought about this more than I have."

Many computer attacks are malicious and designed to harm a computer or its data. Viruses can corrupt computer data, worms are intended to "clog" a computer and slow it to a crawl, and logic bombs are written to erase critical company data. These types of attacks are similar to vandalism, where the goal is to deface or destroy.

Another type of attack that has been rapidly proliferating is now one of the most feared. Instead of destroying data on the computer, these attacks are designed to steal personal information and use it for financial gain. For example, some attacks install software that secretly monitors every keystroke in order to steal passwords or credit card numbers. Other attacks trick users into revealing personal information in response to a fake e-mail. Instead of vandalizing the computer and data, these new attacks are directly aimed at the user's personal security.

In this chapter, we will examine attacks directed at users and their personal security. First, we'll explore what these attacks are and why they are so dangerous. Then, we'll examine the defenses you can use to protect yourself from attacks on your personal security.

Attacks on Personal Security

Attacks on personal security can take many different forms. These attacks include spyware, password attacks, phishing, attacks on users of social networking sites, and identity theft.

What Is Spyware?

Spyware is a general term used to describe software that violates a user's personal security. The Anti-Spyware Coalition defines spyware as tracking software that is deployed without adequate notice, consent, or user control. This software is implemented in ways that impair a user's control over:

- The use of system resources, including what programs are installed on a user's computer

- The collection, use, and distribution of personal or otherwise sensitive information

- Material changes that affect the user experience, privacy, or system security

The Anti-Spyware Coalition is composed of antispyware software companies, hardware vendors, academic institutions, and consumer groups including Google, Microsoft, Dell, and Symantec. Their Web site is *www.antispywarecoalition.org*.

Although spyware is often dismissed as just a nuisance, two characteristics of spyware make it dangerous. First, spyware creators are motivated by profit: their goal is to generate income through spyware advertisements or by acquiring personal information they can then use to steal from users, unlike the creators of viruses who sometimes are interested in gaining personal notoriety through the malicious software that they create. Because of this heightened motivation, spyware is often more intrusive than some other types of malware, more difficult to detect, and harder to remove.

Second, harmful spyware is not always easy to identify. This is because not all software that performs these functions is necessarily spyware. With the proper notice, consent, and control, some of these same technologies can provide valuable benefits. For example, monitoring tools can help parents keep track of the online activities of their children while they are surfing the Web, and remote-control features allow support technicians to remotely diagnose computer problems. Vendors that sell software that performs these functions are considered legitimate. Software developers who sell programs that cause pop-up advertisements to appear on Web pages likewise consider themselves to be legitimate and performing a useful function. Whereas there is no question about the creators of a virus performing a malicious act, the line between legitimate businesses that use spyware-like technology and malicious spyware operators is sometimes blurred. This makes it difficult to pinpoint the perpetrators of malicious spyware and to defend against them.

One way to differentiate between a legitimate business that uses spyware-like technology and malicious spyware is that malicious spyware performs functions without appropriately obtaining the user's consent.

Spyware is very widespread. For example:

- Approximately 9 out of 10 computers are infected with some type of spyware.
- The average computer has over 24 pieces of spyware on it.
- Microsoft estimates that half of all computer crashes are due to spyware.
- According to Dell, over 20 percent of all technical support calls involve spyware.

The impact of spyware on an organization is significant. A study by CompTIA (the Computing Technology Industry Association) revealed the following regarding spyware:

- Over 25 percent of end users reported their productivity was affected by a spyware infection.
- Over one-third of end users' computers had been infected multiple times with spyware, while some were infected 10 times or more.
- On average it takes 20 hours from the time of the spyware infection to the time the computer is cleaned.
- The cost of spyware infections to an organization exceeds $8,000 a year, not counting lost revenue.

Table 4-1 lists some of the effects that spyware can have on a computer.

Table 4-1 Effects of spyware

Effect	Explanation
Slow computer performance	Spyware can increase the time to boot a computer or surf the Internet.
System instability	Spyware can cause a computer to freeze frequently or even reboot.
New browser toolbars or menus	Spyware may install new menus or toolbars to a Web browser.
New shortcuts	New shortcuts on the desktop or in the system tray may indicate the presence of spyware.
Hijacked homepage	An unauthorized change in the default homepage on a Web browser can be caused by spyware.
Increased pop-ups	Pop-up advertisements that suddenly appear are usually the result of spyware.

Although attackers use several different spyware tools, two common tools are keyloggers and browser hijackers.

Keyloggers A keylogger is either a small hardware device or a program that monitors each keystroke a user types on the computer's keyboard. As the user types, the keystrokes are collected and saved as text. This information can be later retrieved by the attacker or secretly transmitted to a remote location. The attacker then searches for any useful information in the captured text such as passwords, credit card numbers, or personal information.

As a hardware device, a keylogger is a small device inserted between the keyboard connector and computer keyboard port, as shown in Figure 4-1. Because the device resembles an ordinary keyboard plug and because the computer keyboard port is on the back of the computer, a hardware keylogger is virtually undetectable. The device collects each keystroke and the attacker who installed the keylogger returns at a later time and physically removes the device in order to access the information it has gathered.

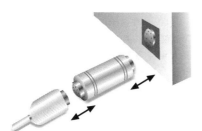

Figure 4-1 Hardware keylogger

Course Technology/Cengage Learning

Software keyloggers are programs that silently capture all keystrokes, including passwords and sensitive information, as seen in Figure 4-2. Software keyloggers do not require physical access to the user's computer but are often unknowingly downloaded and installed as a Trojan or by a virus. Software keylogger programs also hide themselves so that they cannot be easily detected even if a user is searching for them.

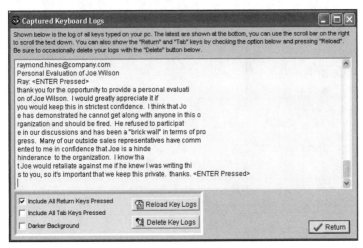

Figure 4-2 Captured information by keylogger

Course Technology/Cengage Learning

Browser Hijackers A **browser hijacker** is a program that an attacker installs on a computer and changes the Web browser's home page and search engine to another site. Whenever the Web browser is launched, instead of accessing the home page Web site the user has configured, the browser is directed to another site. This site typically displays advertisements, pornography, or other unwanted material along with numerous popup ads. In many instances closing one popup ad results in more being displayed, preventing the user from navigating to another Web site.

 Many browser hijackers also record and then report the user's Web browsing habits to a central site. This information is then sold to marketing companies.

Another type of attack does not directly change the browser's home page; instead, it places Internet shortcut links in the user's *Favorites* folder without asking permission. Because Web sites can earn advertising revenue by the number of users who view the site, this attack is designed to increase traffic to the sites as curious users click on links.

 Some browser hijackers are so tenacious that changing settings in the Internet Options does not solve the problem because the program re-hijacks the browser every time the computer reboots.

Passwords

When accessing a computer or a secure Web site, users are typically required to provide information that identifies them and provides proof that they are who they say they are. Each user is assigned a **username**, which is a unique name for identification, such as *SRosser, Traci_Li,* or *Administrator*. Yet virtually anyone could type in a person's username. How can the computer or Web site be certain that the person entering that username is authentic and not an imposter? The process of providing proof that the user is "genuine" or authentic is known as **authentication**. Figure 4-3 illustrates a Web site requesting a username and authentication.

Figure 4-3 Web site username and authentication

Course Technology/Cengage Learning

Authentication can be performed based on one (or a combination of) three entities:

- What you have
- What you know
- What you are

Consider this scenario: Bob stops at the health club to exercise. After he locks his car doors, he walks into the club and is recognized by Alice, the clerk at the desk. Alice chats with Bob and allows him to pass on to the locker room. Once in the locker room, Bob opens his locker using a combination lock using a series of numbers that he has memorized.

Bob has used three different means to authenticate or prove that he is the "real" Bob. First, by locking the doors of his car, its contents are protected by what Bob *has*, namely the car key or wireless key fob. Next, access to the locker room is protected by what Bob *is*. Alice had to recognize Bob's unique characteristics (his hair color, his face, his body type, and his voice) before he could enter the locker room. Those characteristics serve to make Bob who he is and were used to authenticate him. Finally, the contents of Bob locker are protected by what he *knows*, the lock combination.

Computers have typically relied upon authenticating users by what they know through using a password. A **password** is a secret combination of letters, numbers, and/or symbols that serves to validate or authenticate a user by what she knows. Because no other person knows (or should know) that password, the computer can be assured that the user is actually who he or she claims to be.

Despite the fact that passwords are the primary (and often exclusive) means of authenticating a user for access to a computer, a Web site, or a program, passwords are not considered as strong defenses against attackers. This is because passwords can be weak and are subject to different attacks.

Weak Passwords Passwords provide only a weak degree of security. This is because of the "password paradox." For a password to remain secure, it should never be written down but must be committed to memory. A password should also be of a sufficient length and complexity that an attacker cannot easily determine it. However, this creates the paradox: although lengthy and complex passwords should be used and never written down, it is very difficult to memorize these types of passwords.

Compounding the problem is that today users have multiple accounts for computers at work, school, and home, e-mail accounts, banks, and online Internet stores, to name a few, and each account has its own password. Because humans have a limited capacity for retaining precise information, the sheer number of passwords makes it impossible to remember all of them. In addition, passwords are often set to expire after a period of time, such as 60 days, and a new one must be created. And some devices even prevent a previously used password from being recycled and used again, forcing the user to repeatedly memorize multiple passwords for multiple devices.

All of these factors cause many users to use **weak passwords**, or those that compromise security. Characteristics of weak passwords include:

- *A common word used as a password (such as* January*)*—Attackers can use an electronic dictionary of common words to help discover the password.

- *Not changing passwords unless forced to do so*—If a user does not change a password, an attacker who gains access to a device or account would have unlimited access for the foreseeable future.

- *Passwords that are short (such as* ABCD*)*—Short passwords are easier to break than long passwords.

- *Personal information in a password (such as the name of a child or pet)*—These passwords can be easy to guess.

- *Using the same password*—An attacker who secures the password can then gain access to all the user's accounts or devices.

- *Writing the password down*—This can serve as an "open invitation" to enter an account or device.

- *Predictable use of characters*—Many applications have 76 different characters that can be used for passwords, consisting of 26 uppercase and lowercase letters (*A-Z* and *a-z*), 10 digits (*0-9*), and 14 symbols (*!@#$%^&*()-_+=*). One study revealed that 80 percent of password characters used only 32 of the 76 characters (those characters in order of occurrence were *ea1oirn0st2lud!m3hcyg94kSbpM758B*) and ten percent of passwords were composed *only* from the 32 characters.

One reason for weak passwords is that there are several myths regarding passwords. Table 4-2 lists some common password myths.

Table 4-2 Common password myths

Myth	Explanation
P9#6@ is better than *this_is_a_very_long_password*.	Even though the first password is a combination of letters, numbers, and symbols, it is too short and can easily be broken.
The best length for a password is 6 characters.	Because of how systems store passwords, the minimum recommended length is 15 characters.
Replacing letters with numbers, such as "J0hn_ Sm1th", is good.	Automated password "cracking" programs can look for common words (John) as well as variations using numbers (J0hn).
Passwords can contain only letters and numbers.	Most programs can accept passwords with spaces and special characters.

Due to the use of weak passwords and myths about passwords, passwords have become a prime attack target. The results of several recent studies on passwords indicate why passwords are targeted by attackers:

- 70 percent of users do not use a unique password for each Web site login

- 67 percent of users do not want to be forced to change their passwords

- 65 percent of employees either use the same password for different applications or write down the password

- 50 percent of users have never changed the password they use online

- 40 percent of help desk calls are employee requests for password resets (at $100–$350 annual cost per user for an organization to manage passwords)

- 28 percent of online banking customers use their bank password at other Internet sites

Attacks on Passwords Because passwords are so common yet provide weak security, they are a frequent focus of attacks. Yet simply trying to guess a password through combining a systematic combination of characters, called a **brute force attack**, is not feasible. An eight-character password that can use any of 76 characters (uppercase and lowercase letters, digits, and common symbols) would result in 1.11×10^{15} possible passwords. At two or three attempts per second, it would take 5,878,324 years to guess a password. In addition, each variation of the password must be entered into the password login program in order to determine if it is correct. Most computers can be set to disable all logins after a small number (3–5) of incorrect attempts, thus locking out the attacker.

An alternative approach is to decrypt an encrypted password. Passwords typically are stored in an encrypted form called a "hash"; when a user enters her password to log on, it is hashed and compared with the stored hashed version (if it matches then the user can log on). Attackers try to steal the file of hashed passwords and then break the hashed passwords offline. An advantage of decrypting a hashed password is that each variation of the password does not have to be entered into the password login program in order to determine if it is correct.

One common offline password attack is a **dictionary attack**. A dictionary attack begins with the attacker creating hashes of common dictionary words, and compares those hashed dictionary words against those in a stolen password file. This can be successful because users often create passwords that are single dictionary words or simple variations, such as appending a single digit to a word. A dictionary attack is shown in Figure 4-4.

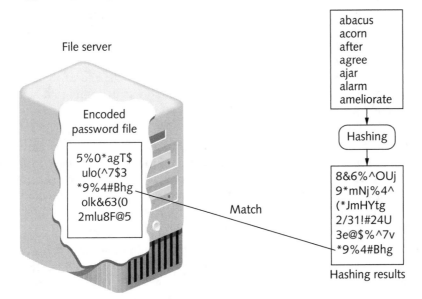

Figure 4-4 Dictionary attack

Course Technology/Cengage Learning

Although brute force and dictionary attacks were once the primary tools used by attackers to crack an encrypted password, today attackers use **rainbow tables**. Rainbow tables make password attacks easier by creating a large pregenerated data set of hashes from nearly every possible password combination. Although generating a rainbow table requires a significant amount of time, once it is created it has three significant advantages: a rainbow table can be used repeatedly for attacks on other passwords, rainbow tables are much faster than dictionary attacks, and the amount of memory needed on the attacking machine is greatly reduced. Rainbow tables are freely available for download from the Internet.

 The maximum time to break a 14-digit password of letters, numbers, and symbols (such as *1A2*3&def456G$*) using a brute force attack is 6.09×10^{12} years, while an attack using a rainbow table would take a matter of minutes.

Phishing

Sometimes the easiest way to attack a computer system requires no technical ability and is usually highly successful. **Social engineering** relies on deceiving someone to obtain secure information. Consider these examples:

- Maria, a customer service representative, receives a telephone call from someone claiming to be a client. This person has a thick accent that makes his speech hard to understand. Maria asks him to respond to a series of ID authentication questions to ensure that he is an approved client. However, when asked a question, the caller mumbles his response with an accent and the representative cannot understand him. Too embarrassed to keep asking him to repeat his answer, Maria finally provides him with the password.

- The help desk at a large corporation is overwhelmed by the number of telephone calls it receives after a virus attacks. Ari is a help desk technician and receives a frantic call from a user who identifies himself as Frank, a company vice president. Frank says that an office assistant has been unable to complete and send him a critical report because of the virus and is now going home sick. Frank must have that office assistant's network password so he can finish the report, which is due by the end of the day. Because Ari is worn out from the virus attack and has more calls coming in, he looks up the password and gives it to Frank. Ari does not know that Frank is not an employee, but an outsider who now can easily access the company's computer system.

- Natasha, a contract programmer at a financial institution, drives past a security guard who recognizes her and waves her into the building. However, the guard does not realize that Natasha's contract was terminated the previous week. Once inside, Natasha pretends that she is performing an audit and questions a new employee, who willingly gives her the information she requests. Natasha then uses that information to transfer over $10 million dollars to her foreign bank account.

These examples are based on actual incidents, and share a common characteristic: no technical skills or abilities were needed to break into the system. Social engineering relies on the friendliness, frustration, or helpfulness of a company employee to reveal the information necessary to access a system. Social engineering is a difficult security weakness to defend because it relies on human nature ("I just want to be helpful") and not on computer systems.

One of the most common forms of social engineering is **phishing**, or sending an e-mail or displaying a Web announcement that falsely claims to be from a legitimate enterprise in an attempt to trick the user into surrendering private information. The user is asked to respond to an e-mail or is directed to a Web site where they are instructed to update personal information, such as passwords, credit card numbers, Social Security numbers, bank account numbers, or other information for which the legitimate organization already has a record. However, the Web site is actually a fake and is set up to steal the user's information.

The word phishing is a variation on the word *fishing*: bait is thrown out knowing many will ignore it yet some will be tempted into biting.

The number of unique phishing Web sites continues to grow rapidly. According to data from the Anti-Phishing Working Group, the number of unique phishing Web sites is between 25,000 and 50,000 each month (in January 2004 there were only 198 phishing sites). In addition, the number of phishing e-mails that point unsuspecting users to these phishing Web sites also continues to increase. During a recent 1-week period a single attacker was responsible for sending out over 5 billion e-mail messages.

The number of users that respond to phishing attacks is considered to be extremely high. Researchers who have conducted controlled tests showing phishing e-mails to users have reported that anywhere from 28 percent to 50 percent of the users were tricked and entered their personal information. In one study conducted among cadets of the U.S. Military Academy at West Point, 80 percent of the 400 cadets who received a phishing e-mail were deceived into following an embedded link regarding their grade report from a fictitious colonel.

Phishing e-mails and fake Web sites appear legitimate. Figure 4-5 illustrates a Web site used in phishing. These messages contain the logos, color schemes, and wording used by the legitimate site so that it is difficult to determine that they are fraudulent.

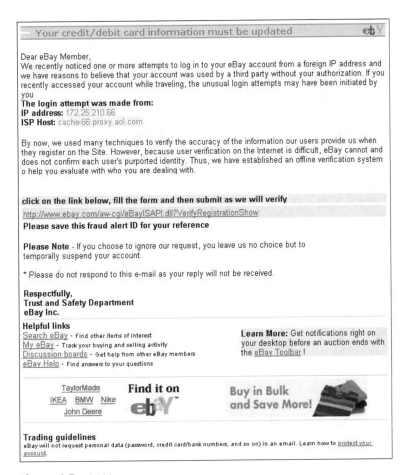

Figure 4-5 Phishing message

Course Technology/Cengage Learning

Studies have also revealed that certain characteristics of the phishing e-mail itself can increase the response rate. E-mail that appears to be intended specifically for the user and is not a bulk e-mail to a large number of users can increase user response. An e-mail that is sent from an organization with which the user normally interacts also can increase user response rates. A third factor is the appearance of the e-mail: if it "looks familiar," this can increase response rates.

Social Networking Attacks

Grouping individuals and organizations into clusters or groups based on some sort of affiliation is called **social networking**. Although social networking is often achieved in person at schools or work, social networking is increasingly performed online. The Web sites that facilitate linking individuals with common interests like hobbies, religion, politics, or school contacts are called **social networking sites** and function as an online community of users. A user who is granted access to a social networking site can read the profile pages of other members and interact with them.

Social networking sites are increasingly becoming prime targets of attacks. The reasons why social networking sites are popular with attackers include:

- *They provide a treasure trove of personal data.* Users often include personal information in their profiles for others to read, such as birthdays, where they live, and their employment history. Attackers may steal this data and use it for malicious purposes.

- *Users are generally trusting.* Attackers often join a social networking site and pretend to be part of the network of users. After several days or weeks, users begin to feel they know the attackers and may start to provide personal information or click on embedded links provided by the attacker that loads malware onto the user's computer.

- *Social networking Web sites are vulnerable.* Because social networking sites have only recently become the target of attackers, many of these sites have lax security measures making it is easy for attackers to break into the sites to steal user information.

Identity Theft

Identity theft involves using someone's personal information, such as a Social Security number, to establish bank or credit card accounts that are then left unpaid, leaving the victim with the debts and ruining their credit rating. The following are some of the actions that can be undertaken by identity thieves:

Identity theft was introduced in Chapter 1.

- Change the mailing address on a credit card account and then charge large purchases to the account. Because the bills are being sent to the new address, the owner of the credit card does not know that there is a problem.

- Produce counterfeit checks or debit cards and then remove all money from the bank account.

- Establish phone or wireless service in the person's name.

- File for bankruptcy under the person's name to avoid paying debts they have incurred or to avoid eviction.

- Provide the name of the real person to police or other law enforcement officers during an arrest. When the suspect does not appear for their court date, an arrest warrant is issued in the name of the identity-theft victim.
- Go on spending sprees using fraudulently obtained credit and debit card account numbers to buy expensive items such as computers that can easily be resold.
- Open a bank account in the person's name and write bad checks on that account.
- Open a new credit card account, using the name, date of birth, and Social Security number of the identity-theft victim. When the thief does not pay the bills, the delinquent account is reported on the victim's credit report.
- Obtain loans for expensive items such as autos and other motor vehicles.

The number of security breaches that have exposed users' digital data to attackers continues to increase. According to the Privacy Rights Clearinghouse, from January 2005 through December 2008 over 246 million data records of Americans containing personal information such as address, Social Security numbers, and credit card numbers were exposed due to weak security, putting them at risk of identity theft.

Security in Your World

Lindsay turned off her cell phone and placed it on the table. "That is so awful!" she said. Maggie set down her book and asked, "What's the matter?" "That call was from my Uncle Ted," said Lindsay. "He just found out that somebody used his credit card number last month and charged over $2,300 in airline tickets to his account." "I'm so sorry to hear that," said Maggie. "I remember when my brother had his identity stolen and it took him over a year to finally get things back to normal. He says he wished that he had ordered a credit report every so often to check on his credit. That would have let him know much sooner that something was wrong."

"That's exactly what Uncle Ted said that he was going to do, but I don't even know what that means. Is ordering a credit report just checking your bank statement each month?" asked Lindsay. "No", said Maggie, "You can order a free credit report to make sure that nobody has tried to take out a loan or open up a credit card under your name and charge stuff to it that you would have to pay for. I order a different credit report three times a year."

Lindsay grinned. "Maggie, you sure know a lot more about this personal security stuff than I do. I never thought about what you told me about Facebook, and now you're talking about checking your credit reports. Where did you learn all of this?"

"I guess it was while my brother was trying to put his life back together after his identity was stolen, and I also had that computer class last year where we talked about a lot of this," said Maggie. "After watching all that my brother had to go through, I sure don't ever want to suffer through that, so I just decided I'm going to be safe and not sorry."

"What else are you safe about?" asked Lindsay.

Personal Security Defenses

To defend against attacks on personal security, there are tools and techniques that should be implemented. These include installing antispyware software, using strong passwords, recognizing phishing attacks, setting social networking defenses, avoiding identity theft, and using cryptography.

Installing Antispyware Software

Just as antivirus (AV) software is one of the best defenses against viruses, another class of defensive software known as **antispyware** software helps prevent computers from becoming infected by different types of spyware. AV and antispyware software share many similarities. First, antispyware software must be regularly updated to defend against the most recent spyware attacks. Second, antispyware can be set to provide continuous real-time monitoring as well as perform a complete scan of the entire computer system. Finally, antispyware can display the name of the spyware, a threat level, a description of the spyware, and recommended action regarding how to handle it.

Several good antispyware products are freely available on the Internet along with reasonably priced commercial packages. Some security experts recommend that you install at least two antispyware products on a computer, because one product may not always detect all of the spyware.

Using Strong Passwords

Because passwords are a widespread and fundamental means of personal security defense, it is essential that **strong passwords**, or passwords that are difficult to break, be used. Successful password attacks can be minimized by following these basic rules for creating strong passwords:

- Passwords should optimally have at least 15 characters.
- Passwords should be a random combination of letters, numbers, and special characters.
- Passwords should be replaced with new passwords at least every 60 days.
- Passwords should not be reused for 12 months.
- The same password should not be duplicated and used for multiple accounts.

Many applications can accept non-keyboard characters, which are created by holding down the *Alt* key while simultaneously typing a number on the numeric keypad (but not the numbers across the top of the keyboard). For example, *Alt + 0163* produces £. To see a list of all the available non-keyboard characters on a Windows computer, click Start and enter *charmap.exe*. Click on a character and the code Alt + 0xxx will appear in the lower-right corner (if that character can be reproduced in Windows).

Different techniques have been suggested to help make passwords easy to remember but hard to break. One technique is to use a phrase or expression instead of a single word, such as an event (Today I passed my final exam), a jingle from a commercial (Yeah, we've got that), or a famous line from a song or speech (Fourscore and seven years ago). Then, replace the spaces between the words with a special character (Today@I@passed@my@final @exam), an alphanumeric character, (1Yeah2we've3got4that5), or a combination (%Four score1and2seven3years4ago%). However, this can quickly become cumbersome.

A more secure approach is to use a **password storage program**. These programs allow the user to enter account information such as username and password, along with other account details, as shown in Figure 4-6. The password storage program is itself protected by a single strong password, and can even require the presence of a file on a USB flash drive before the program will open. Many of these programs allow the user to drag and drop usernames and passwords into these fields without the need to type them.

Figure 4-6 Password storage program

Course Technology/Cengage Learning

Recognizing Phishing Attacks

Because phishing involves social engineering to trick users into responding to an e-mail message or visiting a fake Web site, the first line of defense is for the user to recognize phishing attacks. Some of the ways to recognize these messages include:

- *Deceptive Web links*—A link to a Web site embedded in an e-mail should not have an @ sign in the middle of the address. Also, phishers like to use variations of a legitimate address, such as *www.ebay_secure.com, www.e–bay.com,* or *www.e-baynet.com.* Users should never log on to a Web site from a link in an e-mail; instead, they should open a new browser window and type the legitimate address.

- *E-mails that look like Web sites*—Phishers often include the logo of the vendor and otherwise try to make the e-mail look like the vendor's Web site as a way to convince the recipient that the message is genuine. The presence of logos does not mean that the e-mail is legitimate.

- *Fake sender's address*—Because sender addresses can be forged easily, an e-mail message should not be trusted simply because the sender's e-mail address appears to be valid (such as tech_support@ebay.com). Also, an @ in the sender's address is a technique used to hide the real address.

- *Generic greeting*—Many phishing e-mails begin with a general opening such as "Dear e-Bay Member" and do not include a valid account number. If an e-mail from an online vendor does not contain the user's name, it should be considered suspect. However, because phishers also send customized e-mail messages, the inclusion of a username does not mean that the e-mail is legitimate.

- *Popup boxes and attachments*—Legitimate e-mails from vendors never contain a popup box or an attachment, since these are tools often used by phishers.

- *Urgent request*—Many phishing e-mails try to encourage the recipient to act immediately or else their account will be deactivated.

Despite scrutinizing e-mail, it still can be difficult to recognize phishing attacks. Another approach is to change the overall "philosophy" of e-mail and simply treat e-mail like a picture postcard received from a friend on vacation. The postcard (and e-mail) has these features:

- *Anybody can read it*—Just as anyone can read what is written on a postcard, e-mail likewise can be read as it moves through the Internet. A good idea is to not put anything private in an e-mail that a stranger should not read.

- *You can only read it*—The only thing that can be done with a postcard is read it; it does not have a return envelope to respond back to the sender. E-mail should also be seen as "read only," so users should not click on embedded links or provide requested information.

- *It has nothing else with it*—While a letter in an envelope may also contain other documents a postcard cannot, and e-mail should be treated in the same way. Users should not accept any e-mail attachments unless the sender is known and has provided prior notification.

Setting Social Networking Defenses

Users should be cautious regarding placing personal information on social networking sites. Certain types of information could prove to be embarrassing if read by certain parties, such as a prospective employer. Other information could be used by attackers in a variety of ways. General security tips for using social networking sites include the following:

- *Consider carefully who is accepted as a friend.* Once a person has been accepted as a friend that person will be able to access any personal information or photographs.
- *Show "limited friends" a reduced version of your profile.* Individuals can be designated "limited friends" who only have access to a smaller version of the user's profile. This can be useful for casual acquaintances or business associates.
- *Disable options and then reopen them only as necessary.* Users should disable options until it becomes apparent that option is needed, instead of making everything accessible and restricting access after it is too late.

Tables 4-3 and 4-4 contain recommendations for profile and contact information settings at Facebook, a popular social networking site. Other sites have similar settings and should be configured in the same manner.

Table 4-3   Recommended Facebook profile settings

Option	Recommended Setting	Explanation
Profile	Only my friends	Facebook networks can contain hundreds or thousands of users and there is no control over who else joins the network to see the information.
Photos or photos tagged of you	Only my friends	Photos and videos have often proven to be embarrassing. Only post material that would be appropriate to appear with a resume or job application.
Status updates	Only my friends	Because changes to status such as "Going to Florida on January 28" can be useful information for thieves, only approved friends should have access to it.
Online status	No one	Any benefits derived by knowing who is online are outweighed by the risks.
Friends	Only my friends (minimum setting)	Giving unknown members of the community access to a list of friends may provide attackers with opportunities to uncover personal information through friends.

Table 4-4   Recommended Facebook contact information settings

Option	Recommended Setting	Explanation
Mobile phone, land line, current address	Opt-out (decline to enter)	Users can contact other subscribers through the on-line features of Facebook; there are serious security risks to publishing personal contact information.
Website	Only my friends	A Web site may contain photos or private information that could be used by attackers to identify the user.
Contact e-mail address	No one	Because messages can be sent through Facebook itself it is not necessary to reveal an e-mail address.

Avoiding Identity Theft

Identity theft occurs when an attacker uses the personal information of someone else, such as a Social Security number, credit card number, or other identifying information, to impersonate that individual with the intent to commit fraud or other crimes. Because personal information is stored in numerous locations by employers, banks, credit card agencies, and governments, it is virtually impossible for the user to know if this information is adequately protected. Instead of attempting to completely *prevent* identity theft, it is far more practical to take proactive steps to minimize the risk and *avoid* it.

Avoiding identity theft involves two basic steps. The first step is to deter thieves by safeguarding information. To help safeguard information:

- Shred financial documents and paperwork that contains personal information before discarding it.
- Do not carry a Social Security number in a wallet or write it on a check.
- Do not provide personal information either over the phone or through an e-mail message.
- Keep personal information in a secure location in a home or apartment.

The second step is to monitor financial statements and accounts by doing the following:

- Be alert to signs that may indicate unusual activity in an account, such as a bill that did not arrive at the normal time or a large increase in unsolicited credit cards or account statements.
- Follow up on calls regarding purchases that were not made.
- Review financial and billing statements each month carefully as soon as they arrive.

Legislation has been passed that is designed to help U.S. users monitor their financial information. The **Fair and Accurate Credit Transactions Act (FACTA) of 2003** contains rules regarding consumer privacy. FACTA grants consumers the right to request one free credit report from each of the three national credit-reporting firms every 12 months. Because a credit report can only be ordered once per year from each of the credit agencies, security experts recommend that one report be ordered every 4 months from one of the three credit agencies. This allows the user to view a credit report each quarter without being charged for it.

To access your credit report, go to *www.AnnualCreditReport.com* or call 1-877-322-8228.

TIP

If a consumer finds a problem on her credit report, she must first send a letter to the credit-reporting agency. Under federal law, the agency has 30 days to investigate and respond to the alleged inaccuracy and issue a corrected report. If the claim is upheld, all three credit-reporting agencies must be notified of the inaccuracies so they can correct their files. If the investigation does not resolve the problem, a statement from the consumer can be placed in the file and in any future credit reports.

Although the credit reports are free, the law does not grant consumers free access to their credit score, which is a numerical measurement used by lenders to assess a consumer's creditworthiness. Those reports cost about $10.

TIP

Using Cryptography

SEND SECURE INFORMATION

Another method for protecting personal information is to safeguard sensitive data by "scrambling" it through encryption. Even if attackers break through defenses and reach data, they cannot read the contents. An attacker would be forced to attempt to break the encryption as well, a particularly difficult and time-consuming task. This scrambling is a process known as **cryptography** (from Greek words meaning *hidden writing*). Cryptography is the science of transforming information into a secure form while it is being transmitted or stored so that unauthorized users cannot access it.

Changing original text to scrambled text using cryptography is known as **encryption,** and the reverse process (changing an encrypted document back to the original text) is **decryption**. Data that is in an unencrypted form is called **cleartext** data. Cleartext data is data that is either stored or transmitted "in the clear," without any encryption. Cleartext data that is to be encrypted is called **plaintext**. Plaintext data is input into an encryption **algorithm**, which consists of a procedure based on a mathematical formula used to encrypt the data. A **key** is a mathematical value entered into the algorithm to produce **ciphertext**, or text that is "scrambled." Just as a key is inserted into a lock to open or secure a door, in cryptography a unique mathematical key is input into the encryption algorithm to create the ciphertext. Once the ciphertext is transmitted or needs to be returned to cleartext, the reverse process occurs with a decryption algorithm. The cryptography process is illustrated in Figure 4-7.

Symmetric cryptography uses the same key to encrypt and decrypt a message. A document encrypted with a symmetric cryptographic algorithm by User A can be decrypted by User B. It is therefore essential that the key be kept confidential, because if an attacker secured the key he could decrypt all encrypted messages. For this reason, symmetric encryption is also called **private key cryptography**. Symmetric encryption is illustrated in Figure 4-8 where identical keys are used to encrypt and decrypt the message.

Another cryptography technique is **asymmetric cryptography**, also known as **public key cryptography**. Asymmetric encryption uses two keys instead of one: one to encrypt the message and one to decrypt it. These keys are mathematically related and are known as the public key and the private key. The **public key** is known to everyone and can be freely distributed,

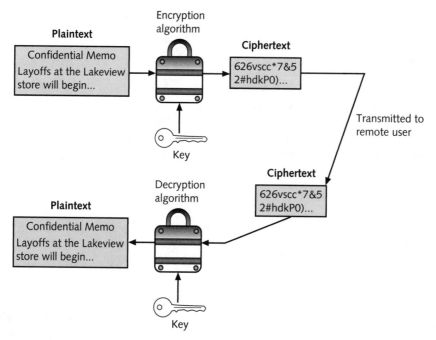

Figure 4-7 Cryptography process

Course Technology/Cengage Learning

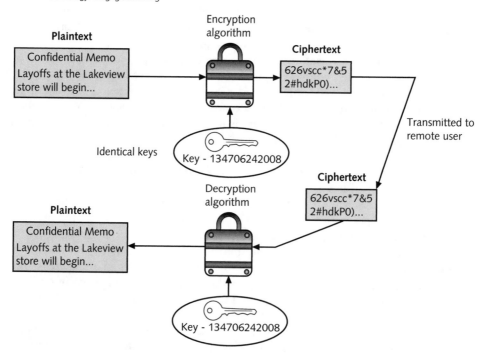

Figure 4-8 Symmetric cryptography

Course Technology/Cengage Learning

while the **private key** is known only to the recipient of the message. When Bob wants to send a secure message to Alice, he uses Alice's public key to encrypt the message. Alice then uses her private key to decrypt it. Asymmetric cryptography is illustrated in Figure 4-9.

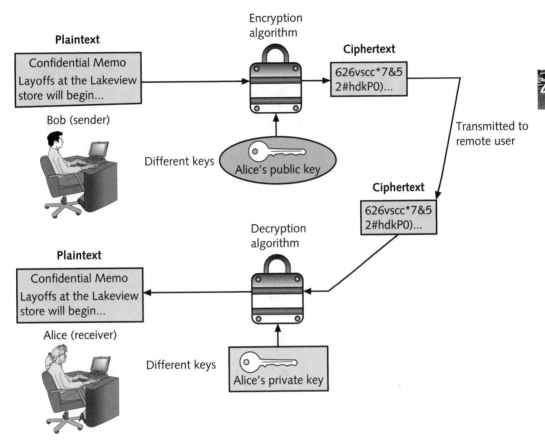

Figure 4-9 Asymmetric cryptography

Course Technology/Cengage Learning

Public keys can be very "public" and freely given to any user, including attackers. This is because a public key is a one-way function: the public key can only encrypt a document and cannot be used to decrypt. Only the private key must be kept confidential. Alice can freely distribute her public key but she must keep her private key confidential.

One way to think about dual keys in asymmetric cryptography is to consider an employee who has an office in a building. Any employee can request a key to the outer door of the building, and each key to the outer door is identical: Bob's key opens the outer door just like Alice's key does. However, each employee also has a second key that will only open the door to his or her office. Each of these keys is unique. When Bob wants to work on the weekend he will use his "public" key to open the outer door to the building—just like any employee can–but only his "private" key will open his office door.

There are several different technologies that use cryptography to provide personal security. Two of the most common are using cryptography on files or disks and digital certificates.

Encrypting Files and Disks Cryptography can be used to protect individual documents or messages by scrambling their contents. However, it can be cumbersome to encrypt and decrypt individual documents, since each may require a separate key. As an alternative, cryptography can also be used to protect groups of files on a computer or even an entire disk.

Protecting groups of files, such as all files in a specific folder, can take advantage of the operating system's existing features for storing, retrieving, and organizing files. Protecting multiple files can be performed by using products such as the Microsoft Windows Encrypting File System (EFS). Because EFS is tightly integrated with the operating system, file encryption and decryption are transparent to the user: any file created in an encrypted folder or added to an encrypted folder is automatically encrypted. When an authorized user opens a file, it is decrypted by EFS as data is read from disk; when a file is saved, EFS encrypts the data as it is written to disk.

Cryptography can also be applied to entire disks. This is known as **whole disk encryption**. Whole disk encryption includes using products such as Microsoft Windows BitLocker. Unlike EFS, BitLocker is a hardware-enabled data encryption feature. It can encrypt the entire hard drive, which includes Windows operating system files as well as user files. BitLocker encrypts the entire disk, including any temporary files that might hold confidential information.

BitLocker and other cryptographic software can take advantage of the **Trusted Platform Module (TPM)**. TPM is essentially a chip on the motherboard of the computer that provides cryptographic services. Because all of this is done in hardware and not through the software of the operating system, malicious software can not attack it. Also, TPM can measure and test key components as the computer is starting up. It will prevent the computer from booting if system files or data have been altered.

With TPM, if the hard drive is moved to a different computer the user must enter a recovery password before gaining access to the data.

Digital Certificates Digital certificates can be used to associate or "bind" a user's identity to a public key. A digital certificate is the user's public key that has itself been "digitally signed" by a reputable source entrusted to sign it. Digital certificates function like passports in that they provide a means of authentication. Unlike a passport, which a traveler should never give away to another person, a digital certificate can be distributed and copied without restriction. This is because certificates do not normally contain any confidential information and their free distribution does not create a security risk.

Server digital certificates are issued from an Internet Web server computer to a Web browser. Server digital certificates typically perform two functions. First, they ensure the authenticity of the Web server. Server digital certificates enable users connecting to the Web server to examine the identity of the server's owner. A user who connects to a Web site that has a server digital certificate can be confident that the data transmitted to the server is usable only by the person or organization identified by the certificate.

Some digital certificates are only entry-level certificates that provide domain-only validation; that is, they authenticate only that an organization has the right to use a particular Web domain name like *www.course.com*. These certificates indicate nothing regarding the individuals behind the site.

Second, server certificates can ensure the authenticity of the cryptographic connection to the Web server. Sensitive connections to Web servers, such as a user entering a credit card number to pay for an online purchase, need to be protected from attackers. Web servers can set up secure cryptographic connections so that all transmitted data is encrypted. Server certificates can verify the authenticity of this connection and provide the server's public key for encryption.

A server digital certificate ensures that the cryptographic connection functions as follows and is illustrated in Figure 4-10:

1. The Web server administrator generates an asymmetric pair of public/private keys for the server and a server digital certificate is created that binds the public key with the identity of the server.

2. A user who clicks on the "Pay Now" button to purchase merchandise needs a secure connection to the Web server.

3. The Web server presents its digital certificate to the user's Web browser. The browser examines the certificate's credentials and verifies that the certificate issuer is one that it recognizes. If the Web browser does not recognize the certificate issuer it will issue a warning to the user.

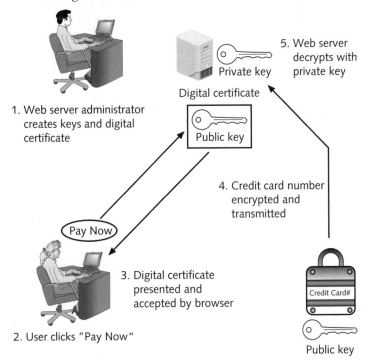

Figure 4-10 Web Server digital certificate

Course Technology/Cengage Learning

4. The Web server's public key connected to the server's digital certificate is used to encrypt the credit card number on the user's computer and then that encrypted data is transmitted to the Web server.

5. When the Web server receives the encrypted credit card data it decrypts it using its private key.

Most server digital certificates combine both server authentication and secure communication between clients and servers on the Web, although these functions can be separate. A server digital certificate that both verifies the existence and identity of the organization and securely encrypts communications displays a padlock icon in the Web browser as seen in Figure 4-11. Clicking the padlock icon displays information about the digital certificate along with the name of the site.

Padlock icon

Figure 4-11 Padlock icon

Course Technology/Cengage Learning

An enhanced server digital certificate is now being utilized. Known as an **Extended Validation Secure Sockets Layer Certificate (EV SSL)**, this type of certificate requires more extensive verification of the legitimacy of the business. In addition, Web browsers can visually indicate to users that they are connected to a Web site that uses the higher-level EV SSL by using colors on the address bar. Figure 4-12 shows a Web site that uses EV SSL with the address bar shaded (in green but not shown in color here) and the site's name displayed (a user does not have to click on the padlock icon to display the name of the site). In addition, Web browsers also now have the ability to display a red address bar if the site is known to be dangerous.

Figure 4-12 EV SSL

Course Technology/Cengage Learning

Internet Explorer 7 was the first browser to display the address in green. Mozilla Firefox and Opera have now added this feature as well.

Chapter Summary

- Spyware is a general term used to describe software that violates a user's personal security by using tracking software that is deployed without adequate notice, consent, or control for the user. Spyware is not always easy to distinguish from legitimate programs that perform spyware-like functions. One common tool of spyware is a keylogger, which is either a small hardware device or a program that monitors each keystroke a user types on the computer's keyboard. Another tool is a browser hijacker program that changes the Web browser's home page and search engine to another site.

- The process of providing proof that the user is "genuine" or authentic is known as authentication. Computers have typically relied upon authenticating users by what they know through using a password, which is a secret combination of letters and numbers. Passwords provide a weak degree of security because of the "password paradox": although lengthy and complex passwords should be used and never written down, it is very difficult to memorize these types of passwords. Because passwords are so common yet provide weak security, they are a frequent focus of attacks. Dictionary attacks and rainbow table attacks are more common than brute force attacks.

- Social engineering relies on deceiving someone to obtain secure information. One of the most common forms of social engineering is phishing. Phishing involves sending an e-mail or displaying a Web announcement that falsely claims to be from a legitimate enterprise in an attempt to trick the user into surrendering private information to a Web site. However, the Web site is actually a fake and is set up to steal the user's information.

- Web sites that facilitate linking individuals with common interests are called social networking sites and function like an online community. Social networking sites are increasingly becoming prime targets of attacks because of the large amount of personal data that can be found there, because users are often too trusting of strangers on these sites, and the sites themselves are not always secured. Users of social networking sites that provide personal information may become the victims of identity theft, which involves using someone's personal information, such as a Social Security number, to establish bank or credit card accounts that are then left unpaid, leaving the victim with the debts and ruining their credit rating.

- There are several defenses against personal security attacks. Defensive software known as antispyware software helps prevent computers from becoming infected by spyware. Because passwords are a widespread and fundamental means of personal security defense, it is essential to use strong passwords, or passwords that are difficult to break. A password storage program allows the user to enter account information such as username and password, along with other account details and relieves the need to memorize numerous passwords. Because phishing involves social engineering to trick users into responding to an e-mail message or visiting a fake Web site, the first line of defense is for the user to recognize phishing attacks.

- Users should be cautious regarding placing personal information on social networking sites. In addition, recommendations for secure profile and contact information settings should be followed. Because personal information is stored in numerous locations by employers, banks, credit card agencies, and governments, it is virtually impossible for the user to know if this information is adequately protected. Instead of attempting to completely prevent identity theft, it is far more practical to take proactive steps to minimize and avoid the risk.

- Another method for protecting personal information is to safeguard sensitive data by "scrambling" it through encryption in a process known as cryptography. One technology using cryptography is to encrypt files or entire disks on computers. Another technology employs server digital certificates, which authenticates the Web server and provides a cryptographic connection between the server and a Web browser.

Key Terms

algorithm   Procedure based on a mathematical formula; used to encrypt data.

antispyware   Software that helps prevent computers from becoming infected by spyware.

asymmetric cryptography   Encryption that uses two mathematically related keys for encryption and decryption.

authentication   The process of providing proof that the user is genuine.

browser hijacker   A program that changes the Web browser's homepage and search engine to another site.

brute force attack   An attack that attempts to guess a password through combining a systematic random combination of characters.

ciphertext   Data that has been encrypted.

cleartext   Unencrypted data.

cryptography   The science of transforming information into a secure form while it is being transmitted or stored so that unauthorized users cannot access it.

decryption   The process of changing ciphertext into plaintext.

dictionary attack   An attack on a password that creates hashes of common dictionary words, and then compares those hashed dictionary words against those in the password file.

digital certificate   A certificate that associates a user's identity to a public key.

encryption   The process of changing plaintext into ciphertext.

Extended Validation Secure Sockets Layer Certificate (EV SSL)   A certificate that requires more extensive verification of the legitimacy of the business.

Fair and Accurate Credit Transactions Act (FACTA) of 2003   A U.S. federal law that contains rules regarding consumer privacy.

identity theft   Using someone's personal information, such as a Social Security number, to establish bank or credit card accounts that are then left unpaid.

key   A mathematical value entered into an encryption algorithm to produce ciphertext.

keylogger   A small hardware device or a program that monitors each keystroke a user types on the computer's keyboard.

password   A secret combination of letters, numbers and/or characters that serves to authenticate a user.

password storage program   A program for entering account information such as username and password, along with other account details.

phishing   Sending an e-mail or displaying a Web announcement that falsely claims to be from a legitimate enterprise in an attempt to trick the user into surrendering private information.

plaintext   Data input into an encryption algorithm.

private key   A cryptographic key that is widely known and can be freely distributed.

private key cryptography   Cryptographic algorithms that use a single key to encrypt and decrypt a message.

public key   A cryptographic key that is only known to the recipient of the message.

public key cryptography   Encryption that uses two mathematically related keys.

rainbow tables   An attack on a password that uses a large pregenerated data set of hashes from nearly every possible password.

server digital certificates   Digital certificates that are issued from an Internet Web server computer to a Web browser.

social engineering   Relying on deceiving someone to obtain secure information.

social networking   Grouping individuals and organizations into clusters or groups based on some sort of affiliation.

social networking sites   Web sites that facilitate linking individuals with common interests.

spyware   A general term used to describe software that violates a user's personal security.

strong passwords   Passwords that are difficult to break.

symmetric cryptography   Encryption that uses a single key to encrypt and decrypt a message.

Trusted Platform Module (TPM)   A chip on the motherboard of the computer that provides cryptographic services.

username   A unique computer name for identifying a user.

weak passwords   Passwords that compromise security.

whole disk encryption   Cryptography applied to entire disks.

Review Questions

1. _____ is a general term to describe software that violates a user's personal security.
   a. Spyware
   b. Malware
   c. Adware
   d. Netware

2. Each of the following is true about keyloggers except _____.
   a. it can be a small device inserted between the keyboard connector and computer keyboard port
   b. it collects only information entered on a Web site
   c. keystrokes are collected and saved as text
   d. software keyloggers are often downloaded and installed as a Trojan

3. A(n) _____ is a program that an attacker installs on a computer and changes the Web browser's home page and search engine to another site.
   a. IE relocator
   b. Internet server redirector
   c. IMAPI
   d. browser hijacker

4. The process of providing proof that the user is "genuine" or authentic is known as _____.

    a. identification

    b. registration

    c. genuinization

    d. authentication

5. Each of the following is a characteristic of a weak password except _____.

    a. short password (fewer than six characters)

    b. complicated password

    c. personal information in a password

    d. not changing the password

6. The least effective type of password attack is a _____.

    a. brute force attack

    b. dictionary attack

    c. rainbow table attack

    d. machine attack

7. Relying on deceiving someone to obtain secure information is known as _____.

    a. social engineering

    b. magic attack

    c. brute force attack

    d. sleight attack

8. The goal of a phishing attack is _____.

    a. to send a fraudulent e-mail to a user

    b. to trick a user into surrendering private information such as a Social Security number

    c. to duplicate a legitimate service

    d. to capture keystrokes

9. Each of the following is a reason why social networking sites are increasingly becoming prime targets of attacks except _____.

    a. social networking sites employ strong security measures

    b. social networking sites contain personal user information

    c. users on these sites are often trusting

    d. birthdays, where the user lives, and their employment history may be found on these sites

10. Each of the following may be performed by an identity thief except _____.

    a. producing counterfeit checks or debit cards and then remove all money from the bank account

    b. filing for bankruptcy under the person's name to avoid paying debts they have incurred or to avoid eviction

    c. opening a bank account in the person's name and write bad checks on that account

    d. sending a worm to a bank's online accounting system

11. Data that is to be encrypted by inputting it into an algorithm is called _____.

    a. clear text

    b. open text

    c. ciphertext

    d. plaintext

12. Symmetric cryptographic algorithms are also called _____.

    a. cipherkey cryptography

    b. public/private key cryptography

    c. public key cryptography

    d. private key cryptography

13. The Trusted Platform Module (TPM) _____.

    a. is only available on Windows computers running BitLocker

    b. includes a pseudorandom number generator (PRNG)

    c. provides cryptographic services in hardware instead of software

    d. allows the user to boot a corrupted disk and repair it

14. Each of the following is required of antispyware except _____.

    a. it must be regularly updated to defend against the most recent spyware attacks

    b. it can provide both continuous monitoring and a complete scan of the entire computer

    c. it can display detailed information about the threat recommended actions

    d. it is only available as a commercial product with an annual subscription fee

15. Each of the following is a characteristic of a strong password except _____.

    a. the same password should be duplicated and used for multiple accounts

    b. passwords should normally have 12-15 characters

    c. passwords should be a random combination of letters, numbers, and special characters

    d. passwords should not be reused for 12 month

16. A phishing attack can have the following characteristics except _____.

    a. deceptive Web links

    b. real sender's address

    c. generic greeting

    d. urgent request for action

17. A reason why "Only my friends" should be considered as a setting for content placed on a social networking site is because _____.

    a. friends cannot be trusted

    b. there is no control over who can join a network to view information

    c. this setting is required

    d. attackers do not pretend to be friends

18. Each of the following is a step to deter identity theft except _____.

    a. carry a copy of a Social Security card in a wallet instead of the original

    b. keep personal information in a secure location

    c. shred financial documents and paperwork that contains personal information

    d. do not provide personal information either over the phone or through an e-mail message

19. A server digital certificate that both verifies the existence and identity of the organization and securely encrypts communications displays a _____ icon in the Web browser.

    a. green checkmark

    b. padlock

    c. blue earth

    d. computer

20. Each of the following is a means of authentication except _____.

    a. what you have

    b. where were you raised

    c. what you know

    d. what you are

Hands-on Projects

Project 4-1: Download and Install a Password Storage Program

The drawback to using strong passwords is that they can be very difficult to remember, particularly when a unique password is used for each account that a user has. As an option there are several password storage programs that allow the user to enter account information such as username and password. These programs are themselves then protected by a single strong password. One example of a password storage program is KeePass Password Safe, which is an open source product. In this project you download and install KeePass.

1. Use your Web browser to go to **keepass.info** and click on **Downloads**.

It is not unusual for Web sites to change the location of where files are stored. If the URL above no longer functions then open a search engine like Google and search for "KeePass".

2. Locate the portable version of KeePass and click it to download the application. Save this file in a location such as your Desktop, or a folder designated by your instructor, or your portable USB flash drive. When the file finishes downloading install the program. Accept the installation defaults.

Because this is the portable version of KeePass it does not install under Windows. In order to use it you must double-click the filename KeePass.exe.

3. Launch KeePass to display the opening screen, as shown in Figure 4-13.

4. Click **File** and **New** to start a password database. Enter a strong master password for the database to protect all of the passwords in it. When prompted enter the password again to confirm it.

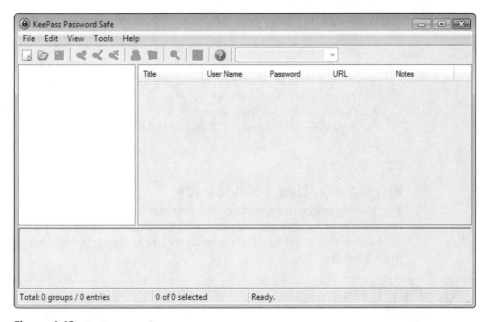

Figure 4-13 KeePass opening screen

Course Technology/Cengage Learning

5. Click **Edit** and **Add Entry**. You will enter information about an online account that has a password that you already use.

6. Under **Group:** select an appropriate group for this account.

7. Enter a title for this account under **Title:**.

8. Under **User name:** enter the username that you use to login to this account.

9. Erase the entries under **Password:** and **Repeat:** and enter the password that you use for this account and confirm it.

10. Enter the URL for this account under **URL:**.

11. Click **OK**.

12. Click **File** and **Save**. Enter your last name as the filename and click **Save**.

13. Exit KeePass.

14. If necessary navigate to the location of KeePass and double-click the file **KeePass.exe** to launch the application.

15. Enter your master password to open it.

16. If necessary, click the group to locate the account you just entered; it will be displayed in the right pane.

17. Double-click under **URL** to go to that Web site.

18. Click **KeePass** in the task bar so that the window is now on top of your browser window.

19. Drag your username from KeePass into the login username box for this account in your Web browser and drop it into the login box.

20. Drag and drop your password from KeePass for this account.

21. Click the button on your browser to log in to this account.

22. Because you can drag and drop your account information from KeePass you do not have to memorize any account passwords and can instead create strong passwords for each account. Is this an application that would help users create and use strong passwords? What are the strengths of these password programs? What are the weaknesses? Would you use KeePass?

23. Close all windows.

Project 4-2: Use a Keylogger

A keylogger program captures everything that a user enters on a computer keyboard. The program runs invisibly in the background and cannot be detected even from the Windows Task Manager. In this project, you download and use a keyboard logger.

The purpose of this activity is to provide information regarding how these programs function in order that adequate defenses can be designed and implemented. These programs should never be used in a malicious fashion against another user.

1. Open your Web browser and enter the URL **www.softdd.com/ keystrokerecorder/index.html.**

The location of content on the Internet such as this program may change without warning. If you are no longer able to access the program through the above URL then use a search engine like Google (www.google.com) and search for "Keyboard Collector".

2. Click **Download Here**.

3. When the File Download dialog box appears, click **Save** and follow the instructions to Save this file in a location such as your Desktop or a folder designated by your instructor. When the file finishes downloading click **Run** and follow the default installation procedures.

Some antivirus software may detect that this program is malware. It may be necessary to temporarily disable the antivirus software in order to download and run the application. Be sure to remember to restart the antivirus software when you are finished.

4. If you are asked for a password click **OK**.

5. Click **Run Keyboard Collector** and then click **OK**.

6. Select the **Always Run** check box, if necessary.

7. Click **Activate/Start**, and then click **Yes** to confirm.

8. Spend several minutes performing normal activity, such as creating a document or sending an e-mail message.

9. Now examine what the keylogger captured. Double-click the **Keyboard Collector Trial** icon on the desktop.

10. When asked to enter a password click **OK**.

11. Click **Run Keyboard Collector** and then click **OK**.

12. Click **View Your Logs**, and then click **OK**. Notice that the text you typed has been captured.

13. Click **Return** and then **Exit**.

14. Now notice that Keyboard Collector is cloaking itself so that it does not appear to be running. Press the **Ctrl+Alt+Delete** keys and click **Start Task Manager**.

15. Click the **Applications** tab to see all of the programs that are currently running. Does Keyboard Collector appear in this list? Why or why not?

16. Close the Windows Task Manager.

17. Remove Keyboard Collector from the computer. Double-click the **Keyboard Collector Trial** icon on the desktop.

18. When asked to enter a password click **OK**.

19. Click **Run Keyboard Collector** and then click **OK**.

20. Click **Deactivate** and then click **OK**.

21. Click **Uninstall** and follow the default procedures to install the program.

22. Close all windows.

Project 4-3: View an Annual Credit Report

Security experts recommend that consumers receive a copy of their credit report at least once per year and check its accuracy to protect their identity. In this project, you access your free credit report online.

1. Use your Web browser to go to **www.annualcreditreport.com**. Although you could send a request individually to one of the three credit agencies, this Web site acts as a central source for ordering free credit reports.

2. Select the state in which you live.

3. Click **Request Report**.

4. Enter the requested information and click **Continue**.

Be sure to check the box, "Click here if, for security reasons, you want no more than the last four digits of your Social Security Number to appear when you view or print your credit report."

5. Click **TransUnion**. Click **Next**.

6. Click **Next**.

7. You may then be asked personal information about your transaction history in order to verify your identity. Answer the requested questions.

8. Follow the instructions to print your report. Review it carefully, particularly the sections of "Potentially negative items" and "Requests for your credit history." If you see anything that might be incorrect, follow the instructions on that Web site to enter a dispute.

9. Follow the instructions to exit from the Web sites.

10. Close all windows.

Project 4-4: Use the Internet Explorer 8 SmartScreen Filter

Phishers create fake, or spoofed, Web sites to look like a well-known branded site such as ebay.com or citibank.com with a slightly different or confusing URL. Internet Explorer (IE) contains a built-in phishing filter. This filter operates in the background as users browse the Internet and analyzes Web pages to determine if they contain any characteristics that might be suspicious. If IE discovers a suspicious Web page it will display a yellow warning to advise the user to precede with caution. In addition, the filter checks sites against a list of known phishing sites that is regularly updated. If a user attempts to access a known phishing site, the filter displays a red warning notifying the user that the site has been blocked. In this project you explore the uses of the IE 8 phishing filter.

1. Launch Internet Explorer 8.

2. First check that the phishing filter is turned on. Click **Tools** and then point to **Internet Options** and then click the **Advanced** tab.

3. Scroll down under the **Security** category to **Enable SmartScreen Filter**.

4. If necessary click **Enable SmartScreen Filter**.

5. Click **Apply** and then **OK**. If you receive a message box click **OK**.

6. Close all windows.

Project 4-5: View Digital Certificates

When entering private information on a Web page, such as a credit card number, it is important to first ensure that the Web site's digital certificate is valid. In this project you view digital certificate information.

1. Use your Web browser to go to **www.google.com**. Because this is the interface to a search engine it generally would not be necessary to have a digital certificate for this site.

2. Note that there is no padlock icon in the browser address bar, indicating that no digital certificates are used with this site. To verify this click **File** and then **Properties**. The **Protocol:** is HyperText Transport Protocol and the **Connection:** is **Not Encrypted**.

3. Click the **Certificates** button. A message appears that there are no digital certificates for this site. Click **OK** and then click **OK** on the **Properties** dialog box.

4. Now use your Web browser to go to **https://gmail.google.com**. This is the Web interface to the Google e-mail facility. Information entered and viewed here is protected with a digital certificate.

5. Note the padlock icon in the browser address bar. Click on the **padlock** icon to view the **Website Identification** window.

6. Click **View certificates**.

7. Note the general information displayed under the **General** tab.

8. Now click the **Details** tab. The fields are displayed for this X.509 digital certificate.

9. Click **Valid to** to view the expiration date of this certificate.

10. Click **Public key** to view the public key associated with this digital certificate. Why is this site not concerned with distributing this key? How does embedding the public key in a digital certificate protect it from impersonators?

11. Click the **Certification Path** tab. Because Web certificates are based on the distributed trust model there is a "path" to the root certificate. Click the root certificate and click the **View Certificate** button. Click the **Details tab** and then click **Valid to**. Why is the expiration date of this root certificate longer than that of the Web site certificate? Click **OK** and then click **OK** again to close the **Certificate** window.

12. Now view all the certificates in this Web browser. Click **Tools** and **Internet Options**.

13. Click the **Content** tab.

14. Click the **Certificates** button.

15. Click the **Trusted Root Certification Authorities** to view the root certificates in this Web browser. Why are there so many?

16. Close all windows.

Case Projects

Case Project 4-1: Phishing Test

Detecting phishing e-mails can often be difficult. Point your Web browser to *http://survey.mailfrontier.com/survey/quiztest.cgi* and then click on *The Mail-Frontier Phishing IQ Test v2.0*. Click on each hyperlink to display an e-mail message or Web site, and then decide whether or not it is phishing. When you are finished your score will be displayed along with an explanation regarding why the example is or is not phishing. Then click on *The MailFrontier Phishing IQ Test* and take another phishing test. Did what you learn on the first test help? Was your score on this test improved? Write a one-paragraph summary on what you learned about phishing in this test.

Case Project 4-2: Anti-Phishing Phil Demonstration

Carnegie Mellon University has created a game that teaches how to detect phishing scams. Point your Web browser to *http://cups.cs.cmu.edu/antiphishing_phil/new/index.html* and play the game. What new antiphishing techniques did you learn? Would you recommend this game for someone to learn about phishing? Why or why not? Write a one-paragraph summary of what you learned.

Case Project 4-3: Antispyware Sites

The Internet contains several good spyware help sites that provide useful information regarding spyware and recent attacks. Use a search engine to locate the top five spyware sites. Record the Web address and write a one or two sentence description of each site and why it is in your list of top five. Share your list with other students. You may want to compile a master list for the class as a resource.

Case Project 4-4: Testing Your Passwords

How strong are your passwords? First, assign the number 1 through 5 to five of the passwords you are currently using and write down the number (not the password) on a piece of paper. Then enter those passwords into an online password testing service such as that found at *https://www.microsoft.com/protect/yourself/password/checker.mspx* (other testers are also available). Record next to each number the strength of that password. Then use the online password tester to modify the password by adding more random numbers or letters to increase its strength. Would you be able to remember these passwords? Create a one-paragraph summary of your work.

Case Project 4-5: Winstead Computer Consultants

A regional temporary employment firm called $700 More was recently the victim of a phishing scheme, in which many of its clients received a fake e-mail claiming to be from $700 More and were tricked into divulging personal information. $700 More wants to provide written material to distribute to its clients about phishing, and has hired Winstead Computer Consultants (WCC), a local information technology company that specializes in security, to help them. WCC has hired you to assist them with this project.

Create a PowerPoint presentation of eight or more slides that covers the basics of phishing attacks. Define what phishing is, how it works, and what defenses should be used. Include in your presentation an image of a fake phishing e-mail from the Internet and point out how it can be identified as phishing.

chapter 5

Wireless Network Security

After completing this chapter you should be able to do the following:

- Explain what a network is and the different types of networks
- List the different attacks that can be launched against a wireless network
- Give the steps necessary to secure a wireless network

Security in Your World

Braden shifted his backpack as he reached forward to ring the doorbell. The door quickly opened. "Braden! Hi there. Come on in," said Mrs. Sumners. Braden had been taking classes with Mrs. Sumners' son Thomas at the community college before Thomas transferred to a university in another part of the state. Braden and Thomas, who both were majoring in Computer Information Systems, were good friends. "How are your classes?" asked Mrs. Sumners. Braden said, "They're fine. I'll graduate at the end of this semester and I'm thinking about transferring to where Thomas is."

"That's great. And thank you very much for coming over," said Mrs. Sumners. Braden had received a phone call from Thomas the previous evening. A severe thunderstorm had come through the Sumners' neighborhood and lightning struck a pole near their home. When the electricity came back on, none of the computers in the house were functioning. "I'm so worried that the lightning blew up all the computers. That's what happened to the Flanagans down the street," said Mrs. Sumners. Braden set down his backpack and said, "We'll hope not. Thomas told me about the setup here in the house. Is it OK if I start checking everything?" "Yes, please do. I'll keep my fingers crossed," said Mrs. Sumners.

In just a short time Braden came into the room where Mrs. Sumners was sitting. "I've got great news, and you can thank Thomas for it. All of the equipment was connected to these expensive surge protectors that Thomas had installed," said Braden. He held up a white box about ten inches long and four inches high. "Surge protectors are designed to stop a spike of electricity from reaching your equipment, and these protectors did their job. In fact, they don't work anymore, so I guess you could say the protectors gave their life for your computers. That's why your equipment wouldn't turn on because these surge protectors are dead."

"Oh, I'm so glad," said Mrs. Sumners. "You know that Thomas had everything set up so that we could all print on the color laser printer upstairs from any computer and we could watch movies on the TV that were sent from the computer. He also said that everything was backed up automatically each night so we didn't have to do that." Braden smiled. "Yes, Thomas and I actually talked in class last semester about the computer network he set up here." Mrs. Sumners frowned. "Network? I didn't know we had a network. Just what does a network do?"

Until fairly recently, computer networks were only found in large businesses and schools. Today, networks are also a standard commodity for consumers. As users install multiple computers in their home offices, bedrooms, kitchens, dens, and children's rooms, a network is essential to tie all of the devices together so that they can share a single Internet connection, printer, and even software. And because most operating systems such as Microsoft Windows come with built-in networking capabilities, creating a small network can be easily accomplished in just a few minutes.

Most home users today opt to set up a wireless network. Wireless networks allow all users within the house or apartment to connect to the Internet simultaneously no matter where they may be located. And because the network signal "floats" through the air it is not necessary to string long cables or reorient furniture so it will be close to a wired network connection.

However, many home wireless computer networks do not have the necessary security features enabled. Wireless computer networks are one of the prime targets of attackers, because once the network is breached, every device on the network may be vulnerable. Creating a secure wireless network does not require advanced technical networking skills. Wireless networks, no matter how large or small, can be defended against attackers with relative ease.

In this chapter, we will examine wireless computer networks. We will first look at the fundamentals of networks and how they function. Next, we will explore attacks on wireless networks. Finally, you will learn how to create a secure wireless network.

How Networks Work

It is important to understand the basics of how a network works in order to secure a wireless network. This includes understanding what a network is, how it transmits data, the different types of networks, and the devices typically found on a home wireless network.

What Is a Computer Network?

A personal computer on a user's desk or lap can perform a broad range of tasks, such as create a document, calculate a complex formula, or draw an image. However, if a computer is not connected to a network, it is isolated from other computers. The functionality of the computer is limited to the software installed on that computer and the hardware that is directly connected to it. Figure 5-1 shows that in an organization, personal computers may each have their own programs (such as a payroll program), data (such as the employee names and telephone numbers), and devices (such as a printer). This configuration results in higher costs (a copy of the payroll program and a printer must be purchased for each user) and increases the risk of errors (a change to an employee's telephone number on one computer may not be changed on all other computers).

The capabilities of a personal computer are greatly improved if it can access other software and hardware. This enhanced access can be accomplished by interconnecting computers and devices together to form a **computer network**. The purpose of a computer network can be summarized in a single word: *share*. As shown in Figure 5-2, instead of

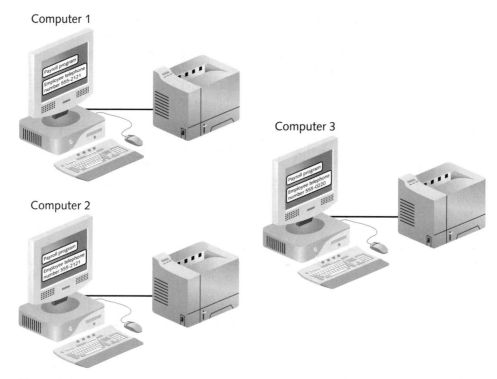

Figure 5-1   Isolated computers

Course Technology/Cengage Learning

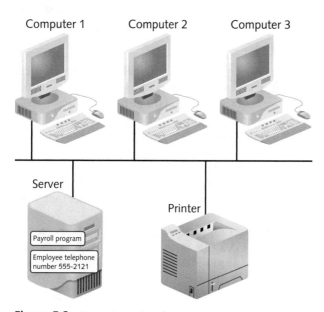

Figure 5-2   Computer network

Course Technology/Cengage Learning

installing a copy of the employee data program on each employee's computer, a single copy is stored on one central network computer (known as the **server**) that all employees can access if they have the proper authorization. Because the data is centralized and can only be changed in one place, the integrity of the information is preserved (there are not multiple copies that are different). Likewise, devices such as printers can be shared across the network.

Although a home computer network would not share payroll programs or employee data, home networks are useful. For example, a home computer network allows a single Internet connection device or printer to be shared by all users. In addition, digital photos, music, and videos can be centrally located in a home computer network instead of stored on each user's own hard drives. This makes it easier to perform backups and distribute material to other users.

Transmitting Across a Network

For data to be transmitted across a network, both the sending and receiving devices must follow the same set of standards (protocols). The most common set of protocols used today on networks is called the Transmission Control Protocol/Internet Protocol (TCP/IP).

Protocols and TCP/IP were introduced in Chapter 3.

Just as a street number in an address uniquely identifies one house on a street, so too each computer on a network has a unique network number. Computers on networks today use two different sets of unique numbers, each for a different purpose. The first number is called the **IP address**. An IP address is a series of four sets of digits separated by periods, such as 198.146.118.20. IP addresses for home users are generally provided by an Internet Service Provider (ISP). These addresses can be permanent (**static addresses**) that do not change, or they can be temporary (**dynamic addresses**) that change whenever the computer is turned on or after a set period of time.

The second unique address used by computer networks is a **Media Access Control (MAC)** address. This address, sometimes called the **physical address**, is 12 characters separated by either dashes or colons, such as 00:15:58:3C:31:C3.

The transmission of data through a computer network is accomplished by dividing the data to be sent into smaller units called **packets**. As shown conceptually in Figure 5-3, the sending computer divides the data into individual packets (on an actual network a packet would contain more than a single word) and labels each packet with information such as the packet number, the sender's IP address, and the destination IP address. These packets are then individually sent through the network. When the receiving computer gets the packets, it reassembles them in the correct sequence.

Types of Networks

Computer networks can be classified in at least two different ways. The first classification is based on the distance between devices. A computer network that has all of the computers

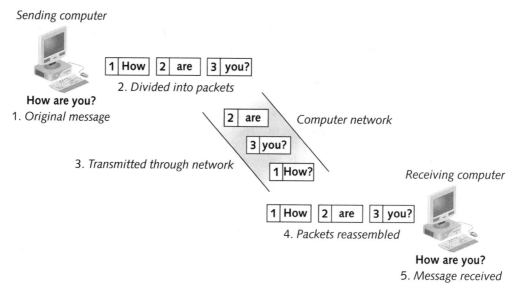

Sending computer

1 How   2 are   3 you?
2. Divided into packets

How are you?
1. Original message

2 are   *Computer network*

3 you?

3. Transmitted through network

1 How?

Receiving computer

1 How   2 are   3 you?
4. Packets reassembled

How are you?
5. Message received

Figure 5-3 Sending data by packets

Course Technology/Cengage Learning

located relatively close to each other is called a **local area network (LAN)**. For example, networked computers that are located on one floor of an office building or in a classroom of a college may be considered a LAN. A **wide area network (WAN)** connects computers and networks over a larger geographical area than a LAN, even spanning regions, countries, or the globe. The technical definition of a WAN is a network that connects computers and LANs that crosses over a public thoroughfare, such as a road, highway, or railroad. A **personal area network (PAN)** generally describes devices other than personal computers that communicate at a distance usually up to 10 feet (3 meters).

A second means of classifying computer networks is by the type of connection. Originally networks were composed of computers that were connected through a cable that attached to each device. However, today wireless connections are often used to connect computers. One type of wireless network that has experienced phenomenal growth is a **wireless local area network (WLAN)**, sometimes called **Wi-Fi (Wireless Fidelity)**. These wireless networks are based on a protocol that transmits data at fast speeds over a distance of up to 375 feet (115 meters). A home wireless network can connect laptop computers, desktop computers, printers, an Internet connection, and even audio and video systems on a single network without using any cables. A home wireless network is illustrated in Figure 5-4.

Network Devices

Different types of network hardware devices may be part of a home network. On the user's computer a hardware device that connects a computer to a wired network is called a **network**

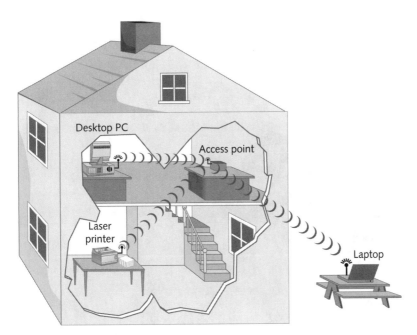

Figure 5-4 Home wireless network

Course Technology/Cengage Learning

interface card (NIC) adapter. It sends and receives data through the network. For desktop and laptop computers connecting to a wired network, an internal NIC is used that has a jack for a cable connection to the network. A NIC for a wireless network performs the same functions as a NIC for a wired network with one major exception: it does not use a jack for a wired connection to the network. In its place is an antenna to send and receive signals, as seen in Figure 5-5. Virtually all laptop wireless NICs are built in and do not have an external antenna.

One hardware device that typically is connected to the network itself is a **router**. A router is responsible for sending packets through the network toward their destination. Because of the number of computers on a network and how the network is configured, a router may not necessarily send the packet directly to the receiving computer; instead, it may send the packet to another router or device that is connected to the destination computer.

Another common network hardware device is designed for security. Known as a **firewall**, this device can repel attacks through filtering the data packets as they arrive at the perimeter of the network. Acting as the gatekeeper to the network, those packets that meet certain criteria are allowed to pass through while packets that fail the test are destroyed. Hardware firewalls usually are located outside the network security perimeter as the first line of defense, as shown in Figure 5-6.

Another device that is increasingly popular for home networks is a central device for backups. This allows all of the computers attached to the network to be backed up automatically to the device. The device commonly used is a **Network Attached Storage (NAS)** device. NAS is a dedicated hard disk-based file storage device that provides centralized and consolidated disk storage available to network users. NAS devices have an IP address and connect to the network like a computer, and even appear to the network as an independent network device.

Figure 5-5 Internal wireless NIC

Course Technology/Cengage Learning

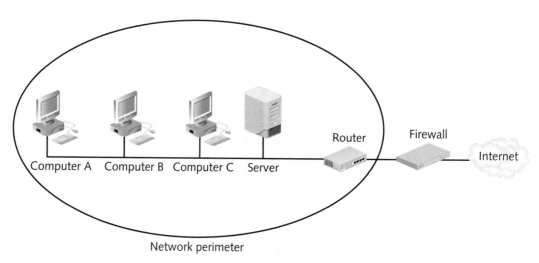

Figure 5-6 Hardware firewall

Course Technology/Cengage Learning

The operating system on NAS devices can be either a standard operating system like Microsoft Windows, a proprietary operating system, or a "stripped-down" operating system with many standard features omitted (these generally include variations of Linux). Because NAS functions at the file system level, a device or program on the network sees files on the NAS as if they were on the user's own computer.

Wireless networks require an **access point (AP)**. An AP has two primary functions. First, an AP acts as the "base station" for the wireless network, in that all of the wireless devices that have a wireless NIC transmit directly to the AP, which in turn redirects the signal to the other wireless devices. Second, an AP acts as a "bridge" between the wireless and wired networks. This allows devices on the wireless network to communicate with devices on the wired network and Internet (and vice versa). A wireless network with an AP is illustrated in Figure 5-7.

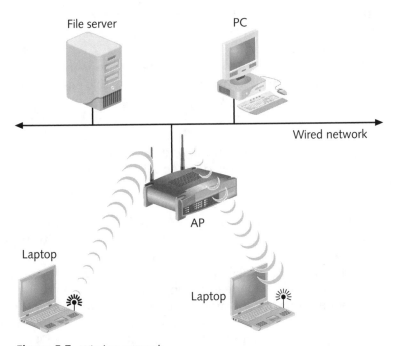

Figure 5-7 Wireless network

Course Technology/Cengage Learning

Wireless networks for home use typically combine the features of an AP, firewall, and router in a single hardware device. Strictly speaking these devices are **wireless gateways**. However, most vendors instead choose to label their products as *wireless broadband routers* or *wireless routers*.

Security in Your World

Braden set his tray on the table. "Thanks, Mrs. Sumners," he said. After determining that the surge protectors were the only items destroyed by the lightning strike, Braden and Mrs. Sumners drove to the local electronics store to pick up replacements. Her daughter, Amy, also had accompanied them to pick up an external mouse for her new laptop computer. Mrs. Sumners insisted that they all stop at a local sandwich shop so she could buy lunch.

"Braden, I love my new laptop," Amy said as she turned it on at the sandwich shop. "Yes, Thomas told me that you were really turning into a geeky computer person just like him!" Braden said. Amy laughed and said, "Oh, I wouldn't go that far. But since our computers at home were dead after the lightning strike I've been coming here to check my e-mail on their free Wi-Fi service."

Amy clicked her mouse and said, "Braden, could you tell me something? Whenever I come here my laptop shows two different wireless networks. This one says 'Sandwich Shop Wi-Fi,' but there's another one that just says 'Free Internet Connection.' But the first has a different symbol than the other one. Does it matter which one I use?"

Braden moved his chair to see Amy's screen. "No, no, don't click on 'Free Internet Connection,'" he said. Amy set down her drink and said, "Why not?" "Well," said Braden, "You were right that the symbol is different. That means it's not a regular wireless network but is one that is just connected to somebody's computer. If you clicked on it you'd be directly connected to their computer. They could then get into your computer and infect it or steal what you have on it." "Can they really?" asked Mrs. Sumners. "I'm afraid so," said Braden. "You have to be careful with these free wireless networks. In fact, the way they are set up someone could actually see everything that you're sending and receiving."

Amy looked up from her e-mail message and said, "Oh, Braden, you're just joking. They can't do that." Braden thought for a moment and then pulled his laptop out of his backpack. After a few minutes he said, "Well, Amy, it looks like you're sending an e-mail to your friend Becky Gregory about her boyfriend Michael. You said that Becky should..." "What?" Amy said. "You really *can* see what I'm doing!" "Yep," said Braden, "And do you want me to tell you what your e-mail password is? It's right here on my screen. You really need to change it to something better."

Mrs. Sumners shook her head. "Braden, I can't believe it's that easy. What else do we need to know about using Wi-Fi?"

Attacks on Wireless Networks

As wireless networks have become more popular, they have come under increasing attacks. Wireless attacks are typically a three-step process: discovering the wireless network, connecting to the network, then launching assaults.

Discovering

At regular intervals (normally every 100 microseconds) a wireless router sends a signal to announce its presence and to provide the necessary information for devices that want to join the network. This process, known as **beaconing**, is an orderly means for wireless devices to establish and maintain communications. Each wireless device looks for the incoming beacon information (known as **scanning**). Once a wireless device receives a beacon it can attempt to join the network.

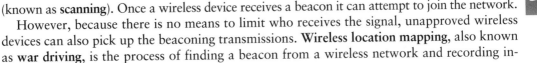

However, because there is no means to limit who receives the signal, unapproved wireless devices can also pick up the beaconing transmissions. **Wireless location mapping**, also known as **war driving**, is the process of finding a beacon from a wireless network and recording information about it.

War driving is derived from the term *war dialing*. In the 1983 movie *War Games*, Matthew Broderick stars as a teen that discovers a back door into a central military computer and accidentally starts a countdown to begin World War III. He finds the back door by having his computer randomly dial telephone numbers until another computer answers the call. This random process of searching for a connection was called war dialing, so randomly searching for a wireless signal was known as war driving.

War driving technically involves using an automobile to search for wireless signals over a large area. However, war driving does not require an automobile—it could be accomplished by carrying a portable computing device while simply walking down the street.

Airplanes have also been used to locate wireless signals and this is called *war flying*.

To conduct war driving, the following tools are necessary:

- Mobile computing device—A mobile computing device used for war driving can be a standard portable computer, a handheld computer, or an advanced technology cell phone (smart phone).
- Wireless NIC adapter—The wireless NIC allows the mobile computing device to detect a wireless signal. For war driving a USB wireless NIC is often used instead of an internal wireless NIC. A USB wireless NIC is connected by a cable to the computer and the NIC can more easily be moved and adjusted to pick up the wireless signal. A USB wireless NIC is shown in Figure 5-8.
- Antenna—Although all wireless NIC adapters have embedded antennas, attaching an external antenna will significantly increase the ability to detect a wireless signal. The most common type of antenna for war driving is an **omnidirectional antenna** that can detect signals from all directions equally.

Figure 5-8 USB wireless NIC

Course Technology/Cengage Learning

- Global positioning system receiver—A **global positioning system (GPS)** receiver uses the GPS system, which was originally developed by the U.S. military in the late 1970s as a navigation system but was later opened to civilian use. It is used to precisely identify the location of a receiver. GPS is composed of 27 earth-orbiting satellites (some satellites are "spares" in case one fails), each of which circles the globe twice a day at a height of 12,000 miles (19,300 km). A GPS receiver allows the user to precisely record where the wireless networks are located.

- Software—Client utilities and integrated operating system tools are available to detect and analyze the signal.

War driving in itself is not an illegal activity. What can be considered illegal in some localities is using that signal to connect to the network without the owner's permission.

Connecting

Once an attacker has identified the location of a wireless network, the next step is to connect to the network. Due to the nature of wireless LANs, if the network has not been configured with the correct security protections, this process is not difficult.

In order for a wireless device such as a laptop computer to be connected to the network, that device needs to know the **Service Set Identifier (SSID)** of the wireless network. The SSID serves as the "network name" and can be any alphanumeric string from 2 to 32 characters. If the wireless device sends to the wireless router the correct SSID of the network it can then be connected to the network. Connecting to a wireless network is illustrated in Figure 5-9.

Wireless networks are designed to freely distribute their SSID. When the wireless router performs beaconing to all wireless devices, by default it sends the SSID. Once a wireless device receives a beacon with the SSID it can then attempt to join the network. Thus there is virtually nothing that an attacker must do other than receive a beacon from the wireless router with the SSID and then return it to the wireless router in order to become connected to the network.

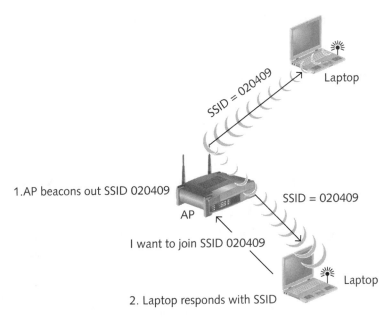

SSID = 020409

Laptop

1.AP beacons out SSID 020409

AP

SSID = 020409

I want to join SSID 020409

Laptop

2. Laptop responds with SSID

Figure 5-9 Connecting to a wireless network

Course Technology/Cengage Learning

For a degree of protection, some wireless security sources encourage users to configure their APs to prevent the beacon from including the SSID but instead require the user to manually enter the SSID on the wireless device (this assumes that only authorized users have been given the SSID). Although not advertising the SSID might seem to provide protection, in reality it does not, because:

- The SSID can be easily discovered even when it is not contained in beaconing because it is found in other transmissions sent by the wireless router.
- It is not always possible or convenient to turn off SSID beaconing.
- Turning off SSID beaconing can also impact the mobility of the user, because it prevents wireless devices from freely moving from one wireless network to another.
- With some versions of Microsoft Windows, a device will not connect to a network that is not broadcasting its SSID if there is another network that is broadcasting its SSID in the vicinity.

Configuring a wireless router not to include the SSID provides virtually no protection. Although it may prevent a "casual" unauthorized user from capturing the SSID and connecting to the network, it can easily be discovered by an attacker with a basic knowledge of wireless technology.

Launching Assaults

After an attacker has discovered the wireless network and connected to it, there are different attacks that can be launched. These attacks include eavesdropping, stealing data, injecting malware, storing illegal content, launching denial of service attacks, and impersonating a legitimate network.

Eavesdropping   The transmissions of a wireless network "float" between devices in the air. With the correct software, attackers can easily view the contents of these transmissions from hundreds of feet away, even if they have not connected to the wireless network. Figure 5-10 illustrates the results of a program used to capture these transmissions, which can then be searched for passwords, credit card numbers, or private information.

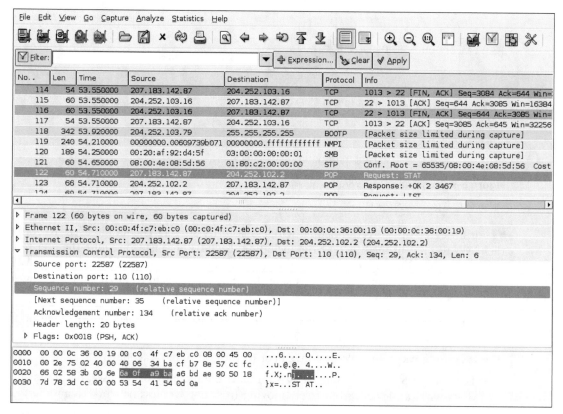

Figure 5-10   Contents of captured transmissions

Course Technology/Cengage Learning

In order to protect against wireless eavesdropping, a standard known as the **Wired Equivalent Privacy (WEP)** was designed to ensure that only authorized parties can view transmitted wireless information. WEP accomplishes this confidentiality by taking unencrypted text (plaintext) and then encrypting it into ciphertext so that it cannot be viewed by unauthorized parties while being transmitted. WEP relies on a "secret key" that is shared between the wireless client device and the wireless router. The same secret key must be installed on both the device and the wireless router in advance and is used to encrypt any information to be transmitted as well as decrypt information that is received.

However, due to the way in which WEP was implemented it contained a serious flaw. Attackers were able to exploit this vulnerability and reveal the shared secret key. Today an attacker can discover a WEP key in less than one minute, revealing the contents of the wireless transmissions.

In 2005 attackers used a laptop computer to capture and then unlock wireless transmissions that were protected by WEP at a Marshalls department store near St. Paul, Minnesota. The information obtained allowed them to access the central online database of the parent company, where they continued to steal sensitive customer data over the next 18 months. By the time the breach was discovered, attackers had stolen information on at least 45.6 million credit and debit cards.

Stealing Data Once an attacker has connected to the wireless network he is treated as a "trusted" user by the network. This allows him to have access to files stored on any computer in the network that are configured to be shared among other users (users often set **file sharing** on folders to allow other users on their network to be able to access their documents or for automatic backups). An attacker who has entered the wireless network could steal files that contain personal contact information, Social Security numbers, credit card numbers, and other sensitive information.

Injecting Malware An attacker who connects to a wireless network as a "trusted" user enters from behind the network's firewall, as shown in Figure 5-11. This allows an attacker to inject malware onto a computer, such as a worm, which can quickly infect all other computers in the network.

Storing Illegal Content Attackers often break into a wireless network in order to use the network to store illegal or harmful content. An attacker who breaks into a wireless network can

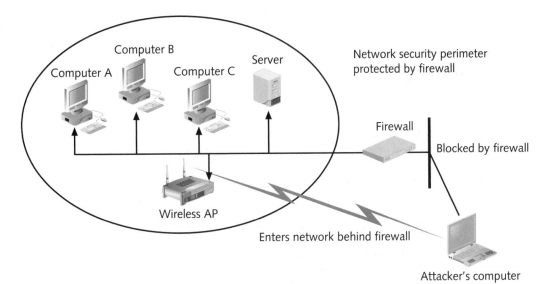

Figure 5-11 Injecting malware behind a firewall

Course Technology/Cengage Learning

set up storage space on the user's computer to download and store child pornography, pirated software, illegal videos, stolen credit cards, and other data, all without the user's knowledge.

If this illicit action is discovered by the authorities, the unsuspecting owner of the computer and network is considered the culprit. In several instances local authorities who have become aware of illegal downloads have arrested the owners instead of the criminals who broke into the wireless network.

Launching Denial of Service (DoS) Attacks A denial of service (DoS) attack is designed to prevent a device from performing its intended function. DoS attacks are common against Web servers. Wireless DoS attacks are different than wired network DoS attacks. Instead of denying service to a server, wireless DoS attacks are designed to deny wireless devices access to the wireless router itself.

Although it is possible to "flood" the wireless frequency with enough radio frequency interference to prevent a device from effectively communicating with the wireless router, these attacks are rare because sophisticated and expensive equipment is necessary to generate enough interference to impact the network. In addition, because a very powerful transmitter must be used at a relatively close range to execute the attack, it is easy to locate the transmitter and identify the source of the attack.

There are several ways to launch a wireless DoS attack. An attacker who has become connected to the wireless network can start a download of an extremely large file from the Internet, such as a video file. This will effectively "tie up" the network and prevent other devices from accessing the network, as seen in Figure 5-12.

Legitimate users who download large files over a wireless network can impact the speed of other users on the network.

Another DoS attack technique is to use a **packet generator**. This program will create fake packets and flood the wireless network with traffic so that legitimate users cannot access the network. Also, an attacker can send fraudulent **disassociation frames**. A **disassociation frame** is a communication from a wireless device that indicates the device wishes to end the wireless connection. An attacker can pretend to be a wireless router and send a forged disassociation frame to a wireless device. This will cause the device to disassociate from the router/access point. By sending continual disassociation frames, an attacker can prevent any device from communicating with the wireless router. This is illustrated in Figure 5-13.

Impersonating a Legitimate Network In many locations, such as restaurants, coffee shops, airports, and libraries, wireless networks are often made available for any user to access. Attackers will often impersonate these legitimate networks by creating their own look-alike network, tempting unsuspecting users to connect with the attacker's network instead.

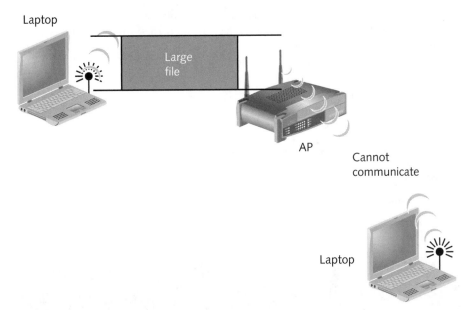

Figure 5-12 A large file transfer can tie up a wireless network

Course Technology/Cengage Learning

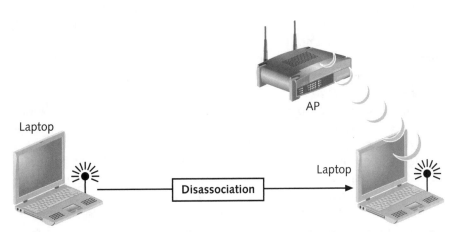

1. Attacker sends disassocation frame   2. Associated device disassociates from AP

Figure 5-13 DoS attack using disassociation frames

Course Technology/Cengage Learning

These look-alike networks do not require that a wireless router be installed. Instead, an attacker can set up an **ad hoc** or **peer-to-peer** network that connects wireless devices directly to another wireless device. An attacker who sets up an ad hoc network will name it "Free

Wireless Network" or "Free Airport Wireless" in the hopes that an unsuspecting user will connect directly to the attacker's computer, even though the wireless icons are different, as seen in Figure 5-14. Once the connection is made, the attacker might be able to directly inject malware into the user's computer or steal data.

Attacker ad hoc network

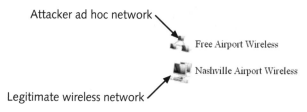

Free Airport Wireless

Nashville Airport Wireless

Legitimate wireless network

Figure 5-14   Different wireless icons

Course Technology/Cengage Learning

Security in Your World

"There, that should do it," said Braden. After installing the new surge protectors and checking that all of the computers were functioning normally, Braden configured Amy's new laptop computer to connect to the Sumners' wireless network. "The way that Thomas set this up, only authorized users can access your network, and all of your transmissions are encrypted so nobody can see them. And you're now part of that network, Amy."

Amy took her laptop computer and opened a Web browser, which immediately connected to the Internet. "Hey, this will be great. I can be anywhere in the house and stay connected," she said. "Yep, that's the great thing about wireless," Braden replied.

"What about my friends who come over? They'll be able to be connected like I am, right?" Amy asked. Braden said, "You'll have to first do a couple of quick things so they can use your wireless network. But you'll only have to do it one time. I'm making notes right now for you, and then I'll let you practice these steps on my laptop while I'm still here so you'll know just what to do."

Amy slumped in her chair. "Braden, that's such a bother. Couldn't we just turn some of this stuff off so I won't have to do that?" she asked. Braden smiled. "Let's see, I think the e-mail I read in the sandwich shop was something about Becky and her boyfriend Michael, and..."

Amy quickly cut him off and laughed. "OK, I see your point. Here, show me what I have to do. I don't want you reading my e-mails again!"

Wireless Network Defenses

Defending against wireless attacks involves two different procedures. The first is to secure the home wireless network, and the second is to use an unprotected public wireless network in the most secure manner possible.

Securing a Home Wireless Network

Making a home wireless network secure involves several steps, but is not difficult. The steps necessary for securing it include locking down the wireless router, limiting users, turning on Wi-Fi Protected Access 2, and configuring the network settings.

Locking Down the Wireless Router The first step in securing a wireless network is to lock down the wireless router by creating a username and password. This prevents attackers from accessing the wireless router and turning off any security settings that have been implemented or even locking out the owner. All wireless routers from a specific vendor are configured with the same default password, and these passwords are well known by attackers.

In addition to a default username and password, wireless routers also are preconfigured with a default SSID. Users should change the SSID to a "generic" name that would not reveal to an attacker the source of the wireless signal. That is, instead of using a last name or street address for the SSID, a nondescript SSID should be entered.

Locking down the wireless router involves determining the IP address of the wireless router and the default password. This information is included in the documentation of the wireless router or is available online at the vendor's Web site, or can be determined by examining the settings of the network. The IP address is then entered into a Web browser on a computer connected to the local network, which then displays the login screen. Once the default password is entered a configuration screen similar to that in Figure 5-15 appears.

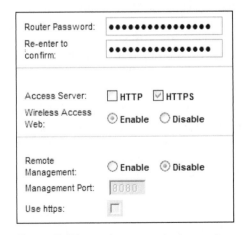

Figure 5-15 Wireless router login security screen

Course Technology/Cengage Learning

The Hands-on Projects at the end of the chapter contain additional useful information about configuring a wireless router.

Typical settings on the wireless router login security screen include:

- Router Password—This is where a new password is entered and confirmed.
- Access Server—The HTTPS option will encrypt the transmissions when configuring the wireless router so that an attacker cannot view them.
- Wireless Access Web—This option allows a wireless device connected to the wireless network to access the wireless router settings. If a wired computer that is connected to the network is available then this setting can be changed to *Disable* for greater security.
- Remote Management—The Remote Management setting allows a user on the Internet to access the wireless router remotely. It is recommended that this be set to *Disable*.

Other security tips for the wireless router include positioning it near the center of the home or apartment instead of near a window to minimize the signal extending outside the building and to turn it off when traveling for an extended period of time.

Limiting Users The next step is to restrict the users who can access the wireless network. This is done by controlling wireless access of devices to the network through the wireless router. Because the wireless router acts as the central "base station" for the wireless network and all of the wireless devices must transmit to it, restricting access to the wireless router will prevent unauthorized users from connecting to the wireless network.

Access to the wireless network can be restricted by entering the MAC address of approved wireless devices into the wireless router (sometimes called a **MAC address filter**). As seen in Figure 5-16, restrictions can be implemented in one of two ways: a device can be allowed into the network ("Let this specific device in") or a device can be blocked from accessing the network ("Keep this specific device out"). MAC address filtering is usually implemented by permitting instead of preventing, since it is not possible to know the MAC address of all of the devices that are to be excluded.

Wireless access control through MAC address filtering should not be confused with *access restrictions*, or limits placed on what users can perform after they are accepted into the network. Access restrictions can limit a user's access to the Internet, what days and times it can be accessed, which Web sites can be visited, or the type of traffic that passes through the wireless router.

A limitation of MAC address filtering is that it requires pre-approved authentication: that is, that the MAC address must first be entered into the MAC address filter on the wireless

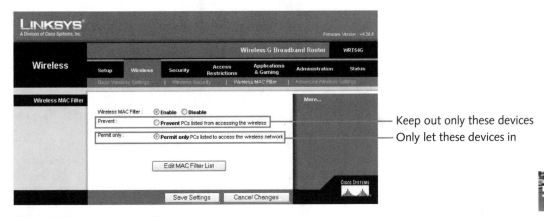

Figure 5-16 MAC address filter

Course Technology/Cengage Learning

router before the device can be authenticated. However, once the MAC address of the device is entered into the filter it does not have to be entered again.

A determined and knowledgeable attacker can circumvent MAC address filtering, so this restriction should be used along with other wireless security settings.

In addition to MAC address filters, other restrictions can be placed on users. Almost all wireless routers distribute IP addresses to network devices using the **Dynamic Host Configuration Protocol (DHCP)**, part of the TCP/IP protocol suite. DHCP "leases" IP addresses to clients to use while they are connected to the network. Properly configuring these settings can provide an additional though limited degree of protection against wireless attackers. These settings are illustrated in Figure 5-17.

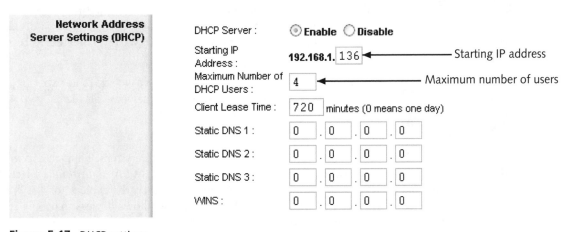

Figure 5-17 DHCP settings

Course Technology/Cengage Learning

First, DHCP distributes addresses to network devices beginning at a specific starting address and incrementing by a value of one for each device. That is, if the starting IP address is 192.168.1.2, then the first device will be given the address 192.168.1.2, the next device will be leased 192.168.1.3, and so on. Attackers who attempt to gain unauthorized access to a wireless network may try to determine the IP address of other network devices by taking the starting address of an IP address range (such as 192.168.1.1) and incrementing by a value of one. However, if the starting IP address is set to a higher number, such as 192.168.1.136, it is more difficult for the attacker to guess a device's IP address.

An even more secure approach is to turn off DHCP entirely and assign to each user a static IP address.

Second, the maximum number of users can be restricted. Wireless users who receive a temporary IP address are given a **DHCP lease**. The maximum number of wireless DHCP users can be limited to the number of authorized devices on the network. That is, if there are four network devices then the maximum number of DHCP users should be set to four. If an attacker is able to breach the wireless security protections and gain access to the network, she would not be leased an IP address since the maximum would already be distributed.

Setting the maximum number of DHCP users is of real value only if all of the approved network devices are currently connected to the wireless network. If one of the wireless users is using a notebook computer that is not connected or if a desktop device is turned off, this leaves an available IP address for an attacker.

Turning on Wi-Fi Protected Access 2 (WPA2) All wireless routers and wireless devices today follow a standard for encrypting transmissions and authenticating users. Known as the **personal security model**, it is designed for single users or small office settings of generally 10 or fewer wireless devices. The personal security model is divided into two parts, **Wi-Fi Protected Access (WPA)** and the updated **Wi-Fi Protected Access 2 (WPA2)**.

WPA2 was introduced in September 2004. Unless a wireless router was manufactured before that time, it will support the newer standard.

Turning on WPA2 is done at the wireless router and involves three steps. First, the *Security Mode* of *WPA2 Personal* is chosen, as seen in Figure 5-18. Next, the *WPA Algorithm* is selected, as seen in Figure 5-19. Depending upon the model of wireless router, the choices for the WPA algorithm are usually *TKIP+AES* or *AES*. The TKIP+AES setting allows devices that only support the weaker WPA to still connect to the wireless network along with devices that use WPA2. The final step is to enter the *WPA Shared Key*. This is the value that is used to encrypt and decrypt wireless transmissions. The rules for creating a WPA Shared Key are similar to those for creating a strong password (it should consist of random letters, digits, and marks of

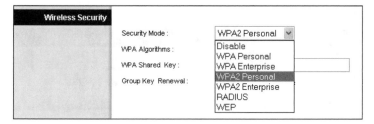

Figure 5-18 Security Mode options

Course Technology/Cengage Learning

Figure 5-19 WPA Algorithms setting

Course Technology/Cengage Learning

punctuation), yet unlike a password the length should be over 20 characters. WPA Shared Keys that are fewer than 20 characters and use common words can easily be broken by attackers.

Although many manufacturers allow WPA Shared Keys as short as eight characters, the developers of this technology clearly state, *"A key generated from a passphrase of less than about 20 characters is unlikely to deter attacks."*

When a wireless device attempts to connect for the first time to a wireless router that is using WPA2, the user is prompted for the WPA Shared Key value. If it is not entered correctly the user will not be accepted into the wireless network.

Configuring Network Settings There are several network settings that also can be used to enhance wireless security. These include network address translation, wireless virtual local area networks, setting up a demilitarized zone, and port forwarding.

Network Address Translation (NAT) "You cannot attack what you cannot see" is the philosophy behind systems using **network address translation** (NAT). NAT hides the IP addresses of network devices from attackers. In a network using NAT, the computers are assigned special IP addresses, which are listed in Table 5-1. Known as **private addresses**, these IP addresses are not assigned to any specific user or organization; instead, they can be used by any user on the private internal network. Private addresses function as regular IP addresses on an internal network. However, if a packet with a private address makes its way to the Internet, the routers drop that packet.

Table 5-1 Private IP addresses

Class	Beginning Address	Ending Address
Class A	10.0.0.0	10.255.255.255
Class B	172.16.0.0	172.31.255.255
Class C	192.168.0.0	192.168.255.255

NAT refers not to a specific device but to a technology.

As a packet leaves a network, NAT removes the private IP address from the sender's packet and replaces it with an alias IP address, as shown in Figure 5-20. The NAT software maintains a table of the special addresses and alias IP addresses. When a packet is returned to NAT, the process is reversed. An attacker who captures the packet on the Internet cannot determine the actual IP address of the sender. Without that address, it is more difficult to identify and attack a computer.

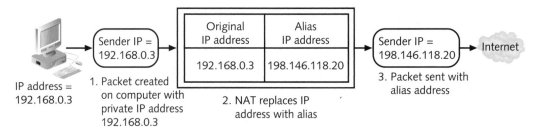

Figure 5-20 Network address translation (NAT)

Course Technology/Cengage Learning

A variation of NAT is **port address translation (PAT)**. Instead of giving each outgoing packet a different IP address, each packet is given the same IP address but a different port number. This allows a single public IP address to be used by several users.

PAT is typically used on wireless routers that allow multiple users to share one IP address received from an ISP.

Wireless Virtual Local Area Network (VLAN) Virtual local area networks (VLANs) are commonly used in organizations to segment users or network equipment in logical groupings. A variation of VLAN is generally available on wireless routers. This creates a separate virtual network for each user of the wireless network. Every wireless

device is given its own virtual network and cannot see any other users or devices on the network. This means that even if an attacker were able to connect to the wireless network, he would not be able to attack any of the devices on the network. A disadvantage of wireless VLANs is that a legitimate user cannot access other equipment on the network, such as a storage device or a shared laser printer.

Wireless VLANs are sometimes referred to as *AP isolation* on a wireless router.

Demilitarized Zone (DMZ) Often the devices most vulnerable to attack are those that provide services to outside users, such as Web servers and e-mail servers. If attackers are able to penetrate the security of these servers, they may be able to access devices on the internal LAN. An additional level of security would be to isolate these services in their own network.

A **demilitarized zone (DMZ)** is a separate network that sits outside the secure network perimeter. Outside users can access the DMZ but cannot enter the secure network. Figure 5-21 illustrates a DMZ for an organization that contains a Web server and an e-mail server that are accessed by outside users. Placing these servers in a DMZ limits outside access to the DMZ network only. Because this DMZ has two firewalls, an attacker would have to breach two separate firewalls to reach the secure internal LAN.

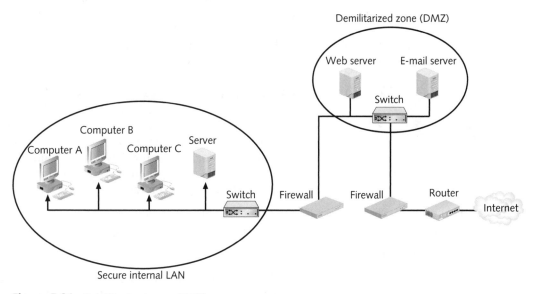

Figure 5-21 Demilitarized zone (DMZ)

Course Technology/Cengage Learning

A demilitarized zone in military warfare is a buffer space between two enemies.

Many wireless routers claim to support a DMZ. However, it is not a true DMZ. Instead it allows one local device to be exposed to the Internet for Internet gaming or videoconferencing by forwarding all the ports at the same time to that one device. The use of a DMZ is not recommended unless it is absolutely required.

Port Forwarding A more secure alternative to a DMZ is **port forwarding**. A DMZ opens all the ports of one computer, effectively exposing the entire computer so that anyone on the Internet can see it. Port forwarding is more secure because it opens only the ports that need to be available.

A computer whose port is being forwarded cannot use DHCP. Instead, it must have a static IP address assigned to it.

Using a Public Wireless Network Securely

Using a public wireless network requires an extra degree of vigilance in order to stay secure. This is because public wireless networks do not attempt to be secure. Although this makes it easy for any user to connect to the network, it poses security risks. The most common steps when using a public wireless network include turning on a personal firewall and using a virtual private network.

Turning on a Personal Firewall When using a public wireless network it is essential that a personal firewall be turned on. A firewall is designed to prevent malicious packets from entering the network, and can be either software-based or hardware-based. A personal software firewall runs as a program on the user's local computer. A firewall operates according to a **rule base**. The rule base establishes what action the firewall should take when it receives a packet. The three typical options are:

- Allow—Let the packet pass through and continue its journey.
- Block—Prevent the packet from passing to the network by dropping it.
- Prompt—Ask the user what action to take.

Packets can be filtered by a firewall in one of two ways. **Stateless packet filtering** looks at the incoming packet and permits or denies it based strictly on the rule base. Although a stateless packet filter does provide some degree of protection, attackers can easily bypass the protection. With a stateless packet filter an attacker only has to discover a valid internal IP address on the computer network. Then she can send an attack using that IP address and falsely change the packet to indicate it is an HTML document.

The second type of firewall provides a greater degree of protection. **Stateful packet filtering** keeps a record of the state of a connection between an internal computer and an external server and then makes decisions based on the connection as well as the rule base. For example, a stateless packet filter firewall might allow a packet to pass through because it is intended for a specific computer on the network. However, a stateful packet filter would not let the packet pass if that internal network computer did not first request the information from the external server.

Although hardware firewalls are considered the most secure, personal software firewalls have strong functionality. Early personal software firewalls performed only inbound filtering: they examined all incoming traffic and blocked any incoming traffic that was not received in response to a request of the computer (solicited traffic) or that has been specified as allowed (excepted traffic). Most personal software firewalls today also filter outbound traffic. This outbound filtering protects users by preventing malware from connecting to other computers and spreading. In addition, today's personal software firewalls have an expanded rule base.

One disadvantage of a personal software firewall is that it is only as strong as the operating system of the computer. Attackers that can exploit operating system weaknesses might be able to bypass the firewall.

Virtual Private Networks (VPNs) A virtual private network (VPN) uses an unsecured public network, such as wireless network in a coffee shop, as if it were a secure private network. It does this by encrypting all data that is transmitted between the remote device and the network. This ensures that any transmissions that are intercepted will be indecipherable. A VPN is illustrated in Figure 5-22.

Apple Mac OS, Linux, and Microsoft Windows include a built-in VPN client.

There are several advantages of VPN technology. These include:

- *Full protection*—The VPN encrypts all transmissions from the client and not just certain applications.
- *Transparency*—Once a VPN is set up it is basically invisible to the user.
- *Authentication*—The VPN can ensure that only authorized users have access to information.
- *Industry standards*—VPNs can take advantage of industry-wide protocol standards.

Using a VPN when accessing a public wireless network will encrypt all transmissions. This will prevent an attacker from viewing any information.

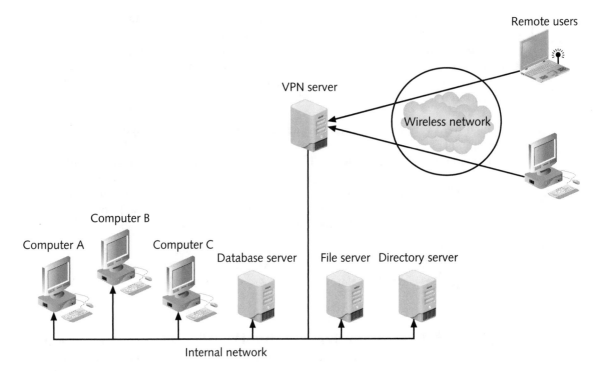

Figure 5-22 Virtual private network (VPN)

Course Technology/Cengage Learning

Another tip when using a public wireless network is to set your computer to not automatically connect to an open wireless network. Some operating systems, such as Microsoft Windows Vista, will never automatically connect to an unprotected or ad hoc network, reducing the risk of automatically connecting to a malicious wireless router.

Chapter Summary

- Home computer networks are common today. Most home users install wireless networks. These networks allow users to share hardware, data, and programs. The transmission of data through a computer network is accomplished by dividing the data to be sent into smaller units called packets. Individual packets contain the information to be transmitted along with the packet number, the sender's IP address, and the destination IP address. A local area network (LAN) is an interconnection of computers that are typically located on one floor of an office building or in a classroom of a college. Wireless LANs are based on a protocol that transmits data at fast speeds over a distance of up to 375 feet (115 meters). A network interface card (NIC) adapter is a hardware device connected to a computer that sends and receives data through the network. A NIC for a wireless network uses an antenna for transmission. A router is a network hardware device that is responsible for sending packets through the network towards their destination. Wireless networks for home use typically combine several features and are often called wireless routers.

■ Attacking a wireless network involves three main steps. The first is to discover the existence of the wireless network. Wireless location mapping, also known as war driving, is the systematic approach of identifying wireless networks. The second step is for the attacker to attempt to connect to the wireless network. The Service Set Identifier (SSID) of the wireless network, which serves as the "network name," is the only identification necessary for a device to attach to an unsecured wireless network. Finally, once an attacker has connected to the wireless network she can launch different types of attacks. One attack is to eavesdrop on the wireless transmissions and view their contents. Another attack is to steal data. Once an attacker has connected to the wireless network he is treated as a "trusted" user by the network. This allows him to have access to files stored on any computer in the network that are configured to be shared among other users. An attacker can also inject malware onto a computer, such as a worm, which can quickly infect all other computers in the network. Attackers also break into wireless networks to store illegal content without the owner's knowledge. A wireless denial of service (DoS) attack can also be launched against wireless users. Finally, it is possible to impersonate a legitimate wireless network and trick users into connecting to it.

■ Securing a home wireless network involves several steps, none of which are difficult. First it is important to secure the wireless router itself. This includes setting a password on the device before anyone can access the settings, as well as prevent Internet users and wireless users from changing the settings. The next step is to restrict the users who can access the wireless network, which is done by controlling wireless access of devices to the network through the wireless router. MAC address filtering is usually implemented by permitting a specific wireless device based on its MAC address.

■ One of the most important steps in securing a wireless network is to turn on Wi-Fi Protected Access 2 (WPA2). Turning on WPA2 is done at the wireless router and involves only three steps. When a wireless device attempts to connect to a network protected by WPA2 the user must first enter the correct shared key value, which is used to both encrypt and decrypt the transmissions. This prevents an attacker from viewing their contents.

■ Many wireless routers support what is called a demilitarized zone (DMZ). It allows one local device to be exposed to the Internet for Internet gaming or videoconferencing by forwarding all the ports at the same time to that one device, setting up a demilitarized zone. A more secure alternative to a DMZ is port forwarding.

■ An extra degree of vigilance is needed to stay secure while using a public wireless network. The most common steps when using a public wireless network include turning on a personal firewall and using a virtual private network.

Key Terms

access point (AP)   The "base station" for the wireless network that redirects signals to other wireless devices and connects to a wired network.

ad hoc   A wireless network that connects wireless devices directly to another wireless device; also called peer-to-peer.

beaconing   The process of a wireless router sending signals at regular intervals to announce its presence and to provide the necessary information for devices to join the network.

computer network   An interconnection of computers and devices to share resources.

demilitarized zone (DMZ)   A separate network that sits outside the secure network perimeter that provides Internet access to certain services.

denial of service (DoS)   An attack designed to prevent a device from performing its intended function.

DHCP lease   A lease of an IP address to a network user.

disassociation frame   A communication from a wireless device that indicates the device wishes to end the wireless connection.

dynamic address   An IP address that changes.

Dynamic Host Configuration Protocol (DHCP)   Part of the TCP/IP protocol suite that leases IP addresses to clients to use while they are connected to the network.

file sharing   Allowing other users to access documents.

firewall   A network device that can repel attacks through filtering the data packets.

global positioning system (GPS)   A system which was originally developed by the U.S. military in the late 1970s as a navigation system but was later opened to civilian use to determine geographic locations.

IP address   A series of four sets of digits separated by periods that uniquely identifies the computer.

local area network (LAN)   A computer network that has all of the computers located relatively close to each other.

MAC address filter   Restricting access to the wireless network by entering the MAC address of approved wireless devices into the wireless router.

Media Access Control (MAC) address   A unique address of 12 characters separated by either dashes or colons used by computer networks to identify the computer.

network address translation (NAT)   A technology that hides the IP addresses of network devices from attackers.

Network Attached Storage (NAS)   A technology that uses a dedicated hard disk-based file storage device to provide centralized and consolidated disk storage available to network users.

network interface card (NIC)   A hardware device that connects a computer to a wired network adapter.

omnidirectional antenna   An antenna that can detect signals from all directions equally.

packet   A unit of data that is transmitted through the computer network.

packet generator   A program that creates fake packets and flood a wireless network with traffic.

peer-to-peer   A wireless network that connects wireless devices directly to another wireless device; also called ad hoc.

personal area network (PAN) A computer network that describes devices other than personal computers that communicate at a distance up to 10 feet (3 meters).

personal security model A model of security designed for single users or small office settings of generally 10 or fewer wireless devices.

physical address A unique address of 12 characters separated by either dashes or colons used by computer networks to identify the computer.

port address translation (PAT) A technology that assigns each packet the same IP address but a different port number.

port forwarding A technology that opens only specific ports that need to be available.

private addresses IP addresses are not assigned to any specific user or organization.

router A network device responsible for sending packets through the network towards their destination.

rule base A set of rules for the action that a firewall should take when it receives a packet.

scanning The process of a wireless device looking for an incoming beacon.

server A central computer on a network that provides files or services on the network.

Service Set Identifier (SSID) The "network name" of a wireless network.

stateful packet filtering A firewall that keeps a record of the state of a connection between an internal computer and an external server and then makes decisions based on the connection as well as the rule base.

stateless packet filtering A firewall that examines an incoming packet and takes action based strictly on the rule base.

static address An IP address that does not change.

virtual local area networks (VLANs) Networks that are commonly used in organizations to segment users or network equipment in logical groupings.

virtual private network (VPN) Using an unsecured public network, such as a wireless network in a coffee shop, as if it were a secure private network.

war driving The process of finding a beacon from a wireless network and recording information about it; also known as wireless location mapping.

wide area network (WAN) A computer network that connects computers and networks over a relatively large geographical area.

Wi-Fi (Wireless Fidelity) A wireless network based on a protocol that transmits data at fast speeds over a distance of up to 375 feet (115 meters).

Wi-Fi Protected Access (WPA) One part of the personal security model that is less secure than Wi-Fi Protected Access 2.

Wi-Fi Protected Access 2 (WPA2) An update to the Wi-Fi Protected Access security model.

Wired Equivalent Privacy (WEP) A technology designed to ensure that only authorized parties can view transmitted wireless information yet is not considered secure.

wireless gateway Wireless network device for home users that combines the features of an AP, firewall, and router in a single hardware device.

wireless local area network (WLAN) A wireless network based on a protocol that transmits data at fast speeds over a distance of up to 375 feet (115 meters).

wireless location mapping The process of finding a beacon from a wireless network and recording information about it; also known as war driving.

Review Questions

1. A network can be used to share each of the following except:
   a. laser printer
   b. Internet connection
   c. mouse
   d. software

2. A centralized network computer on which programs and data can be stored is called a _____.
   a. server
   b. client
   c. Web proxy
   d. Network device authentication (NDA)

3. A(n) example of an IP address is _____.
   a. $419$586$893
   b. 14102009
   c. 00:15:59:3B:30:C3
   d. 192.168.18.2

4. A network that crosses a public thoroughfare is called a(n) _____.
   a. WAN
   b. LAN
   c. PAN
   d. WPAN

5. A(n) _____ can repel attacks through filtering the data packets as they arrive at the perimeter of the network.
   a. network interface card adapter
   b. router
   c. firewall
   d. NAS

6. A wireless router combines each of the following features except:
   a. network attached storage
   b. access point
   c. firewall
   d. router

7. _____ is the process of a wireless router sending a signal to announce its presence.

   a. Beaconing

   b. Signaling

   c. Broadcasting

   d. Informing

8. Each of the following is used in war driving except:

   a. USB wireless NIC

   b. omnidirectional antenna

   c. mobile computing device

   d. audio speakers

9. The Service Set Identifier (SSID): _____.

   a. is the wireless network identifier

   b. cannot be changed

   c. is never transmitted by the wireless router for security reasons

   d. must be fewer than 4 characters on a wired network

10. The standard that attempted to prevent wireless eavesdropping yet contained serious flaws and should not be used today is _____.

    a. WEP

    b. WAP-22

    c. NICW

    d. INFORMATICS

11. A user who has a folder set for _____ can allow other users on the network to see the contents of the folder.

    a. text passing

    b. network authentication

    c. folder distribution

    d. file sharing

12. Wireless denial of service (DoS) attacks _____.

    a. function in an identical fashion to a wired DoS attack

    b. are rarely used by attackers because of their inefficiency

    c. are designed to deny wireless devices access to the wireless router

    d. use disassociation frames to connect to the wired network

13. _____ is a wireless network that attackers use to trick users into connecting to their device instead of to the actual wireless router.

   a. Network Impersonation (NI)

   b. Ad hoc

   c. Freenet

   d. WI-FI TEMP

14. The first step in securing a wireless network is _____.

   a. lock down the wireless router by creating a username and password

   b. disable wireless router network sharing

   c. enable IP address filtering

   d. DMZ recall

15. A secure approach for accessing the setup of a wireless router is for it to be restricted to only _____.

   a. Internet users

   b. a wireless device

   c. a desktop computer connected by a cable to the wireless router

   d. a cell phone

16. A MAC address filter _____.

   a. can either allow a device into the network or block a device from entering

   b. requires knowledge of the IP address of all devices

   c. can be used to block Internet users from accessing the network at a specific time

   d. should only be used as a last resort

17. The purpose of Wi-Fi Protected Access 2 (WPA2) is _____.

   a. to lock down the wireless router by frequently changing the password

   b. to limit the size of downloads

   c. to limit the amount of transmissions by users

   d. to encrypt transmissions

18. Network address translation (NAT) _____.

   a. can only be used on large enterprise networks

   b. cannot be used on wireless networks because it is too complicated

   c. hides the IP addresses of network devices from attackers

   d. provides limited security and is being replaced by MAC address filtering

19. A wireless virtual local area network (VLAN) _____.

    a. creates a separate virtual network for each user of the wireless network

    b. requires the use of MAC address filtering

    c. permits a user to access a shared laser printer

    d. cannot be used on a network with a wireless router

20. A _____ is a separate network that sits outside the secure network perimeter.

    a. demilitarized zone (DMZ)

    b. port replication zone (PRZ)

    c. secure network environment (SNE)

    d. firewalled sandbox (FSB)

Hands-on Projects

HANDS-ON PROJECTS

Project 5-1: Use an Internet Port Scanner

An open port on a computer is an invitation to an attacker to attempt to exploit any vulnerability that may be associated with that port. Attackers will routinely send out "inquiries" over the Internet to computers and networks to determine which ports are open. The most secure configuration is to have the computer or wireless router not respond to these requests. Internet port scanners are available that will probe the ports on a system to determine which ports are open, closed, or blocked (not responding to inquiries). In this project, you perform a port scan using an Internet-based scanner.

1. Use your Web browser to go to **www.grc.com**.

It is not unusual for Web sites to change the location of where files are stored. If the URL above no longer functions then open a search engine like Google and search for "ShieldsUP!".

2. Point to **Services** and click **ShieldsUP!**.

3. Click the **Proceed** button.

4. Click the **All Service Ports** button to scan ports on your computer. A grid is displayed indicating which ports are open (red), closed (blue), or blocked (green). When the scan completes, scroll through the report to view the results. Then print the report.

ShieldsUP! refers to blocked ports as "stealth".

5. Scroll down and click the **File Sharing** button. Shields UP! probes your computer to identify basic security vulnerabilities. Print this page when finished.

6. How many ports are open? How many ports closed but respond to an attacker's inquiry?

7. Close all windows.

Closing or blocking open ports can be done through either the router or firewall to which the computer is attached or through the software firewall running on the computer.

Project 5-2: Identify Shared Network Files

Once an attacker has connected to the wireless network he may have access to files stored on any computer in the network that are configured to be shared among other users. Although file sharing is a useful network feature it can also allow an attacker to steal files that contain personal contact information, Social Security numbers, credit card numbers, and other sensitive information. Often file sharing on a folder is enabled but later forgotten. In this project you discover any shared items on your computer that are open.

1. Use your Web browser Internet Explorer to go to **technet.microsoft.com/en-us/sysinternals/bb897442.aspx**.

It is not unusual for Web sites to change the location of where files are stored. If the URL above no longer functions then open a search engine like Google and search for "Sysinternals ShareEnum".

2. Read the information under **Introduction**.

3. Click **Run ShareEnum** now from Live.Sysinternals.com.

4. When the **File Download - Security Warning** dialog box appears click **Run**.

5. When the **Internet Explorer - Security Warning** dialog box appears click **Run**. If necessary, agree to the license for using this software.

6. When the **ShareEnum - www.sysinternals.com** dialog box appears click **Refresh** to start the scan. If the message **Information may be incomplete because you are not a domain administrator for one or more of the selected domain** appears click **OK**.

7. The output of the scan will appear. Scroll across the output to read about the items that can be shared on this computer. Note under the column **Everyone** what the permissions are (**Everyone** means that all network users—including attackers—can **Read** the information or even **Read/Write** to change it). Did you know that these items were set to be shared? Could the sharing of any of these items be turned off that are no longer being used?

8. Click **Export** to create a copy of this report.

9. Enter a file name and location to save this report.

10. Close all windows.

Closing shared files is done through the operating system and may vary depending upon the version you are using. To find the latest information, open a search engine like Google and search for *disable shared folders XXX*, where *XXX* is the operating system and version you are using.

Project 5-3: Lock Down a Wireless Router

The first step to secure a wireless router is to lock it down by changing some of the default settings. In this project, you perform the steps to secure a wireless router.

The steps in the project are based on the popular Linksys wireless router series WRT54G and WRT54G2. Other wireless routers have similar capabilities and settings.

1. On a computer that is connected to the wireless network, open your Web browser and enter **192.168.1.1,** which is the default IP address of the wireless router.

If that address is not valid it means that it has been changed. To find the new address click **Start** (and then **Run** for Windows XP) and enter **CMD**. When the box opens enter **ipconfig/all** and scroll down to the details listed under the wireless NIC adapter. Record the address of the **Default Gateway** and enter **Exit**. Then enter the IP address into the Web browser.

2. A login screen will appear. Enter **admin** as the default password and click **OK**.

3. Click **Administration**.

4. If necessary click **Management**.

5. Enter a strong password for the wireless router under **Router Password:** and then re-enter it under **Re-enter to confirm:**.

6. Under **Access Server:** check **HTTPS**. The HTTPS option will encrypt the transmissions when configuring the wireless router so that an attacker cannot view them.

7. If a desktop computer that has a wired connection to the wireless router (instead of a wireless laptop) will be used to configure the wireless router under **Wireless Access Web:** check **Disable**. If a wireless laptop will be used to configure the wireless router this setting should be **Enable**.

8. Under **Remote Management:** set this to **Disable** if necessary. This will prevent an attacker from accessing the wireless router through the Internet.

9. Under **UPnP:** change this to **Disable** if necessary.

10. Click **Save Settings**.

11. Click **Wireless**.

12. Under **Wireless Network Name:** enter an SSID that does not identify you or your specific location.

13. Click **Save Settings**.

14. Close the Web browser.

15. Now test the settings. If you set **Wireless Access Web:** to **Disable** in Step 7 above you will use a desktop computer that has a wired connection; if you set it to **Enable** you can use a wireless computer. Open your Web browser and enter **https://192.168.1.1** or the IP address of the wireless router (note that this is **https** and not http).

16. When the login screen appears enter your password and click **OK**.

17. Close the Web browser.

18. If you set **Wireless Access Web:** to **Disable** you can also test that wireless devices cannot access the wireless router. From a laptop computer that is connected to the wireless network open a Web browser and enter **https:// 192.168.1.1**. You should receive an error message that you cannot access the settings.

19. Close all windows.

Project 5-4: Limit Users

Another important step in wireless security is to restrict the users who can access the wireless network. Access to the wireless network can be restricted by entering the MAC address of the approved wireless device into the wireless router through the MAC address filter. In this project you set up a wireless MAC address filter.

A MAC address filter applies only to wireless devices of the network. It does not apply to wired desktop computers that do not use a wireless NIC adapter.

1. Identify the MAC address of a wireless laptop that will be part of this wireless network. On the laptop click **Start** (and then **Run** for Windows XP) and enter **CMD**. When the box opens enter **ipconfig/all** and scroll down to the details listed under the wireless NIC adapter. Record the **Physical Address** under the wireless NIC adapter. Do this for each wireless laptop that will be part of the network.

2. If **Wireless Access Web:** is set to **Disable** you must use a desktop computer that has a wired connection to the wireless router for these configurations;

if it is set to **Enable** you can use a wireless computer. Open your Web browser and enter **https://192.168.1.1,** which is the default IP address of the wireless router.

If that address is not valid it means that it has been changed. To find the new address click **Start** (and then **Run** for Windows XP) and enter **CMD**. When the box opens enter **ipconfig/all** and scroll down to the details listed under the wireless NIC adapter. Record the address of the **Default Gateway** and enter **Exit**. Then enter the IP address into the Web browser.

3. A login screen will appear. Enter the password and click **OK**.

4. Click **Administration** if necessary.

5. Click the **Wireless** tab to display the Wireless settings.

6. Click **Wireless MAC filter**.

7. Under **Permit only:** click **Permit only PCs listed to access the wireless network**.

8. Click the **Edit MAC Address Filter List** button.

9. Enter the MAC address of the first wireless device without any marks of punctuation under **MAC 01:**.

10. Repeat this process for each wireless device.

11. Click **Save Settings**.

12. Under Wireless MAC filter click **Enable**.

13. Click **Save Settings**.

14. Close all windows.

15. Reboot the wireless laptop computer(s).

16. Only these devices can have access the wireless network.

Project 5-5: Turn on WPA2

All wireless routers and wireless devices today follow a standard for encrypting transmissions and authenticating users known as WPA2. In this project you set WPA2 on both the wireless router and wireless devices.

1. If **Wireless Access Web:** is set to **Disable** you must use a desktop computer that has a wired connection to the wireless router for these configurations; if it is set to **Enable** you can use a wireless computer. Open your Web browser and enter **https://192.168.1.1,** which is the default IP address of the wireless router.

If that address is not valid it means that it has been changed. To find the new address click **Start** (and then **Run** for Windows XP) and enter **CMD**. When the box opens enter **ipconfig/all** and scroll down to the details listed under the wireless NIC adapter. Record the address of the **Default Gateway** and enter **Exit.** Then enter the IP address into the Web browser.

2. A login screen will appear. Enter the password and click **OK.**

3. Click **Wireless** to display the Wireless settings.

4. Click **Wireless Security.**

5. Under **Security Mode** click the down arrow to reveal the options.

6. Select **WPA2 Personal.**

7. Under **WPA Algorithms:** select **TKIP+AES.**

8. Under **WPA Shared Key:** enter **1234567890abcdefghijklmnnop.**

9. Click **Save Settings.**

10. Close all windows.

11. Reboot the wireless laptop.

12. Double-click on the wireless icon on the lower part of the screen and select the setting to connect to wireless networks.

13. Click on the SSID of the wireless network.

14. When prompted enter the Network key and if necessary confirm it.

15. As an option you can elect to save these settings.

16. Close all windows.

Case Projects

Case Project 5-1: Wireless Router Comparison

Use the Internet to identify four different brands of wireless routers. Create a table or chart that lists each device, its features, and costs. Below the table, write a paragraph describing which you would choose for your home use and why.

Case Project 5-2: Routers and Packets

Use the Internet and other sources to research routers and packets, the foundation of how information is carried through the Internet. What are the advantages of a network that uses routers and packets? The disadvantages? Write a one-page paper on your findings.

Case Project 5-3: WEP Weaknesses

The Internet contains several good resources regarding WEP and why it should not be used. Write a one- paragraph summary of WEP, what it does, and why it should not be implemented in a wireless network.

Case Project 5-4: Survey of Wireless Users

Create a short survey to administer to wireless users regarding how they would typically use a free wireless network in a restaurant or coffee shop. Include questions such as, "Do you know the difference between an ad hoc and a secure wireless network?" "What precautions do you take when using a free wireless network?" "Can you list the dangers in using an open wireless network?" "Do you ever purchase anything that requires you to type in a credit card number while using a free wireless network?". Ask five friends or acquaintances for their responses. Based on these responses, give a grade of "A" through "F" to each wireless user. Now take the test yourself and give yourself a similar rating. What improvements can you make in using a free wireless network?

Case Project 5-5: Winstead Computer Consultants

New Technologies is a regional computer retailer. As an informational service they hold free classes once each month to help computer users learn about technology. New Technologies has contracted with Winstead Computer Consultants (WCC), a local information technology company, to teach these classes for them. WCC has hired you to assist them with this project.

Create a PowerPoint presentation of eight or more slides that covers the basics of how to make a wireless network secure. Include the types of attacks that a home wireless user may face along with the steps to make a wireless network secure.

chapter 6

Enterprise Security

After completing this chapter you should be able to do the following:

- Define business continuity
- Explain how redundancy planning and disaster recovery planning benefit an organization
- Explain what a policy is and how it is used
- List the different types of security policies

Security in Your World

Caitlin opened the door and walked over to Hunter, who was sitting at the table. This was Hunter's first day on the job working for a large organization after graduating from the local college. He had completed his orientation with the human resources assistant director and now was waiting to meet Caitlin, the IT associate director.

"Hi, Hunter. I'm Caitlin, and I'll be handling the next part of your orientation," she said. "I apologize for being late. Things have been rather hectic here this morning." "I saw all of the commotion when I came in this morning," said Hunter. "It's because of last night's wind storm, isn't it?" "Yes," said Caitlin as she sat down. "We experienced some pretty severe damage to Building D. Several windows were blown out by the high winds and rain came in on all three floors facing the west side. It's pretty much of a mess over there, but I'm glad the damage is no worse than it is. At 5:00 this morning our IRT was called in." Hunter looked puzzled. "I'm sorry, you haven't had time to learn all of our acronyms around here yet," laughed Caitlin. "IRT stands for Incident Response Team. Those are the people who coordinate assessing our damages in a case like this and start the process of getting things back to normal."

Hunter set down his pen. "If you don't mind me asking," he said, "what was your role in the situation?" Caitlin motioned to a large manual sitting on the table. "I launched our IT disaster recovery plan. I called my staff and they were out here by 6:30 AM to start implementing it. Oh, there's my cell phone. Will you excuse me a minute?" Hunter picked up the manual and looked through it while Caitlin spoke with one of her staff members. "Sorry for the interruption," she said. "There was a minor problem with our redundant power, but it's fixed now."

Hunter closed the disaster recovery plan manual. "This is really detailed," he said. "I'll bet it's a lot of work to come up with a plan to keep the business going when something like this happens. How do you create a plan like this?"

Security for the enterprise has many similarities to personal security at home. Viruses, worms, logic bombs, Trojans, and spam are all as much a threat to a business as to a single user. However, there are significant differences. For example, the time to recover from an attack is much more critical to an enterprise than to a home user. Although an hour of downtime to a personal user may be an inconvenience, to a business it can result in of hundreds of thousands or even millions of dollars in lost revenue. Also, an attack that is successful on a home user's computer might impact one or two individuals, while a successful attack on an organization can result in hundreds of users being affected, poor publicity for the organization, and in some instances monetary fines from regulatory agencies.

In this chapter we will explore enterprise security. You will first learn how business continuity is designed to help the organization recover from a security disaster and return to its normal state as quickly as possible. Then, you will study security policies and how they are used by organizations.

Business Continuity

Business continuity is defined as the ability of an organization to maintain its operations and services in the face of a disruptive event. This event could be a computer attack (infection by a worm), natural disaster (hurricane), or any event that would interrupt the organization's normal operations. Although business continuity is critical for all organizations, it remains sadly lacking. Many organizations are either unprepared or have not tested their plans.

In a recent survey only 37 percent of finance professionals reported that their organization is well prepared to handle an event like a hurricane, while only 24 percent said their business or organization had recently tested business continuity plans. Fifty percent had no plans to do so in the near future.

There are at least three common elements of business continuity. These include redundancy planning, disaster recovery procedures, and incident response procedures.

Redundancy Planning

One of the primary ways to ensure business continuity is to use redundancy planning, which involves building excess capacity in order to protect against failures. Redundancy planning can involve redundancy for servers, storage, networks, power, and even sites.

Servers Network server computers, such as Web servers and file servers, play a key role in an organization's infrastructure, to the point that a "crash" of the server that supports a critical application—like the organization's Web site—can have a significant impact. To protect against this **single point of failure**, where the loss of one entity would adversely affect the whole organization, some organizations stockpile spare hardware parts (such as a server's power supply) or keep entire **redundant servers** as stand-bys. However, the time it takes to install a new part or add a new server to the network and then load software and back up data may be more than the organization can tolerate.

Another approach is for the organization to design the network infrastructure so that multiple servers are incorporated into the network yet appear to users and applications as a single computing resource. One way to do this is by using a **server cluster**. A server cluster is the combination of two or more servers that are interconnected to appear as one, as shown in Figure 6-1.

There are two types of server clusters. In an **asymmetric server cluster**, a standby server exists only to take over for another server in the event of its failure. The standby server performs no useful work other than to be ready in the event that it is needed. In a **symmetric server cluster**, every server in the cluster performs useful work. If one server fails, the remaining servers continue to perform their normal work as well as that of the failed server.

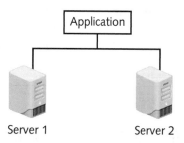

Server 1   Server 2

Figure 6-1 Server cluster

Course Technology/Cengage Learning

 Symmetric clusters are more cost-effective because they take advantage of all of the servers and none sit idle; however, if the servers are not powerful enough in the event of a failure, the additional load on the remaining servers could tax them or even cause them to fail.

Storage Because most hard disk drives are mechanical devices, they often are the first component of a system to fail. Some organizations maintain a stockpile of hard drives as spare parts to replace those that fail. Or, instead of waiting for a hard drive to fail, organizations may implement RAID (Redundant Array of Independent Drives) technology, which uses multiple hard disk drives for increased reliability and performance.

 RAID was introduced in Chapter 2.

One of the most common levels for personal computer users is RAID Level 1. For organizations more advanced levels of RAID are usually installed.

Networks Because connectivity is critical today, redundant networks may also be necessary. A redundant network waits in the background during normal operations and uses a replication scheme to keep its copy of the live network information current. In the event of a disaster, the redundant network automatically launches in a way that is transparent to users. A redundant network ensures that network services are always accessible.

Virtually all network components can also be duplicated to provide redundancy. Some manufacturers offer network equipment that has a primary active connection as well as a standby fail-over network connection for physical redundancy. If a special packet is not detected in a specific time frame on the primary connection, then the fail-over connection automatically takes over. Also, multiple redundant hardware devices such as routers can be integrated into the network infrastructure.

 Some organizations even contract with more than one Internet Service Provider (ISP) for remote connectivity. In case the primary ISP is no longer available, the secondary ISP will be used.

Power Maintaining electrical power is also essential when planning for redundancy. An **uninterruptible power supply (UPS)** is a device that maintains power to equipment in the event of an interruption in the primary electrical power source.

There are two primary types of UPS. An **off-line UPS** is the least expensive and simplest solution. During normal operation the equipment being protected is served by the standard primary power source. The off-line UPS battery charger is also connected to the primary power source in order to charge its battery. If power is interrupted the UPS will quickly (within a few milliseconds) begin supplying power to the equipment. When the primary power is restored the UPS automatically switches back into standby mode.

An **on-line UPS** is always running off its battery while the main power runs the battery charger. An advantage of an on-line UPS is that it is not affected by dips or sags in voltage. An on-line UPS can "clean" the electrical power before it reaches the server to ensure that a correct and constant level of power is delivered to the server. The UPS can also serve as a surge protector, which keeps intense spikes of electrical current, common during thunderstorms, from reaching systems.

A UPS is more than just a large battery. UPS systems can also communicate with the network operating system on a server to ensure that an orderly shutdown occurs. Specifically, if the power goes down, a UPS can complete the following tasks:

- Send a message to or telephone the network administrator to indicate that the power has failed.
- Notify all users that they must finish their work immediately and log off.
- Prevent any new users from logging on.
- Disconnect users and shut down the server.

Because a UPS can supply power for only a limited amount of time, some organizations turn to using a **backup generator** to create power. Backup generators can be powered by gas, diesel, natural gas, or propane gas to generate electricity. Unlike portable residential backup generators, commercial backup generators are permanently installed as part of the building's power infrastructure. They also include automatic transfer switches that can detect in less than one second the loss of a building's primary power and switch to the backup generator.

Sites Just as redundancy can be planned for servers, storage, networks, and power, it can be planned for the entire site itself. A major disaster such as a flood or hurricane can inflict such extensive damage to a building that it may require the organization to temporarily move to another location. Many organizations maintain redundant sites in case this occurs. There are three basic types of redundant sites: hot sites, cold sites, and warm sites.

A **hot site** is generally run by a commercial disaster recovery service that allows a business to continue computer and network operations to maintain business continuity. A hot site is essentially a duplicate of the organization's main production site and has all the equipment needed for it to continue running, including office space and furniture, telephone jacks, computer equipment, and a live telecommunications link. Data backups of information can be quickly moved to the hot site, and in some instances the production site automatically synchronizes all of its data with the hot site so that data is immediately accessible. If the organization's data processing center becomes inoperable, it can move all data processing operations to a hot site, typically within an hour.

A **cold site** provides office space but the customer must provide and install all the equipment needed to continue operations. In addition, there are no backups of data immediately available at this site. A cold site is less expensive, but takes longer to get an enterprise in full operation after the disaster.

A **warm site** has all of the equipment installed but does not have active Internet or telecommunications facilities, and does not have current backups of data. This is much less expensive than constantly maintaining those connections as with a hot site; however, the amount of time needed to turn on the connections and install the backups can be as much as half a day or more.

Businesses usually have an annual contract with a company that offers hot and cold site services for a monthly service charge. Some services also offer data backup so that all company data is available regardless of whether a hot site or cold site is used.

Disaster Recovery Procedures

Whereas business continuity addresses anything that could affect the continuation of "business as usual," disaster recovery is generally more narrowly focused and is considered a subset of business continuity. **Disaster recovery** is defined as the procedures and processes for restoring an organization's operations following a disaster. Generally disaster recovery focuses on restoring computing and technology resources to their former state.

Disaster recovery procedures include planning, disaster exercises, and performing enterprise data backups.

Planning A **disaster recovery plan (DRP)** is a written document that details the process for restoring computer and technology resources following an event that causes a significant disruption in service. Comprehensive in scope, a DRP is intended to be a detailed document that is updated regularly.

There are a variety of different "schemes" or approaches to creating a DRP. One approach is to define different levels of risk to the organization's operations, based on the severity of the disaster. A sample scheme for an educational institution is outlined in Table 6-1.

Table 6-1 Sample educational DRP approach

Risk Level	Description	Impact Areas
Level 1	Central computing resources	The Computer Services building and central computer room which houses the campus servers and routers, and serves as the primary hub for campus electronic and voice communications and connectivity
Level 2	Campus network infrastructure and the telephone public exchange	Central telephone services, 911 emergency services, network infrastructure and services, and cable plant
Level 3	Risks specific to unique applications or functionality	File and print services, student records, e-mail, Web, student residential network, technology enhanced classroom support, and student computer labs

All disaster recovery plans are different, but most address the common features included in the following elements:

- *Purpose and scope*—The reason for the plan and what it encompasses is clearly outlined. Those incidences that require the plan to be enacted should also be listed.

- *Recovery team*—The team that is responsible for the direction of the disaster recovery plan is clearly defined. This part of the plan is continually reviewed as employees leave the organization, home telephone or cell phone numbers change, or new members are added to the team.

It is important that each recovery team member knows his or her role in the plan and be adequately trained.

- *Preparing for a disaster*—A DRP lists the entities that could impact an organization and also the procedures and safeguards that should constantly be in force to reduce the risk of the disaster.

- *Emergency procedures*—Emergency procedures outlines the step-by-step procedures that should be followed if a disaster occurs.

- *Restoration procedures*—After the initial response has been put in place, restoration procedures allow the organization to continue functioning, and outline how to fully recover from the disaster and return to normal business operations.

It is important that a good DRP contains sufficient detail. A sample excerpt from a DRP is shown in Figure 6-2.

COMMUNICATIONS ROOM

The purpose of a communications room is to provide a central point of contact and coordination. This telephone equipment in this room will include:

- Three wired telephones
- Four full-charged cellular telephones
- One satellite telephone

Media communications in this room will include:

- One television
- One standard radio
- One police radio
- One citizens band radio
- One DVD player/recorder

This room should be isolated from other functional areas and only authorized personnel will be allowed to enter.

Figure 6-2 Sample from a DRP

Course Technology/Cengage Learning

Disaster Exercises Disaster exercises are designed to test the effectiveness of the DRP, such as simulating a sustained power outage. Plans that may look solid on paper often make assumptions or omit key elements that can only be revealed with a mock disaster. The objectives of these disaster exercises are:

- Test the efficiency of interdepartmental planning and coordination in managing a disaster.
- Test current procedures of the DRP.
- Determine the strengths and weaknesses in disaster responses.

Enterprise Data Backups Another essential element in a DRP is data backups. Natural disasters, terrorist attacks, additional government reporting regulations, along with increased data complexity, have all made data backups more important than ever.

Data backups were introduced in Chapter 2.

Data backups for the enterprise are significantly different than those for a home user. Several new technologies make data backups easier to create and information easier to restore. Backing up to a magnetic disk, such as a large hard drive or RAID configuration, is known as **disk to disk (D2D)**. A new backup technology is **continuous data protection (CDP)**. As its name implies, CDP performs continual data backups that can be restored immediately. CDP maintains a historical record of all the changes made to data by constantly monitoring all "writes" to the hard drive. Some CDP products even let users restore their own documents. A user who accidentally deletes a file can search the CDP system by entering the document's name and view the results through an interface that looks like a Web search engine. Clicking on the desired file will restore it.

For security purposes, users may only search for documents for which they have permissions.

Incident Response Procedures

When an unauthorized incident occurs, such as an attacker penetrating network defenses, a response is required. These incident response procedures include using forensic science and properly responding to a computer forensics event.

What Is Forensics? Forensics, also known as **forensic science**, is the application of science to questions that are of interest to the legal profession. Forensics is not limited to analyzing evidence from a murder scene; it can also be applied to technology. As computers are the foundation for communicating and recording information, a new area known as **computer forensics** can attempt to retrieve information—even if it has been altered or erased—that can be used in the pursuit of the attacker or criminal.

Digital evidence can be retrieved from computers, cell phones, pagers, digital cameras, USB drives, and virtually any device that has memory or storage.

The importance of computer forensics is due in part to the following:

- *High amount of digital evidence*—By some estimates, almost 95 percent of criminals leave behind digital evidence that can be retrieved through computer forensics.

- *Increased scrutiny by the legal profession*—No longer do attorneys and judges freely accept computer evidence. Retrieving, transporting, and storing digital evidence is now held up to the same standards as physical evidence.

- *Higher level of computer skill by criminals*—As criminals become increasingly sophisticated in their knowledge of computers and techniques such as encryption, it often requires a computer forensics expert to retrieve the evidence.

Responding to a Computer Forensics Incident When responding to a criminal event that requires an examination using computer forensics, there are four basic steps that are followed, which are similar to those of standard forensics. The steps are to secure the crime scene, preserve the evidence, establish a chain of custody, and examine the evidence.

Secure the Crime Scene The computer forensics response team is contacted whenever digital evidence needs to be preserved and serve as first responders. Organizations instruct their users that if they suspect that a computer or other electronic device contains digital evidence based on an unauthorized event such as an attack, the response team must be contacted immediately.

Waiting even one hour to make a decision to report an incident can result in the digital evidence being contaminated by other users or may give the person time to destroy the evidence.

After the response team arrives, the first job is to secure the crime scene. The physical surroundings of the computer are clearly documented. Photographs of the area are also taken before anything is touched. This helps to document that the computer was working prior to the attack. (Some defense attorneys have argued that a computer was not functioning properly and thus the attacker cannot be held responsible for any damages.) The computer is photographed from several angles, and cables connected to the computer are labeled to document the computer's hardware components and how they are connected.

Because digital pictures can be altered, security professionals recommend that photographs be taken by a standard camera using film.

The team also takes custody of the entire computer along with the keyboard and any peripherals. In addition, USB flash drives and any other storage media are secured. The team then interviews everyone who had access to the system and documents their findings, including what they were doing with the system, what its intended functions were, and how it is affected by the unauthorized actions.

Preserve the Evidence Because digital computer evidence is often electronic, it can easily or unintentionally be altered or destroyed through normal use or even by turning on the computer. Only properly trained computer evidence specialists are allowed to process computer evidence so that the integrity of the evidence is maintained and can hold up in a court of law.

The computer forensics team will first capture any volatile data that would be lost when the computer is turned off and move the data to a secure location. This includes any data that is not recorded in a file on the hard drive or a backup, such as contents of the computer's temporary memory known as **random access memory (RAM)**, current network connections, logon sessions, network configurations, and any open files. After it retrieves the volatile data, the team next focuses on the hard drive. A **mirror image backup**, also called a **bit-stream backup**, is an evidence-grade backup because its accuracy meets evidence standards. A mirror image backup is not the same as a normal copy of the data. Standard file copies or backups include only files. Mirror image backups replicate all areas of a computer hard drive, including all files and any hidden data storage areas. Using a standard copy procedure can miss significant data and can even taint the evidence. For example, copying a file may change file date information on the source drive, which is information that is often critical in a computer forensic investigation.

Mirror image backups are considered a primary key to uncovering evidence because they create exact replicas of the crime scene. Defense teams often focus on mirror image backups: if they can prove that the copy of the data was contaminated or altered in any fashion, then any evidence gathered from the data will likely be dismissed. For this reason, mirror image backup software should only be used by trained professionals and done in a controlled manner, using hardware that does not influence the accuracy of the data it captures.

Establish the Chain of Custody As soon as the team begins its work, it starts and maintains a strict chain of custody. The **chain of custody** documents that the evidence was under strict control at all times and no unauthorized person was given the opportunity to corrupt the evidence. A chain of custody includes documenting all of the serial numbers of the systems involved, who handled and had custody of the systems and for what length of time, how the computer was shipped, and any other steps in the process. In short, a chain of custody is a detailed document describing where the evidence was at all times. Gaps in this chain of custody can result in severe legal consequences. Courts have dismissed cases involving computer forensics because a secure chain of custody could not be verified.

The chain of custody is particularly important when documenting the status of the system from the time it was seized as evidence until the time the mirror copies can be completed.

Examine the Evidence After a computer forensics expert creates a mirror image of a system, the original system is secured and the mirror image is examined to reveal evidence. This includes searching word processing documents, e-mail files, spreadsheets, and other documents for evidence. The cache and cookies of the Web browser can reveal Web sites that have been visited. The frequency of e-mails to particular individuals may be useful. In short, all of the exposed data is examined for clues.

Hidden clues can also be mined and exposed. For example, Microsoft Windows operating systems use a special file as a "scratch pad" to write data when sufficient additional RAM is not available. This file is the **Windows page file**. These files can contain remnants of word processing documents, e-mail messages, Internet browsing activity, database entries, and almost any other work performed during past Windows work sessions.

Another source of hidden data is called **slack**. When a file that is being saved is not of a specific size, then Windows pads the remaining space with data that is currently stored in RAM. This padding creates slack, which can contain virtually any information that has been created, viewed, modified, downloaded, or copied since the computer was last booted. Thus, if the computer has not been shut down for several days, the data stored in slack can come from activity that occurred during that time. Slack is illustrated in Figure 6-3.

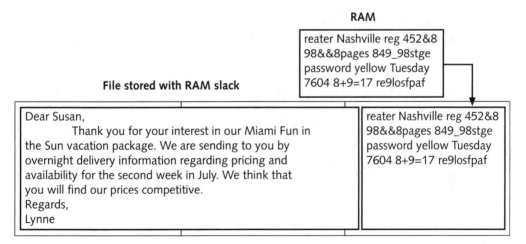

Figure 6-3 Slack

Course Technology/Cengage Learning

An additional source of hidden clues can be gleaned from **metadata**, or data about data. Although some metadata is user-supplied information, most metadata about a file is generated and recorded automatically without the user's knowledge. Examples of metadata include the file type, creation date, authorship, and edit history. Some electronic files may contain hundreds of pieces of such information.

Although metadata can be helpful to authenticate a document or establish facts (such as when a file was accessed), that is not always the case. Often metadata points the wrong way. For example, when an employee uses a word processing program to create a document by using a template created by a supervisor, the metadata for the new document may incorrectly identify the supervisor as the author.

After the evidence is examined a detailed report is required that lists the steps that were taken and any additional evidence that was uncovered in the forensic investigation.

Security in Your World

Caitlin pulled out another thick document from her folder and placed it on the table in front of Hunter. "And this is our acceptable use policy, which outlines what you may and may not do with the computers here. Along with our security and privacy policies that I already gave you, these are probably the three most important documents you'll see today," Caitlin said.

Hunter started to thumb through the document. After looking at several pages he said, "This is much more thorough than the policies we had at our college," he said. "What do you mean?" asked Caitlin. "Well," he replied, "Students had to verify by clicking a checkbox online that we had read all of the policies and would abide by them. But rarely did anyone read them. They were considered just formalities you had to go through so that you can get your computer account activated." Caitlin smiled and shook her head. "I know several organizations that treat their policies that way. But I can assure you it's not that way here. All employees are expected to read and understand the policies and then abide by them on a daily basis. I will tell you that we have even terminated employees because they violated these policies."

Hunter leaned forward and said, "Well, I don't want to follow their example. Can you tell me about this policy before I sign it?"

Security Policies

Because security involves protecting information on the devices that store, manipulate, and transmit that information, security is sometimes viewed as a strictly technical matter. Because we need to protect the information that has been created or is stored by hardware and software, the thinking goes, we should focus on using hardware and software to protect it.

While hardware and software are key elements in providing security, they are not the only elements. Plans and policies must be established by the organization to ensure that people correctly use the hardware and software defenses.

One of the key elements of enterprise security is an organizational security policy. It is important to know what a security policy is, how to balance trust and control, the process for designing a policy, and the different types of security policies.

What Is a Security Policy?

At its core, a security policy is a document that outlines the protections that should be enacted to ensure that the organization's assets face minimal risks. At one level, a security policy can be viewed as a set of management statements that defines an organization's philosophy of how to safeguard its information. At a more technical and detailed level, a security policy can be seen as the rules for computer access and specifically how these will be carried out. In short, a **security policy** is a written document that states how an organization plans to protect the company's information technology assets.

The scope of these definitions is not conflicting but complementary. They reflect the different approaches to viewing a security policy.

Security policies, along with the accompanying procedures, standards, and guidelines, are keys to implementing information security in an organization. Having a written security policy empowers an organization to take appropriate action to safeguard its data.

An organization's information security policy can serve several functions:

- It can be an overall intention and direction, formally expressed by the organization's management. A security policy is a vehicle for communicating an organization's information security culture and acceptable information security behavior.

- It can detail specific risks and how to address them, and provides controls that executives can use to direct employee behavior.

- It can help to create a security-aware organizational culture.

- It can help to ensure that employee behavior is directed and monitored to ensure compliance with security requirements.

Creating a security policy is only an initial step. It is equally important that the policy be tested and implemented, and that users follow the policy. Almost one-third of organizations have never tested their security policies and do not reevaluate them at specified intervals. Some studies indicate that many managers believe that once they have established a security policy, their work is completed. Also, some organizations do not do a good job of following up to ensure that employees are performing as expected in relation to security policies.

Balancing Trust and Control

An effective security policy must carefully balance two key elements: trust and control. There are three approaches to trust:

- *Trust everyone all of the time*—This is the easiest model to enforce because there are no restrictions. However, this is impractical because it leaves systems vulnerable to attack.

- *Trust no one at any time*—This model is the most restrictive, but is also impractical. Few individuals would work for an organization that did not trust its employees.

- *Trust some people some of the time*—This approach exercises caution in the amount of trust given. Access is provided as needed with technical controls to ensure the trust is not violated.

The approach of trusting no one at any time is mostly found in high-security government organizations.

A security policy attempts to provide the right amount of trust by balancing no trust and too much trust. It does this by trusting some of the people some of the time and by building trust over time. Deciding on the level of trust may be a delicate matter: too much trust may lead to security problems, while too little trust may make it difficult to find and keep good employees.

Control is the second element that must be balanced. One of the goals of a security policy is to implement control. Deciding on the level of control for a specific policy is not always clear. The security needs and the culture of the organization play a major role when deciding what level of control is appropriate. If policies are too restrictive or too hard to implement and comply with, employees will either ignore them or find a way to circumvent the controls. Management must commit to the proper level of control that a security policy should address.

Because security policies are a balancing act between trust and control, not all users have positive attitudes toward security policies. Users sometimes view security policies as a barrier to their productivity, a way to control their behavior, or requirements that will be difficult to follow and implement. This is particularly true if in the past policies did not exist or were loosely enforced. Part of the reason for these negative attitudes may actually be the result of how users think of security itself. Table 6-2 summarizes how different groups frequently react to security in an organization.

Table 6-2   Possible negative attitudes toward security

User Group	Attitude Toward Security
Users	Want to be able to get their work done without restrictive security controls
System support personnel	Concerned about the ease of managing systems under tight security controls
Management	Concerned about cost of security protection for attacks that may not materialize

Overcoming pessimistic attitudes about a security policy is sometimes the greatest challenge with a policy. Getting all sides to agree about all parts of a policy may not be practical. Instead, reaching a reasonable consensus is often the best philosophy.

Designing a Security Policy

Designing a security policy involves defining what a policy is and understanding due care. In addition, knowing the security policy cycle is also important.

Definition of a Policy There are several terms used to describe the "rules" that a user follows in an organization. A **standard** is a collection of requirements specific to the system or procedure that must be met by everyone. For example, a standard might describe how to secure a computer at home that remotely connects to the organization's network. Users must follow this standard if they want to be able to connect. A **guideline** is a collection of suggestions that should be implemented. These are not requirements to be met but are strongly recommended. A **policy** is a document that outlines specific requirements or rules that must be met.

A policy generally has these characteristics:

- Policies communicate a consensus of judgment.
- Policies define appropriate behavior for users.
- Policies identify what tools and procedures are needed.
- Policies provide directives for Human Resource action in response to inappropriate behavior.
- Policies may be helpful in the event that it is necessary to prosecute violators.

A policy is considered the correct vehicle for an organization to use when it is establishing security. This is because a policy applies to a wide range of hardware or software (and is not a standard) and a policy is required (it is not just a guideline).

Due Care Security policies typically include statements regarding **due care**. The term due care is used frequently in legal and business settings. It is defined as the obligations that are imposed on owners and operators of assets to exercise reasonable care of the assets and take necessary precautions to protect them. Due care is the care that a reasonable person would exercise under the circumstances. For information security policies, due care is often used to indicate the reasonable treatment that an employee would exercise when using computer equipment. Some examples of due care might include:

- Employees will exercise due care in opening attachments received from unknown sources (a reasonable person should not open an attachment from an unknown source because it may contain a virus or worm).
- Technicians will exercise due care when installing a new operating system on an existing computer (a reasonable person would not set up a "Guest" account or leave the new password written down and affixed to the monitor).

- Students will exercise due care when using computers in a lab setting (a reasonable person would be aware that many students in a crowded lab could see a password that is entered).

 Because the standard of "reasonable treatment" in a due care clause is open to interpretation, security policies frequently include clear and explicit statements regarding conduct, and then state that due care covers implicit measures that are not enumerated (a "catch all" statement).

The Security Policy Cycle Most organizations follow a three-phase cycle in the development and maintenance of a security policy: performing a risk management study, creating a security policy based on the information from the risk management study, and reviewing the policy for compliance.

A risk management study is the systematic and structured approach to managing the potential for loss that is related to a threat. The goal of risk management is to minimize risks to an asset. A risk management study generally involves five tasks:

- *Asset identification*—Asset identification determines the items that have a positive economic value and may include data, hardware, personnel, physical assets, and software. Along with the assets, the attributes of the assets need to be compiled and their relative value.

- *Threat identification*—After the assets have been inventoried and given a relative value, the next step is to determine the threats from threat agents. A threat agent is any person or thing with the power to carry out a threat against an asset.

- *Vulnerability appraisal*—After the assets have been inventoried and prioritized, and the threats have been determined, the next task is to determine what current security weaknesses might expose the assets to these threats. This is known as vulnerability appraisal and in effect takes a snapshot of the security of the organization as it now stands.

- *Risk assessment*—A risk assessment involves determining the damage that would result from an attack and the likelihood that the vulnerability is a risk to the organization.

- *Risk mitigation*—Once the risks are determined and ranked, the final step is to determine what to do about the risks. It is important to recognize that security weaknesses can never be entirely eliminated; some degree of risk must always be assumed.

The second phase of the security policy cycle is to use the information from the risk management study to create the policy. A security policy is a document or series of documents that clearly defines the defense mechanisms an organization will employ to keep information secure. It also outlines how the organization will respond to attacks and the duties and responsibilities of its employees for information security.

The final phase is to review the policy for compliance. Because new assets are continually being added to the organization and new threats appear against the assets, compliance monitoring and evaluation must be conducted regularly. The results of the monitoring and evaluation (such as revealing that a new asset is unprotected) become identified as risks, and the cycle begins again. The security policy cycle is illustrated in Figure 6-4. The security policy cycle is a never-ending process of identifying what needs to be protected, determining how to protect it, and evaluating the protection.

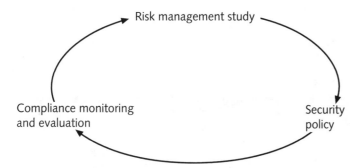

Figure 6-4 Security policy cycle

Course Technology/Cengage Learning

Types of Security Policies

Because a security policy is so comprehensive and is often detailed, most organizations choose to break the security policy down into smaller "subpolicies" that can be more easily referred to. The term *security policy* then becomes an umbrella term for all of the subpolicies included within it.

There are many types of security policies. Some of these are listed in Table 6-3. In addition to the security policies listed in Table 6-3, most organizations have security policies that address acceptable use, security-related human resources, personally identifiable information, disposal and destruction, and ethics.

Acceptable Use Policy (AUP) An acceptable use policy (AUP) defines the actions users may perform while accessing systems and networking equipment. The users are not limited to employees; it can also include vendors, contractors, or visitors, each with different privileges. AUPs typically cover all computer use, including Internet, e-mail, Web, and password security.

An AUP may have an overview regarding what is covered by this policy, as in the following sample:

> *Internet/intranet/extranet-related systems, including but not limited to computer equipment, software, operating systems, storage media, network accounts providing electronic mail, Web browsing, and FTP, are the property of Organization A. These systems are to be used for business purposes in serving the interests of the company, and of our clients and customers in the course of normal operations.*

The AUP usually provides explicit prohibitions regarding security and proprietary information:

> *Keep passwords secure and do not share accounts. Authorized users are responsible for the security of their passwords and accounts. System level passwords should be changed every 30 days; user level passwords should be changed every 45 days.*
>
> *All computers and laptops should be secured with a password-protected screensaver with the automatic activation feature set at 10 minutes or less, or by logging off when the host is unattended.*

Postings by employees from an Organization A e-mail address to newsgroups should contain a disclaimer stating that the opinions expressed are strictly their own and not necessarily those of Organization A, unless posting is in the course of business duties.

Table 6-3 Types of security policies

Name of Security Policy	Description
Acceptable encryption policy	Defines requirements for using cryptography
Analog line policy	Defines standards for use of analog dial-up lines for sending and receiving faxes and for connection to computers
Anti-virus policy	Establishes guidelines for effectively reducing the threat of computer viruses on the organization's network and computers
Audit vulnerability scanning policy	Outlines the requirements and provides the authority for an information security team to conduct audits and risk assessments, investigate incidents, to ensure conformance to security policies, or to monitor user activity
Automatically forwarded e-mail policy	Prescribes that no e-mail will be automatically forwarded to an external destination without prior approval from the appropriate manager or director
Database credentials coding policy	Defines requirements for storing and retrieving database user-names and passwords
Demilitarized zone security policy	Defines standards for all networks and equipment located in the DMZ
Dial-in access policy	Outlines appropriate dial-in access and its use by authorized personnel
E-mail policy	Creates standards for using corporate e-mail
E-mail retention policy	Helps employees determine what information sent or received by e-mail should be retained and for how long
Extranet policy	Defines the requirements for third-party organizations to access the organization's networks
Information sensitivity policy	Establishes criteria for classifying and securing the organization's information in a manner appropriate to its level of security
Router security policy	Outlines standards for minimal security configuration for routers and switches
Server security policy	Creates standards for minimal security configuration for servers
VPN security policy	Establishes requirements for Remote Access Virtual Private Network (VPN) connections to the organization's network
Wireless communication policy	Defines standards for wireless systems used to connect to the organization's networks

Unacceptable use may also be outlined by the AUP, as in the following sample:

The following actions are not acceptable ways to use the system:

- *Introduction of malicious programs into the network or server*
- *Revealing your account password to others or allowing use of your account by others. This includes family and other household members when work is being done at home.*
- *Using an Organization A computing asset to actively engage in procuring or transmitting material that is in violation of sexual harassment or hostile workplace laws in the user's local jurisdiction.*
- *Any form of harassment via e-mail, telephone or paging, whether through language, frequency, or size of messages.*
- *Unauthorized use, or forging, of e-mail header information.*

Acceptable use policies are generally considered to be the most important information security policies. It is recommended that all organizations, particularly educational institutions and government agencies, have an AUP in place.

Security-Related Human Resource Policy A policy that addresses security as it relates to human resources is known as a **security-related human resource policy**. These policies include statements regarding how an employee's information technology resources will be addressed. Security-related human resource policies typically are presented at an orientation session when the employee is hired, and provide the necessary information about the technology resources of the organization, how they are used, and the acceptable use and security policies that are in force. The penalties for violating policies likewise are clearly outlined.

Security-related human resource policies may contain statements regarding **due process**. Due process is the principle of treating all accused persons in an equal fashion, using established rules and principles. A due process statement may indicate that any employee accused of a malicious action will be treated equally and not given preferential treatment. The policy may also contain a statement regarding **due diligence**, or that any investigation into suspicious employee conduct will examine all material facts.

The security-related human resource policy may also typically contain statements regarding actions to be taken when an employee is terminated. For example, the policy may state that:

- When terminating an employee, the employee's access to technology resources should be immediately suspended.
- Once the employee has been informed of the termination, he should not be allowed to return to his office but should be immediately escorted out of the building.
- The IT department should have a list of all user accounts and suspend the appropriate accounts immediately.
- Log files should be routinely scanned to ensure that all the employee's accounts were suspended.

- The supervisor should be responsible for reviewing all employee electronic information and either disposing of it or forwarding it to her replacements.

Personally Identifiable Information (PII) Policy Because privacy is of growing concern, many organizations have a **personally identifiable information (PII) policy** that outlines how the organization uses personal information it collects. A typical PII policy for consumers is seen in Figure 6-5.

In general, you can visit us on the Internet without telling us who you are and without giving any personal information about yourself. There are times, however, when we or our partners may need information from you. You may choose to give us personal information in a variety of situations. For example, you may want to give us information, such as your name and address or e-mail, to correspond with you, to process an order, or to provide you with a subscription. You may give us your credit card details to buy something from us or a description of your education and work experience in connection with a job opening for which you wish to be considered. We intend to let you know how we will use such information before we collect it from you. You may tell us that you do not want us to use this information to make further contact with you beyond fulfilling your request. If you give us personal information about somebody else, such as a spouse or work colleague, we will assume that you have their permission to do so.

Figure 6-5 Sample PII (privacy) policy

Course Technology/Cengage Learning

PII policies in the past were known as privacy policies.

Disposal and Destruction Policy Because of the difficulty in disposing of older computers, often because they contain toxic or environmentally dangerous materials, many organizations recycle older computers by giving them to schools, charities, or selling them online. However, information that should have been deleted from hard drives often is still available on these recycled computers. This is because operating systems like Microsoft Windows do not completely delete files and make the information irretrievable. When a file is deleted, the file name is removed from a table that stores file information, but the content of the file itself remains on the hard drive until it is overwritten by new files. This results in data being accessible to an attacker. Even reformatting a drive may not fully erase all of the data on it.

The risks of not properly erasing data from a hard drive are covered in Chapter 2.

In order to address this potential security problem, most organizations have a **disposal and destruction policy** that addresses the disposal of resources that are considered confidential. This policy often covers how long records and data will be retained. It also involves how to dispose of equipment. For example, hard drives should be erased with third-party software that physically "wipes" the disk clean.

Several companies offer disposal services for IT equipment, guaranteeing the destruction of any data that may have been stored on the system. They will visit the workplace, label the equipment, and then strip it down to the individual component level where it can be sold or given to particular charities on request. If the equipment is faulty and beyond repair, it is then sent for recycling where the components can be reused.

Ethics Policy The corporate world has been rocked in recent years by a series of high-profile scandals. Once-powerful organizations are bankrupt due to "insider trading." In many instances the knowledge and approval of such actions went all the way to the top of the organization. The result was billions of dollars lost by investors and shareholders and thousands of employees suddenly unemployed and left without promised pension benefits. These scandals have resulted in federal legislation in an attempt to force organizations to act in a responsible manner.

Many individuals believe that the only way to reduce the number and magnitude of such scandals is to refocus attention on ethics in the enterprise. Although defining ethics can be difficult, one approach is to compare ethics with values and morals:

- *Values*—Values are a person's fundamental beliefs and principles used to define what is good, right, and just. Values provide guidance in determining the right action to take for a person. Values can be classified as moral values (fairness, truth, justice, and love), pragmatic values (efficiency, thrift, health, and patience), and aesthetic values (attractive, soft, and cold).

- *Morals*—Morals are values that are attributed to a system of beliefs that help the individual distinguish right from wrong. These values typically derive their authority from something outside the individual, such as a higher spiritual being or a terrestrial external authority (such as the government or society). Moral concepts that are based on an external authority may vary from one society to another and can change over time as the society changes.

- *Ethics*—Ethics can be defined as the study of what a group of people understand to be good and right behavior and how people make those judgments. When people act in ways consistent with their moral values, they are said to be acting ethically. Ethics inform people how to act in ways that meet the standards they set for themselves according to their values.

The ethics of decisions and actions is defined by a group, not individually.

It is not the role of the organization to tell an employee what her values should be. However, it is the organization's responsibility to set ethical behavioral standards and train employees so they understand those standards. Many enterprises now have an **ethics policy**, which is a written code of conduct intended to be a central guide and reference for employees in support of day-to-day decision making. This code is intended to clarify an organization's mission, values, and principles, and link them with standards of professional conduct. An ethics policy can be an open disclosure of the way an organization operates and provides visible guidelines for behavior. It also serves as a communication tool that reflects the agreement that an organization has made to uphold its most important values, dealing with such matters as its commitment to employees, its standards for doing business, and its relationship with the community.

Some organizations use the term *code of ethics* instead of ethics policy. They state that a code is a tool to encourage discussions of ethics and to improve how employees deal with the ethical dilemmas, prejudices, and gray areas that are encountered in everyday work. These codes of ethics are meant to complement relevant standards, policies, and rules, and not to substitute for them.

Chapter Summary

- One method for ensuring business continuity is to use redundancy planning, which involves building excess capacity in order to protect against failures. Although it is possible to have redundant servers on hand and press them into production when a server fails, a preferable solution is to design the network infrastructure so that multiple servers are incorporated into the network yet appear to users and applications as a single computing resource. Redundancy for storage can be provided by RAID, which uses multiple hard disk drives for increased reliability and performance. Network redundancy can be accomplished through network design and by duplicating equipment resources.

- Power redundancy can be attained by using an uninterruptible power supply (UPS), which is a device that maintains power to equipment in the event of an interruption in the primary electrical power source, or by using backup generators that can be powered by fossil fuels to generate electricity. Redundancy can also be planned for the entire site itself. A major disaster such as a flood or hurricane can inflict such extensive damage to a building that it may require that the organization temporarily move to another location.

- Disaster recovery is defined as the procedures and processes for restoring an organization's operations following a disaster, specifically restoring computing and technology resources to their former state. A disaster recovery plan (DRP) is a written document that details the process for restoring resources following an event that causes a significant disruption in service. Disaster exercises are designed to test the effectiveness of the DRP. An essential element in any DRP is data backups. One new backup technology performs continuous data backups that can be restored immediately.

- Forensic science is the application of science to questions that are of interest to the legal profession. Computer forensics attempts to retrieve information that can be used in the pursuit of the computer crime. Forensics incidence response is carried out in four major steps. First, the crime scene is secured and documented. Next, the data is preserved by capturing any volatile data and then performing a mirror image backup. A strict chain of custody, or documentation of evidence, must be established at all times. Finally, mirror images must be examined for evidence and a detailed report made.

- A security policy is a written document that states how an organization plans to protect the company's information technology assets. An effective security policy must carefully balance two key elements, trust and control. A security policy attempts to provide a balance between no trust and too much trust. The appropriate level of control is determined by the security needs and the culture of the organization. Most organizations follow a three-phase cycle in the development and maintenance of a security policy. The first phase is a risk management study, the second phase is to use the risk management study to develop the policy. The final phase is to review the policy for compliance.

- Because a security policy is so comprehensive and often detailed, most organizations choose to break the security policy down into smaller subpolicies. The term "security policy" is a general term for all of the subpolicies included within it. An acceptable use policy (AUP) defines the actions users may perform while accessing systems and networking equipment. Policies of the organization that address security as it relates to human resources are known as a security-related human resource policy. Because privacy is of growing concern, many organizations have a personally identifiable information (PII) policy that outlines how the organization uses information it collects. A disposal and destruction policy addresses how confidential resources are disposed of. This policy often covers how long records and data will be retained. An ethics policy is a written code of conduct intended to be a central guide and reference for employees in support of day-to-day decision making.

Key Terms

acceptable use policy (AUP)   A policy that defines the actions users may perform while accessing systems and networking equipment.

asymmetric server cluster   A technology in which a standby server exists only to take over for another server in the event of its failure.

backup generator   A separate generator powered by diesel, natural gas or propane gas to generate electricity.

bit-stream backup   A backup copy of each bit on a computer hard drive. Also known as mirror image backup.

business continuity   The ability of an organization to maintain its operations and services in the face of a disruptive event.

chain of custody   A process of documentation that shows that the evidence was under strict control at all times and no unauthorized individuals were given the opportunity to corrupt the evidence.

cold site A remote site that provides office space; the customer must provide and install all the equipment needed to continue operations.

computer forensics Using technology to search for computer evidence of a crime.

continuous data protection (CDP) Continuous data backups that can be restored immediately.

disaster recovery The procedures and processes for restoring an organization's IT operations following a disaster.

disaster recovery plan (DRP) A written document that details the process for restoring IT resources following an event that causes a significant disruption in service.

disk to disk (D2D) Backing up to a magnetic disk, such as a large hard drive or RAID configuration.

disposal and destruction policy A policy that addresses the disposal of resources that are considered confidential.

due care The obligations that are imposed on owners and operators of assets to exercise reasonable care of the assets and take necessary precautions to protect them.

due diligence The principle of investigation that examines all material facts available.

due process The principle of treating all accused persons in an equal fashion, using established rules and principles.

ethics policy A policy intended to be a central guide and reference for employees in support of day-to-day decision making; sometimes called a code of ethics.

forensics (forensic science) The application of science to questions that are of interest to the legal profession.

guideline A collection of suggestions that should be implemented.

hot site A remote site that contains all equipment, supplies, and telecommunications business needs and is ready immediately in the event of a disaster.

metadata Data about data.

mirror image backup A backup copy of each bit on a computer hard drive. Also known as bit-stream backup.

off-line UPS An uninterruptible power supply in which the battery charger is connected to the primary power source in order to charge its battery.

on-line UPS An uninterruptible power supply which is always running off its battery while the main power runs the battery charger.

personally identifiable information (PII) policy A policy that outlines how an organization uses personal information it collects.

policy A document that outlines specific requirements or rules that must be met.

random access memory (RAM) Temporary computer memory that is erased when the computer is powered off.

redundant server A stand-by server that is manually added to the network if a primary server fails.

security policy A written document that states how an organization plans to protect the company's information technology assets.

security-related human resource policy Policy that addresses security as it relates to human resources.

server cluster A combination of two or more servers that are interconnected to appear as one.

single point of failure A component or entity which, should it fail, would adversely affect the entire system.

slack Hidden data on a hard drive.

standard A collection of requirements specific to the system or procedure that must be met by everyone.

symmetric server cluster A technology in which every server in the cluster performs useful work and if one server fails the remaining servers absorb the load.

uninterruptible power supply (UPS) An external device that provides electrical power when normal power is interrupted.

warm site A remote site that contains computer equipment but does not have telecommunication access constantly running.

Windows page file A temporary or permanent file on a hard drive used by Microsoft Windows operating systems that serves as additional memory when RAM is not available.

Review Questions

1. A standby server exists only to take over for another server in the event of its failure is known as a(n) _____ .
   a. failsafe server
   b. rollover server
   c. symmetric server cluster
   d. asymmetric server cluster

2. A(n) _____ is always running off its battery while the main power runs the battery charger.
   a. on-line UPS
   b. off-line UPS
   c. backup UPS
   d. protected UPS

3. A UPS can perform each of the following except:
   a. Disconnect users and shut down the server.
   b. Prevent any new users from logging on.
   c. Notify all users that they must finish their work immediately and log off.
   d. Prevent certain applications from launching that will consume too much power

4. A _____ is essentially a duplicate of the production site and has all the equipment needed for an organization to continue running.
   a. warm site
   b. hot site
   c. cold site
   d. resource site

5. Which of the following is NOT a characteristic of a disaster recovery plan (DRP)?

    a. It is a private document only used by top-level administrators for planning.

    b. It is written.

    c. It is detailed.

    d. It is updated regularly.

6. When an unauthorized event occurs, the first duty of the computer forensics response team should be to _____.

    a. log off from the server

    b. secure the crime scene

    c. back up the hard drive

    d. reboot the system

7. Which of the following is not an approach to trust?

    a. Trust authorized individuals only.

    b. Trust everyone all of the time.

    c. Trust some people some of the time.

    d. Trust all people all the time.

8. Which of the following characterizes the attitude that system support personnel generally have toward security?

    a. They want to be able to get their work done without restrictive security controls.

    b. They are concerned about the ease of managing systems under tight security controls.

    c. They are concerned about cost of security protection for attacks that may not materialize.

    d. They want to manage how users react to security policies.

9. A _____ is a collection of suggestions that should be implemented.

    a. standard

    b. code

    c. policy

    d. guideline

10. Which of the following is not a characteristic of a policy?

    a. Policies may be helpful in the event that it is necessary to prosecute violators.

    b. Policies identify what tools and procedures are needed.

    c. Policies define what appropriate behavior for users is.

    d. Policies communicate a unanimous agreement of judgment.

11. Each of the following is a step in the risk management study except:

    a. threat identification

    b. threat appraisal

    c. risk mitigation

    d. asset identification

12. _____ is defined as the obligations that are imposed on owners and operators of assets to exercise reasonable care of the assets and take necessary precautions to protect them.

    a. Due obligations

    b. Due process

    c. Due diligence

    d. Due care

13. A(n) _____ defines the actions users may perform while accessing systems and networking equipment.

    a. Internet use policy

    b. user permission policy

    c. end user policy

    d. acceptable use policy

14. A personally identifiable information (PII) policy _____.

    a. is identical to an AUP

    b. outlines how the organization uses information it collects

    c. is required on all Internet Web sites

    d. must be certified before it can be used

15. _____ may be defined as the study of what people understand to be good and right behavior and how people make those judgments.

    a. Ethics

    b. Morals

    c. Values

    d. Principles

16. The one entity that the loss of which would adversely affect the entire organization is known as a _____.

    a. single point of failure

    b. choke point

    c. funnel neck

    d. network restriction point (NRP)

17. The enterprise backup technology that performs constant backups and allows the user to restore their own documents is called _____ .
    a. RAID Level 1024
    b. client backup and restore (C-BAR)
    c. disk to disk (D2D)
    d. continuous data protection (CDP)

18. _____ is the application of science to questions that are of interest to the legal profession.
    a. Scientific type III research
    b. Due clause
    c. Due care
    d. Forensic science

19. A _____ backup is an evidence-grade backup because its accuracy meets evidence standards.
    a. full
    b. RAM storage
    c. bit-stream
    d. mirror slack

20. Each of the following is a type of security policy except:
    a. user policy
    b. acceptable encryption policy
    c. anti-virus policy
    d. e-mail policy

Hands-on Projects

HANDS-ON PROJECTS

Project 6-1: Entering and Viewing Metadata

Although most file metadata is not accessible to users, there are some types of metadata that users can enter and change. In this project, you view and enter metadata in a Microsoft Word document.

1. Use Microsoft Word to create a document containing your name. Save the document as **Metadata1.docx**.

2. Click the **Office Button** and then point to **Prepare** and then click **Properties** to display the Document Information Panel, as shown in Figure 6-6.

3. Enter the following information:
   • Subject—**Metadata**
   • Author—The name of your instructor or supervisor

Figure 6-6   Document Information Panel

Course Technology/Cengage Learning

- Category—**Computer Forensics**
- Keywords—**Metadata**
- Comments—**Viewing metadata in Microsoft Word**

4. Save **Metadata1.docx**

5. Click the down arrow next to **Document Properties** and click **Advanced Properties** . . .

6. Click the **Statistics** tab and view the information it contains. How could a computer forensics specialist use this metadata when examining this file?

7. Click the **Custom** tab. Notice that there are several predefined fields that can contain metadata.

8. In the **Name:** box enter **Reader**.

9. Be sure the **Type:** is set to **Text**.

10. Enter your name in **Value:** and then click **Add**.

11. Select three predefined fields and enter values for each field. Save your document when you are finished.

12. Close the **Document Properties Information** panel and return to **Metadata1.docx**.

13. Erase your name from **Metadata1.docx** so you have a blank document. However, this file still has the metadata. Enter today's date and save this as **Metadata2.docx**.

14. Close **Metadata2.docx**.

15. Reopen **Metadata2.docx**.

16. Click the **Office Button** and then point to **Prepare** and then click **Properties** to display the Document Properties Information panel. What properties carried over to **Metadata2.docx** from **Metadata1.docx**, even though the contents of the file was erased? Why did this happen? Could a computer forensics specialist use this technique to examine metadata, even if the contents of the document were erased?

17. Close all windows.

Project 6-2: Viewing Windows Slack and Hidden Data

RAM slack, drive slack, and other hidden data can be helpful to a computer forensics investigator searching for information. In this project you download and use a program to search for hidden data.

1. Use your Web browser to go to **www.briggsoft.com**.

It is not unusual for Web sites to change the location of where files are stored. If the URL above no longer functions then open a search engine like Google and search for "Directory Snoop".

2. Scroll down to the current version of **Directory Snoop** and click **Download**.

3. Follow the default installation procedures to install Directory Snoop.

4. Click **Start** and point to **All Programs** and open **Directory Snoop 5.0**.

5. Depending on the file system on your computer, click **FAT Module** or **NTFS Module**.

6. Under Select Drive, click **C:** or the drive letter of your hard drive.

7. Click to select a file and display its contents. Scroll under **Cluster Data** to view the contents that you can read.

8. Select other files to look for hidden data. Did you discover anything that might be useful to a computer forensics specialist?

9. Create a text document using Notepad. Launch Notepad.

10. Enter the text **Now is the time for all good men to come to the aid of their country**.

11. Save the document on your desktop as **Country.txt**.

12. Exit Notepad.

13. Now delete this file. Right-click **Start** and click **Explore** and navigate to **Country.txt**.

14. Right-click on **Country.txt** and then click **Delete**.

15. Now search for information contained in the file you just deleted. Return to **Directory Snoop** and click the top-level node for the **C:** drive and click the **Search** icon.

16. Click **Files**.

17. Enter **aid** as the item that you are searching for.

18. Click **Search in slack area also**.

19. Click **OK**. Was the program able to find this data? Why or why not?

20. Close all windows.

Project 6-3: Erasing Data

Many security breaches have occurred because data was left on the hard drive of a computer that was sold or donated to charity. Deleting files in Windows does not physically remove the data, meaning it can be retrieved. A recommendation is to use a third-party product to perform a true erase of the data. In this project, you download a product to securely wipe data so that it cannot be retrieved.

1. Use your Web browser to go to **www.heidi.ie/node/6**.

It is not unusual for Web sites to change the location of where files are stored. If the URL above no longer functions then open a search engine like Google and search for "Eraser".

2. Click **Download**.
3. Click **Download** next to the latest version of Eraser.
4. Click **EraserSetup32.exe** for x32 systems or **EraserSetup64.exe** for x64 systems.
5. Follow the default instructions to install Eraser.
6. Be sure the box **Run Eraser now** is checked and click **Finish**. This will open the Erase main menu.
7. Minimize Eraser.
8. Create a file to be deleted. Launch Notepad.
9. Enter the text **We the people**.
10. Save the document as **People.txt**.
11. Exit Notepad.
12. Restore Eraser.
13. Click **File** and then **New Task**.
14. Click the **File** button and then click the **ellipse** button.
15. Navigate to **People.txt** and click **OK**.
16. Click **OK**.
17. Click **Task**.
18. Click **Run All** and then **Yes** to delete the file.
19. Is this program easy to use? Would you recommend it to others?
20. Close all windows.

Project 6-4: Creating a Disk Image Backup

One of the trends in backups today is to use a disk image program for performing backups. A disk image file is created by performing a complete sector-by-sector copy of the hard drive instead of backing up using the drive's file system. It creates a replicated image of the entire drive into a single file, including the operating system and all user files. In this project you will download Macrium Reflect to create an image backup.

1. Use your Web browser to go to **www.macrium.com/download.asp**.

It is not unusual for Web sites to change the location of where files are stored. If the URL above no longer functions then open a search engine like Google and search for "Macrium Reflect".

2. Click **Download Now**. At the download site also click **Download Now**.

3. Accept the default settings to download and install this program onto your computer.

4. Launch Macrium Reflect and select the 30 day evaluation to display the Reflect screen as seen in Figure 6-7.

5. Click **Backup**.

6. Click **Create Image** to launch the Create Backup Wizard. Click **Next**.

7. Click **Full** and select the disk or partition to backup. If you are unsure check the **Active** partition. Click **Next**.

8. Select the location to store the backup. Click **Local Hard Disk** and click **Browse for folder** ... to select the location on the hard drive to store the backup. Click **Next**.

Reflect can also backup to a Network drive. Click Network folder ... to select the network location to store the backup.

9. Review the settings that are displayed. Note that depending on the size of the data to be backed up and the speed of the computer it will take several minutes to perform the backup. As a general rule of thumb a 50 GB backup may take up to 30 minutes to complete.

10. Click **Finish** and then **OK**.

11. Leave Macrium Reflect open for the next project.

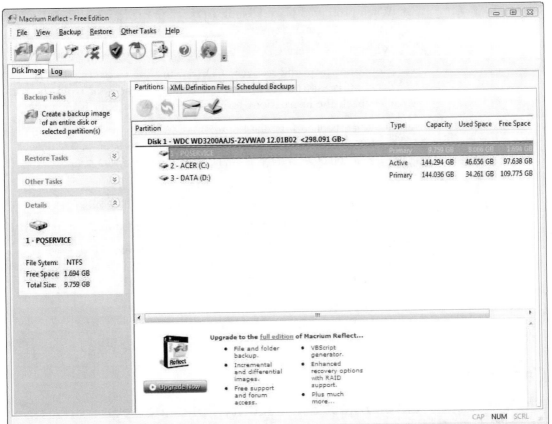

Figure 6-7 Macrium Reflect screen

Course Technology/Cengage Learning

Project 6-5: Restoring a Disk Image Backup

It is important to test the steps necessary to restore a disk image in the event that a hard drive stops functioning. In this project you will go through the steps of restoring the Macrium Reflect image backup created in Hands-On Project 6-4, although you will stop short of actually restoring the image.

1. Once the backup has finished you will create a Rescue CD. This CD will allow you to boot your computer in the event that the hard drive becomes corrupt and restore the backup. Click **Other Tasks** and then **Create Rescue CD**.

2. Select **Linux-Select this option to create a Linux based recovery CD**. Click **Next**.

3. Click **Finish**.

4. When prompted place a blank CD disk in the tray and click **OK**. Reflect will now create a recovery CD.

5. When the recovery CD has been created close all windows.

6. Now boot from the recovery CD. Be sure the recovery CD is in the disk drive and restart your computer. If it does not boot from the recovery CD check the instructions for your computer to boot from a CD.

When booting from the Linux CD a USB mouse may not always be recognized. If you are using a USB mouse you will want to shut down your computer and replace the USB mouse with a PS/2 mouse.

7. When the Restore Wizard dialog box appears click **Next**.

8. In the left pane click the location of where you stored the image backup.

9. In the right pane select the backup image that appears.

10. If you were actually restoring your image backup you would continue to proceed. However, click **Cancel**.

11. Remove the CD.

12. Click **OK** to reboot your computer.

Case Projects

Case Project 6-1: Security Policy Review

Locate the security policy for your school or organization. How difficult was it to locate? Are users required to review it periodically? Based on what you now know about security, is it sufficient? Does it adequately address security for the organization? Is it up to date? What changes would you suggest? Write a one-page paper on your findings.

Case Project 6-2: Acceptable Use Policy

Create your own acceptable use policy for the computers and network access for your school or organization. Be sure to cover computer use, Internet surfing, e-mail, Web, and password security. Compare your policies with other students in the class. Finally, locate the acceptable use policy for your school or organization. How does it compare with yours? Which policy is more strict? Why? What changes would you recommend? Write a one page paper on your findings.

Case Project 6-3: Home UPS

UPS devices are becoming more commonplace in homes as well as in organizations. Use the Internet to research home UPS devices. Identify five different models and create a table listing their features and costs. Which would you recommend and why?

Case Project 6-4: Personal Disaster Recovery Plan

Create a one-page document of a personal disaster recovery procedure for your home computer. Be sure to include what needs to be protected and why. Also include information about where your data backups are stored and how they can be retrieved. Does your DRP show that what you are doing to protect your assets is sufficient? What if any changes should be made?

Case Project 6-5: Winstead Computer Consultants

Valentino's is a local chain of Italian restaurants and a new client of Winstead Computer Consultants (WCC), a local information technology company. Valentino's has asked WCC to help them develop a written security policy, and WCC has hired you to assist them with this project.

Create a PowerPoint presentation of eight or more slides that covers the basics of what a security policy is and how they are created. Include suggestions for Valentino's regarding what elements should be included in the policy.

Glossary

acceptable use policy (AUP) A policy that defines the actions users may perform while accessing systems and networking equipment.

access point (AP) The "base station" for the wireless network that redirects signals to other wireless devices and connects to a wired network.

ActiveX A set of technologies developed by Microsoft for creating special features in an HTML document; also called add-ons.

ActiveX controls A specific way of implementing ActiveX.

ad hoc A wireless network that connects wireless devices directly to another wireless device; also called peer-to-peer.

Address Space Layout Randomization (ASLR) A Windows feature that randomly assigns executable operating system code to one of 256 possible locations in RAM.

adware A software program that delivers advertising content in a manner that is unexpected and unwanted by the user.

algorithm Procedure based on a mathematical formula used to encrypt data.

antispyware Software that helps prevent computers from becoming infected by spyware.

antivirus (AV) Software that can scan a computer's hard drive for infections as well as monitor computer activity and scan all new documents that might contain a virus.

archive bit A file setting that indicates whether a file has been backed up.

asset An entity that has value.

asymmetric cryptography Encryption that uses two mathematically related keys for encryption and decryption.

asymmetric server cluster A technology in which a standby server exists only to take over for another server in the event of its failure.

attachments Documents that are connected to an e-mail message.

authentication The process of providing proof that the user is genuine.

availability Ensures that data is accessible to authorized users.

backup generator A separate generator powered by diesel, natural gas or propane gas to generate electricity.

Basic Input/Output System (BIOS) A coded program embedded on a processor chip that recognizes and controls different devices on the computer system.

Bayesian filtering A sophisticated e-mail filtering technique.

beaconing The process of a wireless router sending signals at regular intervals to announce its presence and to provide the necessary information for devices to join the network.

bit-stream backup A backup copy of each bit on a computer hard drive; also known as mirror image backup.

blacklist A list of senders for which the user does not want to receive any e-mail.

boot virus A virus that infects the Master Boot Record (MBR) of a hard disk drive.

bot herder An attacker who controls several botnets.

botnet A group of zombie computers that are under the control of an attacker.

browser A program that displays HTML documents.

browser hijacker A program that changes the Web browser's home page or search engine to another site.

brute force attack An attack that attempts to guess a password through combining a systematic random combination of characters.

buffer overflow An error that occurs when a computer process attempts to store data in RAM beyond the boundaries of a fixed-length storage buffer.

business continuity The ability of an organization to maintain its operations and services in the face of a disruptive event.

California Database Security Breach Act A state act that requires disclosure to California residents if a breach of personal information has or is believed to have occurred.

cellular telephones (cell phones) Portable communications devices that function in a manner unlike wired telephones.

chain of custody A process of documentation that shows that the evidence was under strict control at all times and no unauthorized individuals were given the opportunity to corrupt the evidence.

channels Internet Relay Chat (IRC) discussion forums.

Children's Online Privacy Protection Act (COPPA) A U.S. federal act that requires operators of online services or Web sites directed at children under the age of 13 to obtain parental consent prior to the collection, use, disclosure, or display of a child's personal information.

ciphertext Data that has been encrypted.

cleartext Unencrypted data.

cold site A remote site that provides office space; the customer must provide and install all the equipment needed to continue operations.

companion virus A virus that adds a program to the operating system that is a copycat "companion" to a legitimate program.

computer forensics Using technology to search for computer evidence of a crime.

computer network An interconnection of computers and devices to share resources.

confidentiality Ensures that only authorized parties can view the information.

continuous data protection (CDP) Continuous data backups that can be restored immediately.

cookie A computer file that contains user-specific information.

copy backup A backup that only copies selected files to a new location and does not reset the archive bit.

cryptography The science of transforming information into a secure form while it is being transmitted or stored so that unauthorized users cannot access it.

cybercrime Targeted attacks against financial networks, unauthorized access to information, and the theft of personal information.

cybercriminals A loose-knit network of attackers, identity thieves, and financial fraudsters that are more highly motivated, less risk-averse, better funded, and more tenacious than other attackers.

cyberterrorism Attacks launched by cyberterrorists that could cripple a nation's electronic and commercial infrastructure.

cyberterrorist An attacker motivated by ideology to attack computers or infrastructure networks.

data backup The process of copying data from a computer's hard drive onto other digital media and then storing it in a secure location.

Data Execution Prevention (DEP) A Windows feature that prevents attackers from using buffer overflow to execute malware.

decryption The process of changing ciphertext into plaintext.

demilitarized zone (DMZ) A separate network that sits outside the secure network perimeter that provides Internet access to certain services.

denial of service (DoS) An attack designed to prevent a device from performing its intended function.

device lock A steel cable and a lock used to secure a laptop computer against theft.

DHCP lease A lease of an IP address to a network user.

dictionary attack An attack on a password that creates hashes of common dictionary words, and then compares those hashed dictionary words against those in the password file.

differential backup A backup that copies all files changed since the last full backup.

digital certificate A certificate that associates a user's identity to a public key.

disassociation frame A communication from a wireless device that indicates the device wishes to end the wireless connection.

disaster recovery The procedures and processes for restoring an organization's IT operations following a disaster.

disaster recovery plan (DRP) A written document that details the process for restoring IT resources following an event that causes a significant disruption in service.

disk mirroring A RAID technology for copying data to two disks simultaneously.

disk to disk (D2D) Backing up to a magnetic disk, such as a large hard drive or RAID configuration.

disposal and destruction policy A policy that addresses the disposal of resources that are considered confidential.

drive-by downloads Infections that occur by only passively viewing a Web page.

due care The obligations that are imposed on owners and operators of assets to exercise reasonable care of the assets and take necessary precautions to protect them.

due diligence The principle of investigation that examines all material facts available.

due process The principle of treating all accused persons in an equal fashion, using established rules and principles.

dynamic address An IP address that changes.

Dynamic Host Configuration Protocol (DHCP) Part of the TCP/IP protocol suite that leases IP addresses to clients to use while they are connected to the network.

embedded hyperlinks A hyperlink typically contained in an e-mail message or other document.

encryption The process of changing plaintext into ciphertext.

ethics policy A policy intended to be a central guide and reference for employees in support of day-to-day decision making; also called a code of ethics.

exploit To take advantage of a vulnerability.

Extended Validation Secure Sockets Layer Certificate (EV SSL) A certificate that requires more extensive verification of the legitimacy of the business.

Fair and Accurate Credit Transactions Act (FACTA) of 2003 A U.S. federal law that contains rules regarding consumer privacy.

file infector virus A virus that infects program executable files with an .EXE or .COM file extension.

file sharing Allowing other users to access documents.

firewall A network device that can repel attacks through filtering the data packets.

first-party cookie A cookie created from the Web site that a user is currently viewing.

flashing The process for rewriting the contents of the BIOS.

forensics (forensic science) The application of science to questions that are of interest to the legal profession.

geometric variance Spam that uses "speckling" and different colors so that no two spam e-mails appear to be the same.

GIF layering Image spam that is divided into multiple images.

global positioning system (GPS) A system which was originally developed by the U.S. military in the late 1970s as a navigation system but was later opened to civilian use to determine geographic locations.

Gramm-Leach-Bliley Act (GLBA) A U.S. federal act that requires private data to be protected by banks and other financial institutions.

guideline A collection of suggestions that should be implemented.

hacker (1) Anyone who illegally breaks into or attempts to break into a computer system; (2) A person who uses advanced computer skills to attack computers but not with malicious intent.

Health Insurance Portability and Accountability Act (HIPAA) A U.S. federal act that requires healthcare enterprises to guard protected health information.

hot site A remote site that contains all equipment, supplies, and telecommunications business needs and is ready immediately in the event of a disaster.

hyperlink A notation in an HTML document that allows the user to jump from one area to another.

Hypertext Markup Language (HTML) A language that allows text, graphic images, audio, video, and hyperlinks to be combined into a single document.

Hypertext Transport Protocol (HTTP) A set of standards for transmitting HTML documents.

identity theft Using someone's personal information, such as a Social Security number, to establish bank or credit card accounts that are then left unpaid, leaving the victim with the debts and ruining their credit rating.

image spam Spam that uses graphical images of text in order to circumvent text-based filters.

IMAP (Internet Mail Access Protocol, or IMAP4) An advanced e-mail protocol.

incremental backup A backup that copies all files changed since the last full or incremental backup.

information security The tasks of guarding information that is in a digital format. More specifically, that which protects the integrity, confidentiality, and availability of information on the devices that store, manipulate, and transmit the information through products, people, and procedures.

integrity Ensures that the information is correct and no unauthorized person or malicious software has altered that data.

Internet A worldwide, interconnected set of computers, servers, and networks.

Internet Relay Chat (IRC) An open communication protocol that is used for real-time "chatting" with other IRC users over the Internet. Also used to remotely control zombie computers in a botnet.

Internet Service Provider (ISP) A business from which users purchase Internet access.

IP address A series of four sets of digits separated by periods that uniquely identifies the computer.

Java A complete programming language that can be used to create standalone applications.

Java applet A separate program for creating special features in an HTML document.

JavaScript A programming language for creating special features in an HTML document.

key A mathematical value entered into an encryption algorithm to produce ciphertext.

keylogger A small hardware device or a program that monitors each keystroke a user types on the computer's keyboard.

local area network (LAN) A computer network that has all of the computers located relatively close to each other.

logic bomb   A computer program or a part of a program that lies dormant until it is triggered by a specific logical event.

MAC address filter   Restricting access to the wireless network by entering the MAC address of approved wireless devices into the wireless router.

macro   A series of commands and instructions that can be grouped together as a single command.

macro virus   A virus written in a scripting language.

malware   Malicious software.

Master Boot Record (MBR)   An area on a hard disk drive that contains the program necessary for the computer to start up and a description of how the hard drive is organized.

Media Access Control (MAC) address   A unique address of 12 characters separated by either dashes or colons used by computer networks to identify the computer.

metadata   Data about data.

metamorphic virus   A virus that alters how it appears in order to avoid detection.

mirror image backup   A backup copy of each bit on a computer hard drive; also known as bit-stream backup.

network address translation (NAT)   A technology that hides the IP addresses of network devices from attackers.

Network Attached Storage (NAS)   A technology that uses a dedicated hard disk-based file storage device to provide centralized and consolidated disk storage available to network users.

network interface card (NIC)   A hardware device that connects a computer to a wired network adapter.

off-line UPS   An uninterruptible power supply in which the battery charger is connected to the primary power source in order to charge its battery.

omnidirectional antenna   An antenna that can detect signals from all directions equally.

on-line UPS   An uninterruptible power supply that is always running off its battery while the main power runs the battery charger.

packet   A unit of data that is transmitted through the computer network.

packet generator   A program that creates fake packets and flood a wireless network with traffic.

partition table   A table on the hard drive that describes how the hard drive is organized.

password   A secret combination of letters, numbers and/or characters that serves to authenticate a user.

password storage program   A program for entering account information such as username and password, along with other account details.

patch   A general software security update intended to cover vulnerabilities that have been discovered after the program was released.

peer-to-peer   A wireless network that connects wireless devices directly to another wireless device; also called ad hoc.

personal area network (PAN)   A computer network that describes devices other than personal computers that communicate at a distance up to 10 feet (3 meters).

personal security model   A model of security designed for single users or small office settings of generally 10 or fewer wireless devices.

personally identifiable information (PII) policy   A policy that outlines how an organization uses personal information it collects.

phishing   Sending an e-mail or displaying a Web announcement that falsely claims to be from a legitimate enterprise in an attempt to trick the user into surrendering private information.

physical address   A unique address of 12 characters separated by either dashes or colons used by computer networks to identify the computer.

plaintext   Data input into an encryption algorithm.

policy   A document that outlines specific requirements or rules that must be met.

polymorphic virus   A virus that changes how it appears and also encrypts its contents differently each time.

popup   A small Web browser window that appears over the Web site that is being viewed.

popup blocker   A separate program or a feature incorporated within a browser that limits or blocks most popups.

port address translation (PAT)   A technology that assigns each packet the same IP address but a different port number.

port forwarding   A technology that opens only specific ports that need to be available.

port number   A number that identifies what program or service is being requested.

Post Office Protocol (POP or **POP3)**   A protocol that handles incoming e-mail.

private addresses IP addresses are not assigned to any specific user or organization.

private key A cryptographic key that is widely known and can be freely distributed.

private key cryptography Cryptographic algorithms that use a single key to encrypt and decrypt a message.

PROM (Programmable Read Only Memory) A chip in which the contents can be rewritten to provide new functionality.

protocol A set of standards.

public key A cryptographic key that is only known to the recipient of the message.

public key cryptography Encryption that uses two mathematically related keys.

rainbow tables An attack on a password that uses a large pregenerated data set of hashes from nearly every possible password.

random access memory (RAM) Temporary computer memory that is erased when the computer is powered off.

Read Only Memory (ROM) A chip that cannot be reprogrammed.

reading pane A feature in an e-mail client that allows the user to read an e-mail message without opening it.

Redundant Array of Independent Drives (RAID) A technology for using multiple hard disk drives for increased reliability.

redundant server A stand-by server that is manually added to the network if a primary server fails.

removable storage Devices, such as USB flash drives, that can store data from a computer and then be disconnected.

resident virus A virus that is loaded into random access memory and can interrupt almost any function executed by the computer operating system and alter it.

risk The likelihood that a threat agent will exploit a vulnerability.

rootkit A set of software tools used by an intruder to break into a computer, obtain special privileges to perform unauthorized functions, and then hide all traces of its existence.

router A network device responsible for sending packets through the network towards their destination.

rule base A set of rules for the action that a firewall should take when it receives a packet.

sandbox A restrictive area that surrounds a program and keeps it away from private data and other resources on a local computer.

Sarbanes-Oxley Act (Sarbox) A U.S. federal act that enforces reporting requirements and internal controls on electronic financial reporting systems.

scanning The process of a wireless device looking for an incoming beacon.

script kiddie An unskilled user who downloads automated attack software to attack computers.

scripting language A language that is similar to a computer programming language that is "interpreted" into a language the computer can understand without the need of a special computer program.

security policy A written document that states how an organization plans to protect the company's information technology assets.

security-related human resource policy Policy that addresses security as it relates to human resources.

server A central computer on a network that provides files or services on the network.

server cluster A combination of two or more servers that are interconnected to appear as one.

server digital certificates Digital certificates that are issued from an Internet Web server computer to a Web browser.

Service Set Identifier (SSID) The "network name" of a wireless network.

signature files Files that contain the pattern of a virus that antivirus software uses to identify malware.

signed Java applet A Java applet with a digital signature that proves the program is from a trusted source and has not been altered.

Simple Mail Transfer Protocol (SMTP) A protocol that handles outgoing e-mail.

single point of failure A component or entity which, should it fail, would adversely affect the entire system.

slack Hidden data on a hard drive.

social engineering Relying on deceiving someone to obtain secure information.

social networking Grouping individuals and organizations into clusters or groups based on some sort of affiliation.

social networking sites Web sites that facilitate linking individuals with common interests.

spam Unsolicited e-mail.

spam filters Special filters that look for evidence of e-mail spam.

spy A person who has been hired to break into a computer and steal information.

spyware A general term used to describe software that violates a user's personal security.

standard A collection of requirements specific to the system or procedure that must be met by everyone.

stateful packet filtering A firewall that keeps a record of the state of a connection between an internal computer and an external server and then makes decisions based on the connection as well as the rule base.

stateless packet filtering A firewall that examines an incoming packet and takes action based strictly on the rule base.

static address An IP address that does not change.

strong passwords Passwords that are difficult to break.

symmetric cryptography Encryption that uses a single key to encrypt and decrypt a message.

symmetric server cluster A technology in which every server in the cluster performs useful work and if one server fails the remaining servers absorb the load.

third-party cookie A cookie that is not created by the Web site that attempts to access the cookie.

threat An event or action that may defeat the security measures in place and result in a loss.

threat agent A person or thing that has the power to carry out a threat.

Transmission Control Protocol/Internet Protocol (TCP/IP) A set of standards for Internet transmissions.

Trojan horse (Trojan) A program advertised as performing one activity but actually does something else, or it may perform both the advertised and malicious activities.

Trusted Platform Module (TPM) A chip on the motherboard of the computer that provides cryptographic services.

uninterruptible power supply (UPS) An external device that provides electrical power when normal power is interrupted.

unsigned Java applet A Java applet that does not come from a trusted source.

USA Patriot Act A U.S. federal act that broadens the surveillance of law enforcement agencies to enhance the detection and suppression of terrorism.

username A unique computer name for identifying a user.

virtual local area networks (VLANs) Networks that are commonly used in organizations to segment users or network equipment in logical groupings.

virtual private network (VPN) Using an unsecured public network, such as a wireless network in a coffee shop, as if it were a secure private network.

virus A program that secretly attaches itself to a document or program and then executes when that document is open or program is launched.

vulnerability A weakness that allows a threat agent to bypass security.

war driving The process of finding a beacon from a wireless network and recording information about it; also known as wireless location mapping.

warm site A remote site that contains computer equipment but does not have telecommunication access constantly running.

weak passwords Passwords that compromise security.

whitelist A list of senders from whom a user wants to receive e-mail messages.

whole disk encryption Cryptography applied to entire disks.

Wi-Fi (Wireless Fidelity) A wireless network based on a protocol that transmits data at fast speeds over a distance of up to 375 feet (115 meters).

Wi-Fi Protected Access (WPA) One part of the personal security model that is less secure than Wi-Fi Protected Access 2.

Wi-Fi Protected Access 2 (WPA2) An update to the Wi-Fi Protected Access security model.

wide area network (WAN) A computer network that connects computers and networks over a relatively large geographical area.

Windows page file A temporary or permanent file on a hard drive used by Microsoft Windows operating systems that serves as additional memory when RAM is not available.

Wired Equivalent Privacy (WEP) A technology designed to ensure that only authorized parties can view transmitted wireless information yet is not considered secure.

wireless gateway Wireless network device for home users that combines the features of an AP, firewall, and router in a single hardware device.

wireless local area network (WLAN) A wireless network based on a protocol that transmits data at fast speeds over a distance of up to 375 feet (115 meters).

wireless location mapping The process of finding a beacon from a wireless network and recording information about it; also known as war driving.

word splitting Separating words in a spam message so that they can still be read by the human eye.

World Wide Web (WWW) A system of Internet server computers that provide online information in a specific format.

worm A program that is designed to take advantage of a vulnerability in an application or an operating system in order to enter a system.

zero day attack An attack that occurs when an attacker discovers and exploits a previously unknown flaw, providing "zero days" of warning.

zero pixel IFrame An HTML element used in drive-by downloads that allows malicious code to be embedded in an HTML document.

zombie Computer under the control of an attacker.

Index

Note: Page numbers in boldface indicate pages where key terms are defined.